Isaac Taylor Tichenor

RELIGION AND AMERICAN CULTURE

Series Editors
David Edwin Harrell Jr.
Wayne Flynt
Edith L. Blumhofer

Isaac Taylor Tichenor. Courtesy of the Auburn University Libraries.

Isaac Taylor Tichenor

The Creation of the Baptist New South

MICHAEL E. WILLIAMS SR.

THE UNIVERSITY OF ALABAMA PRESS
Tuscaloosa

∞

The paper on which this book is printed meets the minimum requirements of American National Standard for Information Science——Permanence of Paper for Printed Library Materials, ANSI Z39.48-1984.

Library of Congress Cataloging-in-Publication Data

Williams, Michael E. (Michael Edward), 1960–
    Isaac Taylor Tichenor : the creation of the Baptist new South / Michael E. Williams, Sr.
        p. cm. — (Religion and American culture)
    Includes bibliographical references (p.) and index.
    ISBN 0-8173-1474-1 (cloth : alk. paper)
    1. Tichenor, I. T. (Isaac Taylor), 1825–1902. 2. Southern Baptist Convention—History—
19th century. I. Title. II. Religion and American culture (Tuscaloosa, Ala.)
    BX6495.T55W55 2005
    286′.1′092—dc22

                                                              2005002049

To my parents,
Jo and Charles Williams,
with great love and appreciation

Contents

Illustrations

Isaac Taylor Tichenor

Introduction

On November 11, 1825, Isaac Taylor Tichenor was born in Spencer County, Kentucky.[1] Although oblivious to the changes taking place in his homeland at the time of his birth, the child and the man he would become were shaped by these influences. In turn, he would play a major role in shaping his region and his denomination. Tichenor served as an evangelist, pastor, denominational leader, military chaplain, businessman, educator, and—as the crowning achievement of his life—corresponding secretary of the Southern Baptist Convention Home Mission Board. Events on either side of his birth year were the harbingers of momentous changes in the United States.

In 1825 the United States of America was still in its infancy. The Constitution of the young country was not quite four decades old, and the birth of the nation had occurred less than five decades earlier. The Louisiana Purchase, doubling the size of the nation, dated only from 1803, and the 1820 census revealed that the population of the fledgling nation was not quite ten million. To the southwest of this new nation, Mexico, another upstart, had recently achieved its independence from Spain. This revolution would set into motion events that would climax with the independence of a northernmost province of Mexico, Texas, eventual statehood for the Lone Star Republic, and the Mexican War. This war resulted in the acquisition of the remainder of the American Southwest and California.

The Erie Canal opened for business in October 1825, steamboats were beginning to navigate the major rivers of the West, and in less than ten years the first trains would begin running. The term *manifest destiny* would not be widely used until 1845, but the focus of the United States continued to shift westward. The Missouri Compromise of 1820 resulted in the addition of Maine and Missouri as the twenty-third and twenty-fourth states of the Union, but the compromise proved to be only a temporary respite from a situation just beginning to divide the nation along sectional lines. The year 1831 marked the beginning of the organized abolitionist movement with the publication of William Lloyd Garrison's the *Liberator*. The Nat Turner slave uprising in Virginia would erupt the same year. One year later the Nullification Crisis between South Carolina and Andrew Jackson's presidential administration brought to the forefront the issue of states' rights. These latter events served notice of the coming crisis that would shatter the nationalism and optimism brought on by the westward expansion of the nation. Simultaneously, these events cultivated the seeds of sectionalism already planted in the soil of the young nation, especially in the South.

American Christianity in 1825 was also in the midst of significant change and optimism. Building upon the advances of the great awakenings, denominations like the Presbyterians and Methodists had seen their influence expand. For instance, the membership of American Presbyterianism had grown almost six-fold between 1800 and 1820. From 1820 to 1837, American Presbyterians tripled in communicants, and the total number of churches more than doubled again. The Methodist church experienced even more phenomenal growth. In the sector west of the Alleghenies, Methodists grew in membership from fewer than 3,000 members in 1800 to more than 175,000 in 1830. Missionary, publication, and education societies also sprang up on the heels of the awakenings, and America's developing denominations were caught up in the prevailing confidence of the day.[2]

American Baptists shared the dominant mood of the 1820s. Slightly more than a decade earlier, Baptists had formed their Triennial Convention. Organized as a convention, in reality it was a society to promote foreign missions. While the Baptist Home Mission Society would not actually be formed until 1832, the Baptist home missions effort had already begun in 1817 with the work of John Mason Peck in the Missouri territory and the creation of mission efforts in New Orleans and Indiana.[3] These efforts prepared the way for a concentrated effort in home missions endeavors. No doubt, these Baptists felt deeply the optimism of their day. At the same time as Americans were claiming a continent for the young nation, Baptists were claiming that same continent for Christianity as part of their own manifest destiny. Unfortunately, the same sectionalism that divided the nation would also divide Baptists and result in the creation of two separate entities, North and South, in 1845.

Within two decades this optimism would wane. The virtual Protestant monopoly in the religious domain was challenged after 1825 by the immigration of vast numbers of Roman Catholics, heralding the emergence of an even more pluralistic nation. By the time of the 1850 census, almost one million Irish were reported in the United States.[4] New denominations like the various expressions of the Churches of Christ also formed in the wake of the revivals of the early part of the century, and in subsequent decades sectarian and communitarian groups emerged that further challenged Protestant hegemony. Baptists were joined by Methodists and Presbyterians whose denominations also divided along sectional lines because of the tensions of the impending national crisis.

By century's end, much of the optimism predominant in 1825 had been shattered by the explosion of the American Civil War and rebuilt with the Gilded Age's expansive spirit. The sectional crisis, foreshadowed by events such as the Nat Turner revolt, the birth of radical abolitionism, and the division of America's leading Protestant denominations along sectional lines, erupted at Fort Sumter in 1861. These hostilities took four years, hundreds of thousands of American lives, and more than $15 billion to quell. More than a decade of painful and largely unsuccessful reconstruction followed for the South. Even so, at the end of this era the former slaves remained essentially enslaved by a prejudiced southern society, and "Redeemer" governments had been established.

Also, by 1900 the flood tide of immigration that surged with the Irish immigration of the 1850s reached its zenith with an influx of eastern and southern Europeans in the period from 1870 to 1910. This immigration, coupled with immigration from traditional locations in western and central Europe and a high American birthrate, led to the U.S. population doubling between 1870 and 1900 to more than 80 million persons. This problem was further complicated by the tripling of the urban population of the United States during the same time period. Thus Americans sought to deal with vast social changes on a number of fronts: those brought on by the attempted assimilation of a race that had been held in bondage, by the continued effort to conquer and settle the frontier, and by rapid urbanization, immigration, and industrial revolution. By the end of the century, the United States had emerged from the political backwater of the world to status as a world power in terms of its physical strength, burgeoning industrial might, and vast potential.

In the midst of rapid change, American Christianity struggled to establish its place in the newly materializing American community and to answer questions raised by a swiftly changing society. This radical conversion of American society offered pointed challenges to American churches, especially the Protestant denominations. The decades from 1870–1900 have sometimes been known as the "Golden Age of Liberal Theology," and American churches attempted to define their positions in relationship to the movement or to refute it. At one level were the theories of Charles Darwin, the questions of historical method, and the higher criticism of German scholars. At a second level, the philosophy of positivistic naturalism was on the rise. Many of the nation's denominations found themselves immersed in theological debate.[5]

In the center of an accelerating society undergoing the metamorphosis from a primarily rural, Anglo-Saxon, and Protestant culture to a much more theologically, ethnically, and culturally diverse society, these new ideas "constituted a threat to accepted understandings of the Christian faith." As church historian Winthrop Hudson further observes,

> The psychological and sociological studies tended to reduce religion to a social phenomenon. The accounts of other religions raised questions with regards to the uniqueness of the Christian faith. Both Darwinian biology and the new biblical studies seemed to undermine the authority of the Bible.[6]

Baptists in America were not untouched by this theological crisis. Northern Baptists proved more susceptible to these issues than their southern cousins. Southern Baptists, however, were not entirely insulated from these concerns as controversies involving Crawford H. Toy and William H. Whitsitt suggest. Toy, a professor at Southern Baptist Theological Seminary, resigned under pressure after espousing views indicative of influence from methods of German higher criticism. Whitsitt, professor of church history and president of Southern Seminary, resigned under pressure after using methods of historical investigation that concluded that Baptists originated in the seventeenth century, contrary to the beliefs of Baptists who identified themselves as Landmark Baptists.[7] With these exceptions, however, Southern Baptists were relatively unaffected by issues such as these and, comparatively, were not nearly as affected by immigration and urbanization as Baptists in the North. At the turn of the century, Southern Baptists remained essentially conservative, largely rural, and primarily concerned with building a spiritual empire from which to evangelize the world.

All of these events from 1825 to 1900 profoundly shaped Baptists. At Augusta, Georgia, in 1845, the Southern Baptist Convention, as one of its first acts, formed the Domestic Mission Board. Later renamed the Home Mission Board, as its work came to encompass not only domestic missions but also Native American mission work and the realm of publications, the Home Mission Board has been, along with the Foreign Mission Board, the vanguard of the denomination's work. Despite its important role in the enterprise of domestic missions, the Home Mission Board has had a checkered past. Early in its existence, the board suffered from a lack of stability due to frequent turnover in leadership. Between 1846 and 1871, five individuals served in the crucial role of corresponding secretary, the chief operating officer of the board. Contrasted against this, the Foreign Mission Board had only one corresponding secretary, James B. Taylor, in the same time period.[8]

During this era came four years of Civil War that ravaged the South. The years of Reconstruction that followed were equally disruptive. In the latter half of the 1870s, there was serious talk of dissolving the Home Mission Board and, perhaps, even of reunifying the Baptists in the South with their northern counterparts. The Home Board raised less than $20,000 during the 1879–80 fiscal year; the following year was little better. Only seven of the twenty-one conventions and general associations represented in the Southern Baptist Convention "were co-operating with the Home Board." The Home Mission Board employed only forty missionaries; there was virtually no Southern Baptist work west of the Mississippi River with the exception of the Indian Territory, and four of the five Texas Baptist organizations were receiving their support from the Northern Baptist Home Mission Society.[9]

In 1882 the Southern Baptist Convention made two decisions pertaining to the Home Mission Board that dramatically altered the course of the convention's history. The first decision was to move the board from Marion, Alabama, to Atlanta, Georgia, to distance it from its largely rural, agricultural past and associate it with the city that embodied the "New South." The second decision was to appoint a new board and hire a new corresponding secretary.[10] Two weeks later the newly elected board met in Atlanta and chose Isaac Taylor Tichenor to fill this significant position.

I. T. Tichenor was no stranger to Southern Baptists or to southerners in 1882. In his young adulthood, he had represented the Indian Mission Association, a partial forerunner of the Home Mission Board, as a regional representative in what was then the southwestern part of the United States.[11] Also in those years, he served pastorates in Mississippi and Kentucky and became actively involved in the early years of the Southern Baptist Convention. While still a young man, he became pastor of the First Baptist Church of Montgomery, Alabama, one of the most strategic congregations in the Deep South. In those years he was intimately involved with some of Southern Baptists' most important enterprises revolving around missions and education at both the state and the regional level. He came to value the immense importance of cooperative efforts by a people who jealously defended local church autonomy. It was also in this period that Tichenor was exposed to the strong sectionalism pervasive in the late antebellum South and became fully a "southern man."

When the American Civil War came, Tichenor distinguished himself as a combat chaplain at the battle of Shiloh, an experience that served as a defining moment not only in his ministry but also for his entire life. After the end of the war, finding prospects in the Reconstruction era pastorate insufficient to provide for his family, he launched himself into the mining enterprise and laid much of the groundwork for the future success of coal and iron mining enterprises in the north-central Alabama region. During this period, Tichenor became vitally interested in New South concepts that were taking hold in some segments of southern Reconstruction society. He fully embraced the New South upon his acceptance of the presidency of Alabama's land-grant university at Auburn, then known as Alabama A & M. As president of A & M, Tichenor not only adopted New South ideals in higher education but also promoted them for the South as a whole. Several years before Atlanta editor Henry Grady popularized the term New South, Tichenor, with prophetic insight, recognized the industrial and agricultural potential that the economically languishing South held and served as an early spokesman for the New South that he and others sought to create. He also pioneered the integrating of revolutionary New South concepts with changing models in higher education and sought to develop a comprehensive system of education for the state of Alabama that would be best represented by A & M.

As corresponding secretary of the Home Mission Board from 1882 to 1899, Tichenor served essentially as the chief operating and executive officer of the board. As such, he played the primary role in developing a denominational identity among Southern Baptists at a time when Southern Baptists were searching desperately for one as well as for a continued purpose and mission. Much in the same way that he had transformed a small denominational liberal arts college at Auburn into a New South land grant college, Tichenor transformed the Southern Baptist Convention from a denomination in retreat to one racing to the forefront of America's denominations. In doing so, he led the development of a religious subculture within southern subculture. His efforts fused various ideas about who Southern Baptists were into a coalition that was as southern as it was Baptist. He defined for Baptists in the South what territory should be considered southern territory, and he rose to defend it when he believed it was threatened. He also utilized language and methods common in the broader American expansionist philosophy of that day to claim additional territory as Southern Baptist domain. More than any single individual, Tichenor influenced the development of Southern Baptists as they marched toward becoming what church historian Martin Marty has identified as the twentieth-century "Catholic Church of the South." Baptist historian Walter Shurden identifies Tichenor, along with William B. Johnson, as the personification of the "Georgia Tradition" of intense sectionalism and cooperative denominationalism. Denominational historian H. Leon McBeth calls Tichenor a "Baptist giant" and writes that "perhaps no better choice could have been made [to serve as corresponding secretary]." Baptist historian Robert Baker writes of Tichenor, "Perhaps he more than any other single individual should be credited with saving the home field." Historian John Franklin Loftis, in a dissertation completed in the 1980s on Southern Baptist ministerial role models, says of Tichenor that he "defined what was 'southern' about the SBC." Earlier Southern Baptist historian William Wright Barnes calls Tichenor "one of the greatest statesmen and most devoted servants the Convention has ever had" and quotes one of Tichenor's successors at the Home Mission Board, B. D. Gray, as saying that Tichenor was entitled "to be called the Father of Cooperation." Baptist Home Mission Board and Sunday School Board writer Joe Burton lists ten contributions Tichenor made to the SBC beginning with the statement, "He saved the Southern Baptist Convention."[12]

My own interest in I. T. Tichenor began in a hallway of the Auburn First Baptist Church of Auburn, Alabama. I was a graduate student in history at Auburn University and was serving on the staff of that church. One day in the hallway of the sanctuary, I noticed a plaque containing the names and tenures of the pastors of the congregation. One name I noticed was that of I. T. Tichenor. Later, I asked the pastor, John Jeffers, if this were the same Tichenor who had served as president of Auburn University in the 1870s. He answered affirmatively, mentioned that Tichenor actually served as a lay leader and frequent interim pastor during those years, and added that Tichenor was a leading Southern Baptist in the nineteenth century.

After completing a master's degree at Auburn and going to Southwestern Baptist Theological Seminary in 1985 as a master of divinity student, two events sparked a renewed interest in Tichenor. One was a chance encounter and conversation with Dr. Robert A. Baker, professor emeritus of church history at Southwestern. Finding that I was an Auburn alumnus, Baker launched into a discussion of Tichenor and his contributions to Baptist and southern history. The second event was my reading H. Leon McBeth's monumental study, *The Baptist Heritage*, which contained insightful commentary on Tichenor's contributions to the Southern Baptist Convention. Upon entering the Ph.D. program at Southwestern in 1989, I asked Dr. McBeth about the possibility of doing a study on Tichenor for my dissertation. His eager response and subsequent interest launched concentrated studies that began in his seminars and resulted in my doctoral dissertation on Tichenor. His assistance throughout the project was crucial.

Upon graduating from the Ph.D. program and beginning to teach Baptist history, American church history, and American history at Dallas Baptist University, I became increasingly convinced that a full-length biography of Tichenor was greatly needed. In the 1950s there were two dissertations concerning his life and work. Neither places him in a broad historical context. Neither dissertation explores fully the cultural influences upon Tichenor nor discusses how he utilized his culture to convince Southern Baptists to rally to the support of its Home Mission Board. Neither work deals at length with the J. S. Murrow controversy or the Fortress Monroe Conference. Both dissertations were completed without the use of the more recently deposited papers of E. L. Compere. Compere, a Home Mission Board appointee to the Indian Territory, corresponded extensively with Tichenor and the Home Mission Board during Tichenor's tenure in office. His considerable correspondence is preserved at the Southern Baptist Historical Library and Archives in Nashville, Tennessee. Both dissertations were completed without consulting the extensive minutes of the Home Mission Board during Tichenor's tenure. Some discussion of Tichenor's role in the resurgence of the Southern Baptist Convention may be found in Joe Burton's *Road to Recovery*, a popular work describing the history of the convention. There is also limited discussion of Tichenor's contributions in developing Southern Baptist identity in John Franklin Loftis's dissertation in 1987. Otherwise, study of Tichenor's contributions has been confined to short descriptions of his work in general histories of Baptists or the Southern Baptist Convention. While this previous study is helpful, more comprehensive analysis needs to focus upon the methodologies used to define and defend the Southern Baptist Convention. This work should include formative influences upon Tichenor's life as well as discussion and analysis of two frequently overlooked but significant portions of his career, years he spent in the coal mining business and the decade he served as president of Alabama A & M, now known as Auburn University.

There was another contributing factor. In recent years a number of works have dealt directly or indirectly with issues that were relevant to Tichenor's life. Paul Gaston's *The New South Creed* and Edward Ayers's *The Promise of the New South* deal with a movement and an ideal with which Tichenor was intimately involved. Charles Reagan Wilson's *Baptized in Blood* speaks to the entire context in which Tichenor worked and ministered and about ideas that Tichenor baptized in his quest to build the Home Mission Board and solidify control of Southern Baptists over southern religious life. Paul Harvey's *Redeeming the South* specifically addresses the "religious cultures and racial identities" in which Tichenor lived and moved. Other works produced in recent years have contributed as well. Seeking to produce a work that would fill a gap in the literature on such a crucial figure, I contacted one of my professors from Auburn, Wayne Flynt, and asked him to read my dissertation for the possibility of publication. His gracious response and detailed insights into Tichenor, various aspects of southern culture and religion, and American history were essential in helping me adapt and expand my dissertation into this present work, as were his patience and suggestions throughout the editorial process. His encouragement and assistance has been essential in my completion of this work.

It is the intent of my study to provide a comprehensive analysis of the life of I. T. Tichenor that examines the overall influence of his life and work and focuses upon his contributions to southern business, education, religion, and culture, as well as the methodologies he used to rally Southern Baptist support around its struggling Home Mission Board. By doing so, he thereby defined the makeup of the Southern Baptist Convention and defended the territory of the convention. His role in shaping Southern Baptists as they became the largest denomination in the South was crucial in determining Southern Baptist identity; furthermore, because of Southern Baptists' pervasive influence throughout the region, Tichenor was highly influential in forming a uniquely southern mindset prior to and at the turn of the century.

Anyone who attempts a study of this scope owes a debt to others far too great to repay. In addition to Leon McBeth and Wayne Flynt, many others have assisted me along the way. Among them are numerous people from libraries and archives: Bill Sumners of the Southern Baptist Historical Library and Archives; Dwayne Cox and Bev Powers of the Auburn University Archives; the staff of the Alabama Department of Archives and History, Montgomery, Alabama; Beverly Carlson of the American Baptist Historical Society Archives, Valley Forge, Pennsylvania; the staffs of the Shelby County Museum and Archives and the Shelby County Courthouse of Columbiana, Alabama; Bill Taylor and Myrta Garrett of the A. Webb Roberts Library, Southwestern Baptist Theological Seminary, Fort Worth, Texas; Elizabeth Wells of Samford University Library; and Mary Fox and library staff of the Collins Learning Center at Dallas Baptist University, especially Carey Moore and Lorraine Walston.

Numerous individuals have also provided crucial assistance. Among them are the staff of The University of Alabama Press; Mindy Wilson for her editorial work; Kenneth Penhale of Helena, Alabama, who provided copies of the Tichenor-Squire correspondence; Jim Day of the University of Montevallo, who shared his fine dissertation on Alabama mining while it was in the final stages of completion; Kenneth Noe of Auburn University, who shared an unpublished paper on Tichenor's experiences at Shiloh; Bart Tichenor, who read a draft of the manuscript in its entirety and provided information on the Tichenor family; and Dr. Lee Allen, retired professor of history at Samford University, who published several small portions of this manuscript in their early stages in the *Alabama Baptist Historian* and provided encouragement throughout the project. Special thanks go to Kathy Maxwell who prepared the index. Colleagues and friends Brenda Bradley, Gary Starnes, Mike Rosato, Deborah McCollister, Alan Lefever, Karen Bullock, and Jan Kennamer read either the entire manuscript or portions of it, making suggestions and offering support. My friends Richard Castleberry, Randall Bradley, Deemie and Davey Naugle, Kathy Knight, and DBU Provost Gail Linam rendered significant encouragement. The faculty of the College of Humanities and Social Sciences at DBU have been patient with me as I have worked on this project and have been very supportive. My administrative assistants at DBU over the past few years, Kit Montgomery, Lee Tincher, Sara Petroff, and Wanda Allen have been especially helpful and encouraging. They have guarded my writing time jealously and helped with minute details that can sometimes overwhelm a dean. Wanda has been especially helpful and supportive throughout the past four years. Thank you, Wanda.

Finally, special gratitude goes to my family for constant blessing in my life. My late aunt, Nita Adams, was a constant source of encouragement. My brother, Gary Williams, and my sister, Alesia Griswald, have encouraged me at various times. I am particularly grateful to my wife, Robbie, and my sons, Michael, Josh, and Carey for their love, patience, companionship, and great joy they bring to my life. Most of all, I wish to thank my parents, Jo and Charles Williams, for instilling a love of learning, providing many opportunities for growth, and for their great support of me through the years. This work is dedicated in their honor.

1

The Emerging Denominationalist

Tichenor as Pastor and Southern Baptist Leader, 1825–60

The family into which Isaac Taylor Tichenor was born in 1825 traced its roots to New England and the early years of colonial settlement in New Haven, Connecticut. Martin Tichenor took the Oath of Allegiance there in 1644. His migration to Connecticut in those years would have placed him in the first decade of settlement in that colony. One family tradition claims that Tichenor came from France and that the family originally came to France from a village in Poland named Tichen. The family drew its name from this tiny village, thus "Tichenors," or the people from Tichen. Some Tichenors claimed Dutch lineage, while other family records discount both traditions to claim that the Tichenors were of English descent, possibly from a place named "Tichen."[1]

From Connecticut Martin Tichenor moved to Newark, New Jersey, where he was among the earliest settlers. Subsequently, he relocated his family to Morris County, New Jersey. Martin's great-grandson Daniel was born there in 1742. In 1790 Daniel exchanged his holdings in New Jersey for new lands in the Green River Valley of Kentucky. Upon moving to the region, however, he found the area unsatisfactory and was forced to purchase lands in Nelson County, about thirty miles south of the new town of Louisville. Daniel Tichenor resided there in 1792 when Kentucky became the fifteenth state of the new nation. Only a decade removed from intense conflict between settlers and Native Americans, Kentucky was still part of the frontier, and Daniel Tichenor and his family would have known the harshness and difficulty of frontier life. They also would have been very aware of the fragility of human life and of the ongoing conflict that continued just north of the Ohio River.

His youngest son, James, was one of three Tichenor sons to marry sisters in the Bennett family. The Bennetts were staunch Baptists who had migrated from Virginia. No little dismay resulted when all the Tichenor children, who had been Presbyterian, converted to the Baptist denomination. It was to the union of James Tichenor and Margaret Bennett that Isaac Taylor was born. He was the fourth son and was named for his parents' Baptist pastor at the time. One nineteenth-century Kentucky Baptist historian recorded that the Tichenors' pastor, Isaac Taylor, "was probably the most popular preacher that ever labored in [that] association."[2]

Young Isaac Taylor Tichenor began his formal education at the relatively early age of four, and his earliest remembrances came from his school experiences. Family tradition indicates that he was converted at age eleven but was not baptized until he was thirteen. He was baptized into the Bloomfield Baptist Church of Nelson County, just south of his birthplace.[3]

The church into which Tichenor was baptized had been constituted in 1791 as Simpson's Creek Church. The congregation had a rich heritage of influence and growth. Recently, it had come through a time of division as its pastor, Jacob Creath, became an early proponent in Kentucky of the primitivist or restorationist movement known as *Campbellism* after its founder, Alexander Campbell. Campbell and his followers rejected mission societies, denominational colleges and institutions, and even denominations themselves as being unbiblical and sought to restore the "primitive" Christian church. Ultimately, the Campbellite movement became the basis of both the Disciples of Christ and the Churches of Christ denominations or movements but at this time divided many Baptist churches, especially in Kentucky and Tennessee. Creath led a large part of the congregation into an eventual split, but despite this, the Bloomfield church remained strong throughout the nineteenth century. It was responsible for many converts and planted numerous congregations in the region. Those Baptists who resisted Campbellism as well as the earlier anti-missions influence of the high Calvinist Primitive Baptists such as Daniel Parker and John Taylor were frequently known in those days as *missionary* Baptists. Typically, those missionary Baptists aggressively supported missions in the same way that those churches that opposed mission boards and the like were aggressively anti-missions.[4] Certainly, Tichenor's home church would have been identified as one such missionary Baptist congregation.

William Vaughan, one of the early prominent Baptist ministers of Kentucky, baptized young Isaac. Vaughan served as pastor of the Bloomfield church from 1836 to 1869. Writing in the 1880s, J. H. Spencer stated that Vaughan was "the strongest and longest link that united the pioneer preachers with those of the present generation and partook largely of the best qualities of both classes." Vaughan baptized Tichenor and a "very fleshy young woman" named Nancy Pulliam on the same day. Apparently, a poor response to his ministry at that time sorely disappointed Vaughan. The baptism of the large young woman attracted a great crowd, who paid little notice to the young teen being baptized.[5]

It is uncertain how much Vaughan and the church at Bloomfield influenced the young Tichenor, but interestingly his conversion and baptism came in a church that had survived the anti-missions and Restorationist controversies and maintained its health and vitality. Furthermore, he was baptized by a leading Baptist minister who had blended the rough, practical nature of the frontier with the more settled environment of the midcentury Kentucky planter. It is also interesting to note that this church participated in associations known for cooperation with other associations and churches and for strong support of the missions movement. Tichenor's later life and ministry reflected these influences.[6]

Isaac Taylor Tichenor was well educated as a child and adolescent. He attended school in Taylorsville, Kentucky, some nine miles north of Bloomfield.[7] He excelled as a student, received training in mathematics, Latin, rhetoric, and logic, and cherished hopes of higher education. His classical education was typical of the educational processes of that day, especially for students preparing for college. When he was sixteen, however, he was stricken with a severe case of measles that also caused a serious throat infection and so weakened him that it prevented his attending college. Throat problems affected him periodically for the rest of his life. In his later years, Tichenor noted that as he got older, his speaking voice grew weaker and did not have the "firmness" of his youth. This deterioration was probably a side effect of his illness as a teenager. Tichenor's later interest in higher education may well have stemmed in part from the fact that his youthful illness denied him formal higher education. Thus, instead of attending college, he stayed in Taylorsville and by age nineteen was teaching school. He was so successful that within a year, he began teaching at Taylorsville Academy with one of his former teachers, Davis Burbank. Burbank, along with his brother Moses, probably had a greater influence on Tichenor than anyone else during these years. Tichenor's classical education, his love of learning, and his wide range of reading, acquired in part from the Burbanks, served him in many ways in the coming years. It was during these years that he was called upon to preach his first sermon, "Search the Scriptures." It is unknown exactly why the pastor chose Tichenor to do so, but the congregation's response to the sermon may be an indication. Afterward, much to Tichenor's chagrin, the pastor of the church moved that Tichenor be licensed to the ministry. This type of action was not uncommon in Baptist churches that often recognized the gifts of some young men before these young men "felt the call." Other opportunities followed, and by the end of that summer he had made such an impact in the surrounding churches that he came to be known as "the boy orator of Kentucky." He was at that time twenty-one years old.[8]

After declining an invitation to the pastorate of the East Baptist Church of Louisville, Kentucky, Tichenor decided to go to Mississippi on behalf of the Indian Mission Association based in Louisville. The Indian Mission Association had been organized in October 1842 and was largely supported by Kentucky Baptists. Its primary purpose was to evangelize the Native American tribes of the Mississippi Valley. Later, this association merged with the Southern Baptist Domestic Mission Board, the forerunner of the Southern Baptist Home Mission Board in which Tichenor would play such a crucial role. The Indian Mission Association sent representatives like Tichenor to various states across the South. A key task of these agents was to raise awareness of autonomous local congregations about the need to support mission endeavors and to combat anti-missionism among Baptists. They also served as fund-raising agents for the association. Undoubtedly, this experience later influenced Tichenor as he lobbied Baptists for a more systematic form of co-operative missions support in the South and among Baptists.[9]

So, in the fall of 1847, Tichenor went by horseback to Mississippi. En route he stopped in Nashville for the annual meeting of the Indian Mission Association. While there he heard Joseph Islands preach. Islands was a full-blooded Creek Indian who served as a missionary among the Creek Indian nation. Tichenor was so impressed by Islands that later in life he wrote an essay entitled "Joseph Islands, Apostle to the Indians." Much of Tichenor's later interest in missions to the Native Americans probably dated from this point. He also stopped in Denmark, Tennessee, and preached twice. Supposedly, one woman was so excited by the effectiveness of his sermons that she responded by saying, "I had rather be that boy than to be Jeems [sic] K. Polk, President of the United States."[10]

Tichenor represented the Indian Association at the November 1847 Mississippi Baptist Convention in Hernando, Mississippi. On Thursday of the convention meeting, he addressed the body in a message described as an "eloquent and feeling appeal to the friends of the Indian." Apparently, he was well received because later in the convention in the report of the Committee on Indian Missions, prominent Baptist leader William Carey Crane recommended him "and solicit[ed] for him the kind regards and the contributions of all brethren favoring this noble subject." This event opened the door for his ministry in the state and marked his first appearance in denominational matters.[11] At the time he was not quite twenty-two years old.

After the convention he traveled for six weeks in the work of the association before coming to Columbus, Mississippi. Delayed there because of the onset of the rainy season and winter, he supplied the pulpit of the local Baptist church. Subsequently, the church called him to serve as the pastor in the spring of 1848. He effectively healed a schism and ministered there for almost two years. An equally young Presbyterian pastor befriended Tichenor and offered him the free use of his library. The library proved to be an indispensable resource, and a lifelong friendship was forged. It could well be that Tichenor's later resistance to the Landmark movement in Baptist life was developed, in part, because of this kindness shown in an ecumenical spirit by the Presbyterian minister. This type of relationship was atypical of denominational rivalries prevalent in the antebellum South and especially along the frontier, and it speaks well of both Tichenor and his unnamed Presbyterian colleague. It also demonstrates how important reading, learning, and preparation were to the young minister, particularly to one lacking formal higher education.[12]

During his brief pastorate, the young minister continued to be involved in association and state convention matters. He attended the 1848 meeting of the Mississippi convention as a representative of the Columbus association and, while there, was appointed to a few responsibilities within the convention. He was also appointed as a delegate-at-large from Mississippi to the Southern Baptist Convention that was to be held in May 1849.[13]

The Southern Baptist Convention had just been formed four years earlier in a meeting in Augusta, Georgia, in 1845. Its formation resulted from increasing tensions between Baptists of the North and South over the question of slavery. While contributing factors were concerns about the amount of money the Home Missions Society was spending in the South as compared to the North and questions about whether the society method was less effective in administering missions than a more structured convention method, the key issue culminating in the division was the question of slavery. When the New York-based Foreign and Home Mission societies failed to eliminate these concerns, southern Baptists, led mainly by Georgia Baptists, organized the Southern Baptist Convention, encompassing the work of a newly created Foreign Mission Board and a Domestic Mission Board. The purpose of these two agencies was to serve as an outlet, exclusively under the control of southerners, for the foreign and home mission efforts of Baptists in the South. The convention met the following year in Richmond, further solidifying Southern Baptist convictions for separation. The 1849 convention was originally scheduled for Nashville, Tennessee, but was adjourned because of the outbreak of a cholera epidemic. Tichenor attended the rescheduled meeting in Charleston, South Carolina.[14]

The young pastor's trip to the 1849 Southern Baptist Convention must have been a highlight of his early life. It was his first trip to the eastern seaboard and his first train ride. Most importantly, it was at this meeting that Tichenor had his first contact with Southern Baptist leaders such as Basil Manly Sr., president of the University of Alabama, and Jeremiah B. Jeter, pastor of First Baptist Church of Richmond, Virginia. Later, Manly would succeed and precede him in pastorates in Montgomery, Alabama. He also met men such as James P. Boyce and Basil Manly Jr., both of whom became part of the founding faculty of the Southern Baptist Theological Seminary and who served as his contemporaries in ministry. Another highlight was the invitation to preach in a service on Sunday afternoon. It is unknown why the convention selected him for this honor. His son-in-law recalled that "this sermon established his reputation in the Convention." It was also in this meeting that he was appointed to his first responsibilities within the SBC, serving on committees, on delegations, and on agencies.[15] While there is no record of Tichenor's making mention of the impression his participation in this early meeting of the SBC made upon him, later commitments in life demonstrate its formative influence. The strong sectionalism pervasive in the origins of the SBC would have been a significant influence upon a young minister. Thus, he probably began to identify himself as a "southerner" if he had not already done so. Likewise, the emphasis placed upon the convention method of cooperation and missions support and the influence of staunch denominationalists like Georgia Baptist William B. Johnson and the pastor of the First Baptist Church of Nashville, Tennessee, R. B. C. Howell, had a lasting effect upon his life. In fact, strong denominationalism blended with strict sectionalism became the key characteristics of his career and ministry later in life. Finally, moving among men such as the Manlys, Jeter, Boyce, and others who were or would become prominent leaders of the South's religion and culture inspired Tichenor to similar ambitions and ideas.

Apparently Tichenor made an impression in more than just denominational matters. A letter from a Matilda James of Pleasant Grove to a Mrs. Wilkinson written in June of that year reveals that young "Mattie" was aspiring to become "Sister Tichenor." She mentioned that Tichenor preached at Second Baptist Church of Charleston the Sunday afternoon of the convention and that the two of them "struck up quite a friendship." Mattie James also inserted that Tichenor was "the dearest little fellow that ever was, a perfect jewel"—obviously she was quite taken with him. The letter also reveals that at least some of the personal charisma demonstrated by Tichenor in later years was present early in his ministry.[16] James's marital aspirations went unrealized, and there is no record of the two ever encountering one another again.

Upon his return to Columbus, Tichenor busied himself with his pastorate and in the denomination. He preached before the 1849 Mississippi Baptist Convention and represented the convention as chairman of the Indian Missions Committee. The Convention selected him chairman of its Temperance Committee. This early involvement in state and convention-wide matters was important in forming Tichenor as a loyal Southern Baptist and in preparing him for later leadership roles.[17]

After two years in Columbus, Tichenor left the church there and traveled to Texas, led revivals in the new state, and then returned to Kentucky. On November 1, 1850, he accepted a unanimous call to the pastorate of the Baptist Church of Hendersonville. The *South Western Baptist* recorded the move, calling Tichenor "a young man of fine promise and great amiability." Less than a year later the same paper recognized Tichenor's participation in the Southern Baptist Convention in Nashville, calling him "one of the most promising and eloquent preachers in the Southwest." Although he was not yet twenty-five years old, the denominational press already recognized and praised his abilities.[18]

Tichenor served only one year as pastor of the church in Hendersonville. During this time, he kept a diary that provides insights into his personality. Also recorded in the diary are several of his sermons. His entries and sermons depict a young man who exhibited fervency and zeal for his calling and who, despite a lack of formal higher education, was well read in the classics and history and was diligently concerned with organization and preparation. His diary is filled with prayers and statements such as his first entry: "Oh, that God may enable me to be there [Henderson] a faithful shepherd rightly dividing the word of truth and giving to each his portion in due season." Another entry shows his diligence in ministry. He writes, "Oh, how much of my time is wasted in idleness or unprofitable labor." The few sermons recorded in the diary reflect a young minister whose social conscience had been awakened. He believed that individuals had a responsibility to improve the community in which they lived. Tichenor believed that Christianity had consistently had a positive influence upon society. While he was careful to add that the church's greatest responsibility lay in spiritual reformation, Tichenor clearly believed that if personal faith and the work of the church resulted in individual change, that change would be reflected in how others were perceived. Individual salvation led to social transformation.[19] Throughout his lengthy career, Tichenor frequently returned to these themes that he undoubtedly adapted from concepts developed as part of the Second Great Awakening.

Tichenor also recorded in his diary an expression of concern and even of veiled ambition, found in the notation recorded on his birthday. "This is my birthday—I am now twenty-five," he wrote. "Half of my life I may reasonably expect to live is already gone, and yet how little I have done for God. Nearly four years since I entered the ministry and how little have I accomplished." This brief diary and the few sermons included indicated Tichenor's sincere desire to see his church members actively participate in making their world a better place and to set high standards for himself.[20]

In fact, Tichenor's life was less than one-third complete, and he had neglected to acknowledge his achievements that were quite impressive for one so young. One may also find in his words a bit of motivation for later accomplishments. His words reflect a sense of higher purpose to his life and also a struggle to please God. Certainly, he had a youthful ambition to accomplish much in his lifetime. These underlying motivations would direct the remainder of his life. His two early pastorates, his brief work on behalf of the Indian Mission Association, his early work in the denomination, and his Kentucky heritage of cooperation and missions provided essential preparation for the challenges that lay ahead. In this period of life, he developed friendships with individuals and ideas that influenced the rest of his life. Also, these years demonstrate Tichenor's zeal for missions, his early concern regarding cooperation, and his intense interest in his denomination, even in the infancy of the Southern Baptist Convention.

After a year at Hendersonville, a reappearance of the persistent throat problem, probably brought on by the cooler climate of his home state, led the young pastor to look southward again for another opportunity of service. The frustration he expressed in his diary regarding his perceived lack of vocational progress may also have prompted him to look for a position of greater responsibility and prominence. This opportunity came in December 1851 when he was called to the Baptist church of Montgomery, Alabama. Isaac Taylor Tichenor began his ministry as the eighth pastor of this church in January 1852. He was then only twenty-six years old, and although he had very limited experience in his two previous pastorates, he served the church at Montgomery ably on two different occasions for a total of fifteen years. He followed Henry Talbird, a prominent Southern Baptist preacher, to the pulpit of First Baptist. Tichenor assumed the ministry at the church with reluctance because of his respect for Talbird.[21]

Other factors may have contributed to his reluctance. Montgomery First Baptist was, perhaps, the most influential Baptist church in the state. The state capital had recently relocated to Montgomery, and the city was strategically located in the Black Belt's heart, on the important artery of the Alabama River, and was experiencing significant growth. By 1860 Montgomery's population had grown to 8,843, still a distant second to Mobile but well ahead of Tuscaloosa, the previous state capital. It had quickly become not only one of the most important cities in Alabama but also one of the most important cities of the Deep South cotton states. "King Cotton" ruled Alabama's economy. Travelers passing through Montgomery in antebellum days found themselves surrounded by bales of cotton onboard the riverboats plying the Alabama river and overwhelmed by cotton conversation among its passengers. At every river stop, one observer wrote, the first question asked was, "What's cotton at?" Certainly, this "cotton fever" would have only worsened in the two decades prior to Tichenor's arrival in Montgomery. The growing city profited greatly from the growth of the cotton kingdom. One historical account of Montgomery on the eve of the Civil War describes it as "a place of wealth, architectural taste, and obvious commercial vigor" and as "the hub of trade in the southern and central Alabama hinterland" that had "a certain vibrancy." It was also a place whose "growth followed the rise and fall in cotton prices." One measure of its significance and strategic location would be the fact that less than a decade later, the seven states that seceded from the Union chose Montgomery for the Confederacy's first capital. An English visitor coming to Montgomery in 1859 wrote that Montgomery was a "pleasant town" and added that "everyone looks clean and well off, schools and churches bright and white as new pennies." However, in 1861 reporter William Howard Russell, another English visitor, was critical of the crowded new Confederate capital as unclean, hot, and infected with insect pests and rodents. No doubt, all of these conditions existed in 1852 when Tichenor arrived. The upstart capital city had a certain charm, but this charm was overshadowed by the bustle of a cotton-driven economy, an incredibly uncomfortable humidity, and the health risks created by the adjacent river area. A yellow fever epidemic erupted about two and a half years after Tichenor came to the city; it was so severe that Montgomery almost had to be abandoned and Tichenor himself became ill.[22]

Tichenor's reluctance to assume the Montgomery pastorate also may have been fostered by some feelings of inadequacy. In this era Baptists in particular increasingly recognized the strategic importance of developing southern cities. They were becoming more socially acceptable and upwardly mobile, and this contributed to a changing context for Baptist pastors. Many Baptist clergymen felt inadequate for the task of ministering in these cities, and Baptist leaders had difficulty locating prime candidates for strategic churches. The recommendation of Tichenor to such a prominent position at a relatively young age may have come as much from the dire shortage of intelligent and qualified urban ministers among Southern Baptists as from his abilities and experience. Perhaps the sermon he preached at Charleston at the 1849 SBC meeting served as a sort of "trial sermon" that demonstrated the elegant style desired in an urban location and hastened his upward mobility.[23]

Furthermore, his reluctance may have originated in the challenges the church itself posed. The church had been a leading supporter of missionary activities at a time when the anti-missions movement was strong among certain Alabama Baptists. The anti-missions movement originated in the 1820s, especially along the American frontier. It was comprised of different facets, including hyper-Calvinism, fears regarding centralization of authority, and primitive church impulses that rejected anything not specifically mentioned in the Bible. Anti-mission sentiments remained strong in Alabama in the 1840s and 1850s. As the pastor of First Baptist, Tichenor was expected to be a leader in promoting missions and combating the anti-missions movement.

He embraced this challenge but as a young pastor may have also been intimidated by it. Tichenor faced additional scrutiny because the church was home to many of the state's most influential political leaders. Consequently, as pastor he was challenged to move in intimate circles with Baptist leaders and prominent Alabama and southern politicians at critical times in the life of the fledgling denomination and in state, regional, and national politics. Finally, the church also had experienced internal tensions. When Tichenor began his pastorate there, the congregation needed a pastor to heal differences within the body.[24]

Apparently the young pastor proved equal to these tasks. As in his Mississippi pastorate, he successfully reconciled some of those involved in the schism that had divided the congregation. The improvements to the church were more than internal. When Tichenor came to Montgomery, the congregation worshiped in an old wooden building, but by 1854 they had built and dedicated an impressive new sanctuary. The building was state of the art for that day. Innovations included gas lighting, cushioned pews, carpeted aisles, and a built-in baptistry under the pulpit. During Tichenor's first pastorate at Montgomery, the white membership almost doubled and the black membership increased substantially. A series of protracted meetings or revivals in 1854 and the start of two preaching points and Sunday schools in other parts of the city stimulated this significant numerical growth. In 1856 he held a successful series of protracted meetings for Montgomery's African-American community. Tichenor later wrote one friend that these preaching points and Sunday schools were initiated and supported by members of First Baptist without "expecting [Tichenor] to do the whole work." This statement demonstrates another side to Tichenor's leadership, depicting him as a leader concerned with a shared ministry, rejoicing in lay leadership and delegating tasks to others.[25]

The congregation's growth was more than numerical. In his time in Montgomery, both the church and its pastor blossomed as state and denominational leaders. Perhaps part of the reason for Tichenor's growth as a minister resulted from the spiritual and intellectual challenge of ministering to a congregation such as the Montgomery church. Some members of his church were already prominent politicians and educators: Thomas H. Watts, leading southern Whig who later served as attorney general of the Confederacy and as Alabama's governor; Henry Bacon, first president of the Alabama Female College in Tuskegee; Noah Davis, a former president of Howard College in Marion and later president of both Alabama's Judson College and Kentucky's Bethel College. Other individuals such as state legislator and future Howard College president Jabez L. M. Curry and William Williams, one of the original faculty of the Southern Baptist Theological Seminary, worshiped regularly at the church. In the 1850s Curry was a state legislator from Talladega County who worshipped at Montgomery's FBC when the legislature was in session. Later he became not only a college president but also a leading southern congressman, both prior to the war, in the Confederate States government, and after Reconstruction. Ultimately, he was appointed U.S. ambassador to Spain. He became a key Baptist educator and noted Baptist statesman. Their pathways would intersect again in the coming years, and Curry is indicative of the quality of individuals with whom Tichenor would have been associated. Among those baptized into the membership in Tichenor's first year as pastor was Albert J. Pickett, Alabama's first historian. Tichenor's later leadership in the state of Alabama, in the South, and in the Southern Baptist Convention can be traced back to his mingling with these and other significant individuals. He observed key political leaders at work, led them in church activities, and honed his oratorical skills in the presence of respected orators.[26]

Like the state itself, Alabama Baptists were growing in dramatic fashion, becoming the largest denomination in the state by 1860. Some of Tichenor's opportunities resulted from his allegiance to the young denomination and to personal leadership skills. For instance, at the 1852 Alabama convention in Marion, Tichenor chaired the committee on periodicals and was appointed as a representative to a subsequent temperance convention in Selma. He assumed an active role as the temperance movement took hold among Baptists in the South. He was also active in the Alabama Baptist Bible Society, which he served as president in 1858. In other years, he served as chairman of the State Temperance Committee, the State of Religion Committee, and the Domestic Missions Committee, among other responsibilities.[27]

Tichenor remained equally active in the biennial meetings of the Southern Baptist Convention during these years. At the 1853 convention in Baltimore, he served on the Board of Managers for the Domestic Mission Board and the convention appointed him to the time, place, and preacher committee. From the latter position, he successfully brought an invitation from Montgomery's First Baptist Church to host the SBC's next meeting.[28]

Hosting the convention in its new sanctuary was a highlight in the young church's history. Likewise, a number of FBC families provided lodging for convention members, which created stronger ties with the young denomination's constituents. Overall, the event cast Tichenor and his congregation in a good light as well as allowing Baptists to make a positive impact upon the growing capital city. This convention was important for Tichenor personally in several other ways. He developed friendships with several prominent Baptist leaders, including A. M. Poindexter, Foreign Mission Board corresponding secretary. Subsequent to the meeting, Poindexter wrote Tichenor concerning the convention's results. Tichenor responded to Poindexter's inquiries with a letter dated June 5, 1855:

> The "impression" made by the Convention on the community was in some respects very favorable. . . . The community were [sic] utterley [sic] surprised at the amount of talent collected together. The impression is that no body of men so able has ever assembled in this place. . . . On the whole the impression is largely for good—Many of the delegates secured the highest esteem of those families in which they tarried and left them with the deepest desire for another Baptist Convention to be held there.[29]

The letter initiated correspondence between the two men regarding Foreign Mission Board matters as well as other concerns. This correspondence continued well into the 1860s. Among items discussed between the two in the 1850s were recommendations of an appointee to the Foreign Mission Board, collections made for the board, and concerns relevant to Tichenor's work in Montgomery.[30]

Tichenor's friendship with Poindexter encouraged the young minister's interest in foreign missions. With Tichenor's leadership the church blossomed in its support of both foreign and home missions. On the foreign fields, First Baptist was active in support of Clara and R. W. Priest in 1856 and 1857 and, after the Priests returned from Africa, in its support of Sarah and John Quincy Adams Rohrer, appointees to Japan. Both these efforts ended tragically. The Priests proved unable to cope with the climate, disease, and hardship of the work in Africa, and the Rohrers perished at sea.[31]

Tichenor, who wrote a report to the *South Western Baptist* on R. W. Priest's ordination, took an intense interest in the Priests, as several letters to Poindexter indicate. He was especially concerned with refuting arguments against the support of African missions. He wrote:

I find some of our brethren are greatly discouraged about the African possession. I mean some of our most influential members. They say that among the *natives* there have not more conversion[s] than *missionaries* sent out in the last fifteen years. They say that the climate has proven to be deathly to white men and that God's providence seems to have closed the field against our efforts. . . . I wish you would write the strongest article you can in refutation of these objections. Give us a comparison between our African Missions and some other new mission, research for example.[32]

This incident in Tichenor's Montgomery pastorate indicates a heightened interest in the missions enterprise and a cooperative spirit in supporting missions. Interest in and sympathy with cooperative mission work became a critical component that shaped Tichenor's opinions and his future. Tichenor's response also shows his desire to obtain as many of the facts as possible in order to argue for the support of missions and denominational interests. It demonstrates a theological rejection of a strong Calvinistic tendency to explain the failure of the African endeavor to "God's providence." It displays a desire to support the denomination's larger work even at the risk of controversy within his church. Perhaps most importantly, it exhibits an individual with a vision of the broader issues involved.

Another reason for the importance of the 1855 convention upon Tichenor's life was the way it increased his and his church's interest in domestic missions. The meeting resulted in the merging of the Indian Missions Association with the Domestic Mission Board and signaled the emergence of support for missionary H. F. Buckner from the Montgomery congregation. The church's first pastor, Lee Compere, had been active in mission work among the Creek Indians, and the Creek people originally had resided in central and eastern Alabama, so this support seemed natural for the mission-minded pastor and his people. Buckner spoke of his work among the Creek Indians in the Indian Territory in the 1855 meeting "with great effect." No doubt, this presentation of the church's historic ties to mission work among these transplanted Alabama Native Americans made the effort attractive to First Baptist Church.[33] It is quite possible that, along with Tichenor's early work for the Indian Missions Association, the support of Buckner and his work influenced him in other ways. It would have demonstrated to Tichenor the need for a more systematic and cooperative form of missions support. This early interest in the Native American mission field also may have helped generate the intensity with which Tichenor would deal with the controversial concerns that developed in the Indian Territory during his later tenure as the Home Mission Board corresponding secretary.

The 1855 meeting in Montgomery was not without controversy. The most intense debate centered upon the issue of resuming the traditional courtesy of extending non-Baptist ministers seats at the convention. The apparent underlying cause of this discussion was the explosive topic of Landmarkism.[34]

Landmarkism was a movement originating in Southern Baptist life in the mid-nineteenth century under the leadership of James Robinson Graves. A Baptist pastor and newspaper editor, Graves was probably one of the most powerful Baptist preachers of that day. He probably influenced Southern Baptist life more than any other single individual in various ways. His constant agitation and angry attacks kept Southern Baptists in almost constant uproar for approximately thirty years. Landmarkism insisted that Baptists had the only true churches and could trace their lineage in an unbroken line to the New Testament. Graves and his allies, J. M. Pendleton and A. C. Dayton, achieved considerable influence throughout the nineteenth century, especially in the old southwestern states of Alabama, Mississippi, Tennessee, Arkansas, and Louisiana. Graves and his followers insisted upon closed communion (only Baptists could participate in the Lord's Supper) and opposed alien immersion (only Baptist baptisms were recognized). Like the earlier movement called the Primitive Baptists and the critiques issued by Alexander Campbell and the Disciples of Christ movement, Graves also questioned the ecclesiological foundations of the SBC and the structure of its mission boards, believing mission boards violated New Testament principles of local church autonomy. The key document of the Landmark movement was the Cotton Grove Resolutions issued in 1851 in Tennessee. Landmarkism came to the forefront of Baptist debate in the 1850s and proved to be a major source of controversy in the new Southern Baptist Convention. In fact, probably no other single internal issue or idea in the SBC created as much conflict as did Landmarkism in the nineteenth century.[35] While the Landmark conflict waned somewhat after the Civil War, outcroppings of Landmarkism occurred on the Baptist landscape throughout the remainder of the nineteenth century and into the twentieth, and Tichenor would be forced to address these outcroppings once he became a denominational leader.

Tichenor apparently referred to this controversy and the ensuing debate in his correspondence with Poindexter when he wrote, "Some of the pedobaptist friends (?) have tried in a quiet way to detract from this [good impression created by SBC meeting in Montgomery] by speaking of the stormy debates, etc." While it cannot be ascertained whether Tichenor took part in the debate, he worked to defuse the volatile nature of the confrontation in the 1859 convention, and later correspondence reveals that Tichenor opposed Graves's agenda in the 1867 Southern Baptist Convention.[36] Likewise, Tichenor had no aversion to preaching in pedobaptist churches and, while not advocating infant baptism, maintained good relations with other Protestant denominations. Tichenor often recalled the Presbyterian minister's friendship in Columbus when he was serving in his first pastorate.

At the 1855 meeting the first discussions were held concerning the founding of Southern Seminary in Greenville, South Carolina. Due to his assistance, Tichenor was considered a proponent of the seminary. Earlier, he had chaired the State Education Committee for the Alabama State Convention and, as a representative of the committee, issued a report that served as an apologetic for the lack of education among Baptist ministers and at the same time defended higher education. It commended the founding of Southern Baptist Theological Seminary by introducing a resolution that stated "that the Convention heartily approves of the objects sought to be accomplished by the establishment of the Southern Baptist Theological Seminary." The report also praised the four original faculty members—Boyce, Broadus, Manly, and Williams—for their "youthful and vigorous minds, and hearts devoted to their Master's cause." It encouraged the Baptists of Alabama to "do their full share towards the establishment of this young and promising Institution." It further called for Baptists to create endowments for both Southern Seminary and Alabama's Howard College. Tichenor's role in issuing such a report is significant because many Southern Baptists retained an anti-education bias, especially with regard to their pastors. Perhaps as much in honor of his support of the school as in recognition of his abilities, Southern Seminary chose him to preach its first commencement address in 1860. His text was "Who is sufficient for these things?" A press report stated that "Tichenor's sermon was full of noble thoughts and delivered in his best style."[37] Tichenor was being increasingly recognized as one of the outstanding public speakers in Southern Baptist life. Also once again, Tichenor's position on a critical issue, ministerial education, placed him at odds with both anti-mission and Landmark Baptist movements in the South.

Tichenor's active involvement in SBC matters set him apart from many Baptist ministers who found the expenses of attending such meetings prohibitive on relatively low salaries. It was not unusual for a typical trip to a convention meeting outside the state to cost more than one month's salary for the average Alabama pastor. His involvement indicates the support and encouragement of his church as well as his own interest. Another factor that discouraged ministers from association with denominational activity was the fiercely independent nature of Baptist polity and a nascent suspicion of denominational hierarchies fostered by national politics and anti-missions, Restorationist, and Landmark controversies. His involvement demonstrates that Tichenor was apparently unconcerned about questions regarding centralization of the missions enterprise or concerns about local church autonomy. Tichenor's participation in denominational matters continued, as he was also active in the 1857 convention meeting in Louisville. He served in several capacities there, as committee member along with James Petigru Boyce and J. H. DeVotie on the work of the Coliseum Place Baptist Church in New Orleans, on the time, place, and preacher committee, and on the important committee to nominate new boards. In 1859 he attended the SBC meeting in Richmond, where he moved a resolution requesting that the religious newspapers publish a previous resolution passed in the convention. This resolution expressed "our earnest conviction that personal controversies among pastors, editors, and brethren should from this time forth be more than studiously avoided." This resolution indicated the SBC's continuing controversy over the Landmark question.[38]

In 1860 Tichenor's wife of seven years, Monimia Clementine, died from disease, leaving him a widower caring for two young daughters, Mary, age six, and Kate, age four. Late in 1860, Tichenor again suffered health problems. As a result of these events, he resigned to take a less strenuous job as Georgia's collecting agent for Southern Seminary and moved his family to Columbus, Georgia. About that time he began to court his second wife, Emily Boykin of the prominent Baptist family from the Columbus, Georgia, area. One of Emily's brothers served as editor of the *Christian Index,* the Georgia Baptist newspaper. The Tichenor genealogy records that "The Boykin family is described in one genealogy as 'a fine old South Carolina family—noted for beautiful women.'" After marrying Emily Boykin in April 1861, Tichenor moved his young family to the Boykin plantation.[39] This series of events ended a very successful pastorate in Montgomery.

During Tichenor's tenure, First Baptist Church had grown and broadened its interest in convention and statewide causes. It supported Henry F. Buckner as missionary to the Indians and built a new sanctuary. Its pastor displayed denominational leadership in a variety of causes: missions, especially domestic missions; periodicals, literature publication, and Bible distribution; temperance; and education. He served as messenger of the Alabama convention to other state conventions, thus giving him exposure in other parts of the South. He ministered to and among some of the state's leading commercial and political figures and developed friendships with the most significant Southern Baptists of his day. Tichenor's involvement in SBC affairs in its formative years was likewise significant for him. He was exposed to individuals responsible for forming the convention who were familiar with the reasons for its origins, both that of strong sectionalism and pro-slavery sentiments and a desire to engage in the convention method of missions support. Tichenor's participation in state convention and SBC affairs was in contrast to other pastors of his era who found such participation cost-prohibitive or contrary to their beliefs regarding the autonomous nature of the local church, or who considered mission boards contrary to the interpretation of the Bible. Tichenor's active participation proved essential to his development as a leader, and the recognition he achieved was important for both him and his church. All of these connections ultimately contributed to his future in significant ways. Perhaps more importantly, the eight years of this pastorate fully transformed Tichenor into a southerner. Serving as pastor in a city later called the "Cradle of the Confederacy" and his role in the early years of the Southern Baptist Convention uniquely molded his attitudes about what it meant to be "southern." In many ways, Tichenor's southernness dated from these formative years as a young minister in Montgomery. Being exposed to a wide variety of political figures, from the more moderate southern Whig, Thomas Watts, to the firebrand secessionist Democrat, William L. Yancey, caused Tichenor to examine his own attitudes. Altogether, his years as pastor of First Baptist Church of Montgomery constituted another step in a pilgrimage of preparation for the tasks that lay before him.

2

The Emerging Sectionalist

Tichenor as Confederate Chaplain and Pastor, 1861–65

When I. T. Tichenor left Montgomery in late 1860, events were already in motion that would drastically alter his future plans. Like the rest of the nation, he had been participating in unfolding events that would result in the cataclysm of the Civil War. The division of the Baptist denomination in 1845 and the creation of the Southern Baptist Convention heralded the coming schism over the question of slavery. An episode during Tichenor's Montgomery pastorate indicated these growing tensions. One Sunday in the spring of 1856 a group of about 250 young southern men on their way to the Kansas Territory stopped for worship at the First Baptist Church. Two years earlier the Kansas-Nebraska Act had opened Kansas for settlement. Though the territory had been closed by law to slavery as a result of the Missouri Compromise, the act allowed settlers in the territory to decide slavery's status there on the basis of popular sovereignty. The result was that in successive years, both radical abolitionists and radical pro-slavery advocates flooded the beleaguered territory in an effort to sway the outcome.

These 250 men passing through Montgomery hoped to claim the newly opened land as slave territory. Ascertaining that many of the young men did not have Bibles, the congregation took up a collection and provided each man a Bible and the entire company a pulpit Bible for use in the Kansas church when they arrived. Tichenor made the presentation, stating that these were true Bibles, unlike the rifles called "Beecher's Bibles" that abolitionists were purported to be shipping to Kansas. One observer wrote that his "address" was made "with such effect, that it was said there was not a dry eye in all the assemblage, and a deep religious impression appeared to be made upon all minds."[1]

Although it is not known whether Tichenor ever clearly stated his exact position on secession prior to the event, once secession came, he embraced its call. Perhaps Tichenor's position was like that of his church member, deacon, and friend, Thomas H. Watts. Watts was born in Butler County, Alabama, and graduated from the University of Virginia. Six years older than Tichenor, Watts practiced law in Greenville, Alabama, until 1847. He moved to Montgomery that year, only a few years before Tichenor. Watts served as a state legislator from both Butler County and Montgomery. He ran unsuccessfully for governor in 1861. As a former Whig and Unionist, Watts originally opposed secession. Certainly Tichenor's roots in Kentucky, the home of Whig leader Henry Clay, might have contributed to his viewpoints as well as his friendship with Watts. Once secession came, however, Watts proved loyal to the southern cause. In the Reconstruction era, he became a committed Democrat. No doubt, there were many others with whom Tichenor associated who were rabid secessionists. It is unclear which position Tichenor held, although later events in his Montgomery pastorate indicated that, like Watts, he became a devoted southern nationalist.[2]

The first shots of southern secession were fired at Fort Sumter on April 12, 1861, and as a result thousands of young men flocked to the banners of the Confederacy. Subsequently, at the public's urging and in recognition of the fact that clergymen already served with the soldiers, the Confederate Congress passed Bill 102 on May 3, 1861, providing for chaplains in the Confederate armies. The bill also gave notice of pay, and a later bill in August granted private's rations to the chaplains. In the following four years, thousands of men responded to this call, and by the spring of 1862, an estimated half of the South's clergy was in Confederate service. This support of the chaplaincy by southern ministers was significant despite the fact that many of these men faced numerous obstacles once they entered service.[3]

When the war began, Tichenor, his health recovered, answered the call for chaplains. Many members of his former church in Montgomery had volunteered for service with the Seventeenth Alabama Regiment under the command of his former church member, Colonel Thomas H. Watts. Watts had just been narrowly defeated in his gubernatorial election bid and formed the Confederate regiment. The Seventeenth Alabama Regiment was primarily composed of companies from Watts's home county, Butler, and his current residence, Montgomery County, but also included companies from six other Alabama counties. Watts appointed Tichenor as chaplain and subsequently the soldiers in the regiment referred to him as "Captain." The title was a result of respect for Tichenor, rather than any official appointment. The Confederate Congress never granted official ranks for chaplains at any time in the war. After organization near Montgomery, the regiment was sent to Major General Braxton Bragg's division at Pensacola, Florida, and participated in the unsuccessful siege and bombardment of Fort Pickens.[4]

As chaplain, Tichenor performed a number of never-ending duties, all considered a part of ministering to the needs of the men. The responsibilities included providing leadership for worship services and prayer meetings, especially when no active campaigning took place, such as was the case at Pensacola. Tichenor, given the speaking ability credited to him at other times in his life, was probably a popular preacher. He also would have provided communion services. Additionally, Tichenor probably provided services such as writing letters for soldiers who were illiterate or too ill to write their families or writing the families of deceased soldiers. Likewise, while at Pensacola he was called upon to assist in the funeral services for a young chaplain, Noble Leslie DeVotie, who accidentally drowned in Mobile Bay while serving with Confederate units at Fort Morgan. Chaplains visited army hospitals and frequently solicited community aid to supplement the meager supplies provided by the Confederate commissary.[5]

By spring 1862, Confederate armies were in full retreat. Confederate forces in Virginia had withdrawn from northern Virginia because of the superior numbers of the Union Army of the Potomac, other Union armies had captured significant portions of the North Carolina coast, and the Confederate army in Arkansas had been defeated at the battle of Pea Ridge and forced to withdraw to the southern portion of that state. Most devastatingly, Union armies had pushed Albert Sydney Johnston's Confederate Army of Tennessee out of Kentucky and, because of defeats at Forts Henry and Donelson, the Confederates abandoned the critical city of Nashville and most of the central part of Tennessee. Because of this drastic turn of events, the Confederate high command determined to concentrate all available forces under Johnston's command and try to strike a blow in southern Tennessee that would turn the tide. The army ordered Bragg's division to Corinth, Mississippi, to combine with Johnston's Army of Tennessee. With Bragg's other regiments, the Seventeenth Alabama moved by rail from Pensacola to Mobile and then north to

Corinth on the Mobile and Ohio Railroad. In transit to the battlefield, the regiment encountered great hardship. Caught in "chilling rains and deep mud" and forced to leave their baggage behind, Colonel Watts and his officers, probably including Tichenor, refused to move the soldiers to the next location, Purdy. Subsequently, Watts and his officers were placed under military arrest. While no direct evidence links Tichenor to this mutiny, the regimental history always listed him with the officers and staff, and years later he recalled that during the Tennessee campaign "the soldiers became so hungry that they would take the corn from the horses' food and eat it." Despite this episode, the troops in Bragg's division were considered among the best disciplined and trained forces in the Army of Tennessee.[6]

While under arrest Watts received his appointment to the Confederate cabinet as attorney general. Lieutenant Colonel Robert Fariss replaced Watts as regimental commander. Under the brigade command of Brigadier General John K. Jackson, in the division of Brigadier General Jones K. Withers and the corps of Major General Braxton Bragg, the regiment participated in the first great battle of the West at Shiloh. The Confederate battle plan placed Bragg's command on the right center in the attack. The overall plan called for the right wing, including Bragg's command, to push Union forces away from the Tennessee River and its line of supply and reinforcement. From almost the beginning of the battle this portion of the plan went awry.[7]

It was at Shiloh that Tichenor gained his only combat experience. This battle gained him the title "The Fighting Chaplain" and earned him a reputation he would carry the rest of his life. In fact, the Confederate chaplaincy proved to be a key experience for many southern ministers. These ministers often referred to episodes in the war as the defining moment of their lives. Tichenor was no exception to this.[8]

On Sunday, April 6, 1862, the battle opened on the left of the Confederate army, and the southerners drove back the Union forces in disarray. On the day prior to the battle, Tichenor went, by request of an officer, with the vanguard of the brigade. Thus, he was in position on Sunday morning to observe and participate in the opening of action as a scout, observing the empty camps of the enemy and reporting back to the command. According to Tichenor's account, he subsequently engaged in the capture of a squad of Union soldiers on the extreme left of the regiment. As he later remembered, "Though I had no command, as no officer was present, the men obeyed my instructions implicitly." A short time later, he also contributed to the capture of a lieutenant colonel of the Fiftieth Illinois. At one point during the battle many of the officers were killed or wounded, and some of the men looked to Tichenor for leadership. Not only did he serve as a leader but also, while attempting to locate some enemy sharpshooters at one point in the battle, one such sharpshooter targeted the chaplain. Armed with a Colt repeating rifle he had gotten from a wounded soldier, the chaplain displayed his skill as a sharpshooter by killing the enemy sniper, the first of several victims of his marksmanship. Later, the newspapers reported that he had killed during the battle "a colonel, a major, and four privates." Tichenor himself originally admitted to killing only two men and wounding another. Apparently, the men respected Tichenor enough that they quickly obeyed his orders despite the fact that he carried no official rank.[9]

As the battle wore on, a minié ball struck the leather belt Tichenor wore. The belt deflected the projectile, and while it knocked him down and badly bruised him, the chaplain escaped serious injury. The projectile was probably spent or nearly spent, as normally a minié ball would have penetrated his abdomen and such a wound would have proved mortal. Tichenor always regarded his survival an act of divine intervention. After this event, Tichenor and the troops continued their advance. The Seventeenth Alabama was engaged on the extreme right of the army, attempting to surround Union soldiers defending the portion of the battlefield later known as the Hornets' Nest. At one point in the fighting there, units on either side of the regiment withdrew. The Alabamians began suffering heavy casualties in the open field in front of the Federal stronghold.[10]

Shortly thereafter, the regiment came under a severe cross fire and faltered. Tichenor recalled,

> During this engagement we were under a crossfire . . . from three directions. Under it the boys wavered. I had been wounded and was sitting down but seeing them waver, I sprang to my feet—took off my hat—waved it over my head—walked up and down the line, and, they say, "preached them a sermon." I reminded them that it was Sunday. That at that hour . . . all their home folks were praying for them; that Tom Watts—excuse the familiar way in which I employed so distinguished a name—had told us he would listen with an eager ear to hear from the Seventeenth; shouting your name loud over the roar of battle, I called upon them to stand there and die, if need be, for their country. The

effect was evident. Every man stood to his post, every eye flashed, and every heart beat high with desperate resolve to conquer or die. They piled that ground high with Yankee slain.[11]

Tichenor added, "I am satisfied—more than satisfied—with my labors as chaplain of the 17th. I feel in my heart the consciousness that in no other position could I have served the cause of my God and my country so well and I am more than recompensed for all my toils and privations."[12]

The type of rhetoric Tichenor used in this episode is consistent with descriptions of southern oratory in the antebellum and Civil War eras. While the war radically modified the South, and soldiers found their lives dramatically altered, one consistent presence throughout both southern culture and army was that of orators. Officers, ministers, politicians, and others consistently utilized spoken rhetoric to motivate their soldiers and the population whether in drill, battle, church, or community. In fact, "some accounts suggest that the Confederate army was as devoted to rhetoric as it was to fighting."[13]

There is no evidence that Tichenor ever displayed any regret over having left the chaplain's usual role of ministering to spiritual and physical needs to move into the front lines. Nor is there any evidence that the chaplain ever demonstrated any remorse for having used a weapon and taken the lives of others. Tichenor may well have considered his efforts self-defense. Certainly, he fired his initial shots at a sharpshooter who had chosen him as a target. He also considered taking a combat role part of his attempt to share in the dangers of the men to whom he was ministering. Clearly, he saw no ethical dilemma in participation in combat in this fashion, including utilization of his own excellent marksmanship. One recent observer has concluded, however, that Tichenor later purposely de-emphasized his martial participation and stressed his rhetorical role when he recalled events.[14]

Several hours later, after the surrender of Federal forces in the Hornets' Nest, the Seventeenth Alabama guarded prisoners briefly before continuing to advance and coming under fire from Union gunboats on the Tennessee. So severe were the regiment's casualties that they were withdrawn from the front and participated little in the second day's fighting. On the subsequent retreat, the regiment made up a part of the rear guard of the army. Withers's reported casualty figures further verify the severity of the fight for the Seventeenth Alabama.[15]

The Confederate attack at Shiloh failed. Arrival of reinforcements turned the tide of battle in the Union's favor on the second day of fighting and forced the southern army to retreat. The battle had been a rude awakening for all Americans, and it especially disheartened the South. The words of a New Orleans resident have been often quoted that after Shiloh "the South never smiled again." More Americans fell at Shiloh than in all previous American wars combined. The dead included Confederate General Johnston. Ultimately, the Seventeenth Alabama's division commander, Braxton Bragg, became commander of the Army of Tennessee. Bragg served in this capacity until after the battle of Chattanooga in November 1863. His brigade commander, John K. Jackson, served with the Army of Tennessee until virtually the end of the war, as did many of the members of the Seventeenth Alabama.[16]

Tichenor withdrew to Corinth with the troops at the close of the battle. Though the Confederates were forced to withdraw at Shiloh, the Seventeenth Alabama and their chaplain had covered themselves with laurels. General Jackson made conspicuous mention of the regiment's bravery and their capture of two stands of Union colors in his report, and the *Religious Herald* reported that "the fighting chaplain" had "fought with the coolness and intrepidity of a veteran." The *South Western Baptist* echoed the Virginia Baptist paper's praises: "We thank God for such a man, and for the preservation of his valuable life." In 1864 when the University of Alabama awarded him an honorary doctor of divinity degree, Tichenor admitted that it was in no small part due "to that little affair at Shiloh." Tichenor's reputation in the South in general, and in Alabama specifically, increased because of his conduct in the battle.[17]

Not everyone approved of Tichenor's conduct at Shiloh. Some claimed he was not nearly as active in combat as originally reported. While he was not alone among Confederate chaplains in assuming a combatant's role in battle and while he contended that he had "the satisfaction of knowing that my conduct on that bloody day met the hearty approval of every officer and private in the regiment," for his participation in the fighting General Jackson "censured [Tichenor] even to the verge of insult." Accordingly, Tichenor submitted his resignation to Secretary of War George W. Randolph. In his resignation letter, Tichenor stated, "I cannot consent to retain my present position in the army, unless I have the privilege of sharing with the men, the dangers of the field, as well as the privations of the camp."[18]

Tichenor's statement was consistent with the observations of later writers about the unique position of the chaplain. If a chaplain were to earn the respect of a unit's men, he had to be willing to confront the perils of combat even though he had permission to remain in the rear.[19] Chaplain H. Clay Trumbull wrote,

A chaplain had a duty to inspire men for the service for their country. If he was himself a coward, or seemed unready to face a soldier's perils, no words from him could have weight with his men. His influence for good was destroyed among them. If . . . their chaplain shared the dangers bravely, his men gave him more than full credit for his courage and fidelity, and were the readier to do their duty under his direct appeals.[20]

Clearly, this was what Tichenor sought to do.

Jackson approved the resignation, stating that "the chaplain was not in the discharge of his proper duty—that instead of adding to the horrors of war, he should have been ministering spiritual consolation to the dying." The new colonel of the Seventeenth Alabama, appointed from outside the regiment, added his approval, stating, "the Regiment does not require a fighting parson." Perhaps there was more to this than simply a difference of opinion regarding the battlefield role of a chaplain. It is quite possible that the absence of his friend Thomas Watts from the command of the Seventeenth Alabama may have both contributed to Tichenor's disenchantment over the situation and denied him an advocate who would have spoken in his behalf. Jackson may have also acted out of lingering resentment toward the regiment due to the aforementioned "mutiny" by the officers, of which Tichenor may have been considered a part. On at least two other occasions in latter battles, subordinate commanders or other men serving under Jackson had substantial and heated disagreements with the general. Jackson's nature may have contributed to the severity of the conflict with Tichenor and led to his resignation.[21] Furthermore, the effects of wounded pride upon Tichenor should not be discounted. As later events in his life would show, he was not always a humble servant. He was a proud man, and his involvement in combat at Shiloh remained a source of great pride for him for years afterward. To have the brigade commander criticize his performance, a role that he believed qualified him for praise rather than reprimand, would have been an unbearable humiliation. No doubt this incident wounded Tichenor's honor terribly. Still, if Tichenor had been most concerned with sharing the burdens of the common soldier, he would have swallowed his pride and remained in his role as chaplain rather than return to the relative comforts of home and family—an option enlisted men did not have.

A few months later the Southern Baptist Convention Domestic Mission Board commissioned Tichenor as a Baptist missionary to the Army of Tennessee. He served for a few months in East Tennessee in this capacity. When his division advanced in support of General Bragg's invasion of Kentucky in the fall of 1862, Tichenor marched with the Thirty-first Alabama regiment. He did not see combat, but he attended actively to the physical and spiritual needs of the army. Some accounts related that the native Kentuckian used his oratorical skills to prod Kentucky residents to join the Confederate cause. Despite seeing no additional active combat, Tichenor gave a thorough report of his activities to the *South Western Baptist.* These accounts demonstrated Tichenor's deep concern for the spiritual welfare of the troops in his care. Unfortunately, family situations forced a return to Columbus, Georgia, where Tichenor remained for the rest of the year.[22]

While his service as a military chaplain and missionary lasted only a little more than a year, Tichenor exhibited personal traits of bravery and boldness, oratorical skills, and coolness in combat. One can see also that his leadership manifested itself in a way not evident prior to this experience. It also demonstrates that he was not personally squeamish about taking human life in self-defense or in defense of a cause he believed to be just. He was not unique among southern ministers in his viewpoints, nor was he exclusive among chaplains who took weapons in hand during combat. Others were similarly given the informal title of "fighting chaplain," and some ministers cast aside all pretense of the chaplaincy to serve as combat soldiers. In his recent book *While God Is Marching On: The Religious World of Civil War Soldiers,* Steven Woodworth documents numerous chaplains who performed similar roles and had similar opinions. Woodworth writes,

The proper role of the chaplain when his regiment went into battle was not clearly defined, and the Civil War saw great variation among chaplains in how they handled this difficult situation. Some did remain safely in the rear, but many did not. A fair number believed that their rightful place was similar to that of the rest of the regimental field and staff officers, a few paces behind the file-closers. There they would walk forward behind the regimental battle line, unarmed, ready to help the wounded when they fell.[23]

Woodworth adds, "Some chaplains actually displayed a surprising propensity for battle and a few even looked more the warrior than the cleric." He gives several accounts of both Union and Confederate chaplains who took weapon in hand either occasionally or regularly, despite the fact that some soldiers believed it "inconsistent for a minister of the gospel to engage in warfare."[24] Tichenor at Shiloh would have fallen into the category of these "warrior-clerics"; apparently his two immediate superiors fell into the latter category who believed his actions inappropriate.

Though brief, Tichenor's service is also significant because it indicates his deep southern loyalties. Undoubtedly, loyal southerners who were Baptists recalled Tichenor's experiences as he attempted to rally them in the years to follow to support the Southern Baptist Convention. At times his rhetoric would rise to heights reminiscent of his battlefield "sermon" to the Seventeenth Alabama at Shiloh. His southern nationalism undoubtedly influenced him to retain the sectional identity of the SBC and to seek to preserve and extend Southern Baptist work. It gave him important credibility in a time when southerners baptized the lost cause in the blood of divine redemption. Later, as president of Alabama A & M and as chief executive of the Home Mission Board, Tichenor made numerous references to the war. He utilized battlefield language in his defense of southern territory from Northern Baptist "invasions." His southern nationalism must have contributed significantly to his sometimes bitter defense of the South and his implication that those who worked with the Northern Baptists were essentially "traitors" to the SBC.

Tichenor's successor at First Baptist, respected Southern Baptist pastor Basil Manly Sr., left the church in late 1862. Finding their former pastor now willing and able to return, the congregation again called Tichenor to begin his second pastorate there in January 1863. The church struggled throughout the war years, and the thirty-seven-year-old pastor worked hard as the ravages of war destroyed the southern economy. Yet, he, like others, remained loyal to "the cause."[25]

Immediately after the removal of the Confederate capital to Richmond in 1861, Montgomery had essentially returned to antebellum normalcy. The impressive sanctuary built in Tichenor's first term as pastor maintained its prominent location on North Court Street. Nearby, the Episcopal Methodist and Protestant Methodist congregations met on Court and Bibb Streets. Presbyterians, Episcopalians, and Roman Catholics all held services regularly in their respective locations. A newly constructed Jewish synagogue occupied a significant spot in the community. Corn and cotton grew close to the city limits, and roaming cattle and hogs posed a problem, even within the city limits. Homes in Montgomery represented the disparate income levels of Montgomerians that indicated the wide range of southern social and economic classes.[26]

By the time Tichenor returned to First Baptist Church, evidence of the war began to be more apparent. Located in the interior of the deep South, Montgomery became a location for several hospitals for wounded and convalescing Confederate soldiers. While not achieving the strategic prominence of other southern cities like Chattanooga, Atlanta, or even southern neighbor Mobile, Montgomery became an important location for storage of army supplies. Both the Alabama River and the rail lines that connected Atlanta with the South and West added to Montgomery's significance, especially as the war crept ever southward. The Confederate Commissary Department utilized the city as a depot for food and uniform storage, the Montgomery arsenal served as storage for firearms, and small factories sprang up to supply war needs. The existing Montgomery Iron Works was already well established. Despite these efforts, the difficulties imposed by the Union blockade, hardships brought on by zealous impressment agents, and the crippling effects of inflation devastated Montgomery's fragile economy. As the cotton kingdom dissolved, so too the economy of Montgomery crumbled.[27] As a citizen of Montgomery and as pastor of one of its more prominent churches, Tichenor was forced to deal with the reality of day-to-day existence. With many local leaders at the front lines or in Richmond, Tichenor would have assumed a more visible role in local leadership.

On August 21, 1863, the Alabama legislature asked Tichenor to bring its "Fast Day" sermon. Both Union and Confederate governments called for periodic days of prayer and fasting throughout the war. The Confederacy was reeling from the twin disasters of the Battle of Gettysburg and the capture of the stronghold of Vicksburg a little more than a month earlier. With these defeats, virtually any Confederate hope of European mediation of the conflict or of alliances with Great Britain or France had died. Tichenor designed his sermon on this occasion to bring a divine message in the midst of political and theological crises. His sermon demonstrated that earlier victories in the war at places like Manassas and Chancellorsville had convinced southerners that God sided with them despite the tremendous odds facing the Confederacy. The recent defeats, like the ultimate defeat of the Confederacy in 1865, caused white southerners loyal to the Confederacy to question God's hand in these events. Tichenor attempted to bring some sense out of the recent major defeats that the South had suffered. This Fast Day message was delivered to the General Assembly of the state and was so popular that he was requested to publish it in the secular press. The text for the sermon was Psalm 46:9, "He maketh wars to cease unto the end of the earth; He breaketh the bow and cutteth the spear in sunder; He burneth the chariot in fire."[28]

Tichenor began the message with an eloquent introduction with which many would have identified. He asked, "When shall we have peace?" He added:

Two weary years of war have wrung this question from the agonized heart of our bleeding country. "Oh! That we could have peace!" exclaims the statesman, as he ponders the problems that demand solution at his hands. "Peace," sighs the soldier, as he wraps his blanket around him and lies down to sleep upon the open field. "Peace!" moans the widow, as she reads the fatal news of her heroic husband fallen on some bloody field, and bitterly thinks of the darkened future in store for herself and her orphaned children. The prayer of the land is for peace. You may hear it in the sanctuary, at the fireside, around the family altar, in the silent chamber, on the tented field. *When will it come?*[29]

The three points of his response to the question were "God Governs the Nations," "The Purposes for Which God Afflicts a Nation," and "The Call for Humiliation and Prayer before the God of Nations." He argued from biblical passages with a rhetorical line of questions and then stated:

If God governs the world, then his hand is in this war in which we are engaged. It matters not that the wickedness of man brought it upon us, that it was caused by the mad attempts of fanaticism to deprive us of our rights, overthrow our institutions, and impose upon us a yoke which, as freemen, we had resolved never to bear.[30]

Tichenor, along with many other southerners, believed that the North had forced the war upon them. Obviously, "overthrow our institutions" is a reference to slavery. Like others, Tichenor apparently believed the southern states had the constitutional right to secede in order to preserve slavery. He did not admit that the South precipitated the war by secession or by firing the first shots at Fort Sumter, nor did he theorize that secession was illegal and slavery immoral. He simply held the beliefs common among many other white Alabamians and southerners. He concluded one section of the sermon with a telling statement: "While the storm-cloud sweeps over our land, let us remember that God rides upon the wings of the tempest, and subjects it to his will. God in his own way will save our Southland."[31]

Tichenor went on to discuss two reasons for the current suffering of the South. He believed that they were "punishment for sin" and "development of national character and resources, so as to qualify a people for some high and holy mission which he designs to commit to their trust." Increasingly in 1863 and 1864, southern ministers called their congregations to repentance, claiming that such repentance would restore God's favor. Unlike Abraham Lincoln, who in his second inaugural address less than two years later also suggested that the war punished the nation for the evil of slavery, the pastor did not criticize his fellow southerners for the peculiar institution. He did criticize, however, the "most crying of our national sins" as being "the covetousness of our people." In this indictment he especially spoke against the use of money for "selfish gratification." He also attacked those who engaged in black market type activities and hoarding. He especially chided those who "have sought to monopolize articles of prime necessity, and by withholding them from market to enhance their price, and fatten themselves upon the sufferings of their country." Confederate government inspector Colonel Eugene E. McLeon cited speculation in Montgomery as a major problem in the report of his visit in March 1864. This would have been a popular sentiment with many suffering the inflationary travail inherent in the Confederate economy. Hoarding and similar activities seriously contributed to starvation and other shortages by midwar, and Tichenor's censure of those elements unquestionably resonated with many of his hearers and subsequent readers.[32]

The Montgomery pastor also condemned pride as another aspect of national sin. He believed that southerners at the beginning of the war held "a vain confidence in our national strength; we placed a high estimate on the valor of our people, and held in contempt the martial qualities of our foes."

This pride had manifested itself in a "boastful self-reliance," said Tichenor. He spoke accurately of the Confederate mindset in 1861:

> We expected no defeat, and thought that nothing but victory could await us on any battlefield. We confidently believed that our agricultural products in which the world is so much interested would bring us recognition by the nations of the earth, defeat the purpose of our enemies to blockade our coasts, and insure our independence. COTTON was our hope. Cotton was not only our *king*, but it was enthroned the god of our confidence, and worshiped as our national deliverer.[33]

Early battlefield victories further contributed to this confidence in Confederate prospects. Early successes convinced Confederates of their martial abilities, of the justness of their cause, and of its ultimate success. Tichenor ended the appraisal of Confederate arrogance with language that suggested that he considered this confidence the equivalent of idolatry, which could only be solved by repentance, a dependence upon God for the future, and "a fresh appeal to arms."[34]

Next, Tichenor criticized some aspects of slavery. As typical of his generation's white southern evangelicals, Tichenor never criticized slavery as an institution but chose rather to condemn its abuses. He raised no questions about the contradiction of denying freedoms to slaves that the South was determined to defend. Rather, he declared, "We have failed to discharge our duties to our slaves." Certainly, the Baptist pastor held a paternalistic view of African Americans. Unlike some who believed slaves to be only property, Tichenor believed them to be inferior beings to be cared for by their masters. While he would not have gone as far as J. D. B. DeBow, a New Orleans editor, in stressing the superiority of southern society and slavery, Tichenor was quick to defend slavery.[35] He stated, "I entertain no doubt that slavery is right," but added, "there are abuses of it which ought to be corrected." He even enumerated these abuses:

> Marriage is a divine institution, and yet marriage exists among our slaves dependent upon the will of the master. "What God has joined together let no man put asunder," yet this tie is subject to the passion, caprice, or avarice of their owners. The law gives the husband and the father no protection in this relation. The remorseless creditor may avail himself of

the power of the law to separate husband and wife, parent and child. This is an evil of no minor magnitude, and one which demands an immediate remedy.[36]

Tichenor also mentioned another abuse—the lack of missionary effort among the slaves. He reprimanded, "Too little attention has been paid to their moral and religious culture." He acknowledged that slave labor had resulted in agricultural prosperity. "By their labor our fields have been made white with abundant harvests," Tichenor admonished, "and the wealth they have produced has been spent with lavish hands," and yet, "scarcely a pittance has been given to furnish them with the bread of life."[37] Many had made this identical criticism prior to the Civil War. Throughout his ministry, Tichenor demonstrated a concern regarding African-American religion. His sermon, however, links the failure to provide adequately for the spiritual condition of slaves with God's punishment of the South.

It is significant that Tichenor made no mention of masters and overseers who abused their slaves physically or the fact that most states forbade slaves to read and write when those skills would have aided them in understanding the message of the gospel. Earlier in his career, Tichenor had been extremely critical of slave preaching that he witnessed. As a young pastor, he recorded in his diary that a slave minister's preaching was harmful, and the lack of substance to the message appalled him. Nowhere, either in his early diary or in this Fast Day sermon, does Tichenor acknowledge or even allude to the fact that the cause of the perceived poor quality of slave preaching, the slave's lack of understanding of orthodox Christian doctrine, and his weak biblical comprehension might have resulted from limitations placed upon slave preachers by southern law and society.

Nor did Tichenor criticize antebellum viewpoints that considered slaves genetically and intellectually inferior. This viewpoint had been advocated by many of those who defended slavery. Utilizing language and methodologies promoted as science, poor biblical interpretation and theology, and an incomplete understanding of history, individuals like Dr. Samuel Cartwright and the aforementioned DeBow promoted rationales for white racial superiority that went unchallenged by Tichenor.[38]

Finally, the Montgomery pastor failed to mention a moral problem that diarist Mary Chesnut noted privately prior to the onset of the war. Chesnut wrote,

God forgive *us,* but ours is a *monstrous* system & wrong & iniquity. . . .
This *only* I see: like the patriarchs of old our men live all in one house
with their wives & their concubines, & the Mulattoes one sees in every
family exactly resemble the white children. . . . & all the time they seem
to think themselves patterns—models of husbands & fathers.[39]

Tichenor could not have been unaware of these other abuses, but the fact
that he neglected to address them demonstrates again that he was a product
of his culture. Even in his attempt to speak in a prophetic voice, he ignored
the opportunity to criticize slavery and its worst abuses.

Tichenor ended his sermon with additional pleas for repentance and prayer.
He held out General Robert Lee as a model Christian warrior and man of
prayer. In third person, he recalled his own battle experiences at Shiloh and
insisted that "it was the thought that prayer was then ascending for [the Seventeenth Alabama] that nerved their arms, and made them heroes in that
fearful hour." He presented an idea to which he returned upon many occasions in the days to come: "It may be that God has for the South a world
mission, and that by these sufferings he is preparing them for that trust." He
asserted,

I confidently believe that in leading us through this fiery trial God is
preparing a chosen people for a great mission. He wants a people purified, a people with a proper understanding and regard for all human
rights; he wants a people, above all things, who will set the glory of God
and the good of the race above all self-centering ambitions.[40]

Certainly, the irony of his own words regarding human rights was lost upon
both Tichenor and his listeners.

The Fast Day sermon gives tremendous insight into Tichenor's speaking
skills and beliefs. The basic content for Tichenor's sermon showed a pastor-
theologian of moderate Calvinist beliefs, convinced of the sovereignty of
God, and at the same time, willing to acknowledge the responsibility of human beings. The power of his oratory comes through clearly. It is no wonder
that Tichenor was regarded as one of the most outstanding preachers of his
day. He moved from the concept of divine chastisement to a call for repentance while at the same time holding out optimistic hopes regarding the future
of the South. The sermon reveals him as a product of his culture with his

defense of slavery and sectionalism, but despite his own prejudices, he maintained a semblance of a prophetic role. His sermon did not merely defend the southern cause and assure that all would be well. While there were obvious and crucial areas that he neglected, he did speak with a critical voice at points. Tichenor's sermon was consistent with other messages preached and proclamations issued during this time.[41] It demonstrates that at this point in the conflict, southerners believed that they could, by repentance and commitment, restore God's favor upon the South. At this moment, and for some years to come, Tichenor, like most of his southern contemporaries, could not perceive that it might be God's will that the South be defeated. In fact, Tichenor remained one Montgomerian who would continue to encourage others to resist almost to the bitter end.[42] Most important was the development of a theme to which he would frequently return in the years to come. As university president at Auburn and as chief executive of the Southern Baptist Home Mission Board, he would repeat many times figuratively and often literally the theme that God had "for the South a world mission."

In Tichenor's Fast Day sermon, one also observes tendencies of what historian Paul Gaston has described as southern mythmaking. Such tendencies were already present in the South prior to the Civil War, but the concepts were not fully developed in 1863. Reading Tichenor's sermon carefully reveals that this mythmaking was developing beyond what Gaston calls an "embryonic" stage.[43] Unknowingly, Tichenor was one of those who laid the foundation for a theology that could both cling to the myth of the Old South while embracing the concepts of a New South.

Tichenor's appearance before the Alabama legislature must have been a highlight of his ministry in Montgomery during the war years. He also would have been heartened by the return of his friend, church member, and deacon Thomas H. Watts to the capital. Watts resigned as Confederate attorney general upon his election as governor of Alabama in the fall of 1863 and took the gubernatorial oath of office in December of that year. Alabamians elected Watts governor even though he had not actively campaigned for the office. Despite his lack of activity and the fact that he had been narrowly defeated two years earlier, voters elected Watts by an overwhelming three-to-one margin. Watts accepted this position despite the fact that he had apparently been somewhat successful as Confederate attorney general and had enacted reforms that made the office more accessible to the public and eliminated unnecessary red tape. Unfortunately for Watts, the problems in Alabama that he faced when he returned to Montgomery only worsened with the declining fortunes of the Confederate cause and eclipsed anything that he had experienced in Richmond in the Justice Department. While Watts originally opposed secession in 1860, by 1863 he completely embraced the Confederate cause, declaring that he was "a war man all over." Watts dealt with food shortages, "disloyal" regions of Alabama, and provided for the defense of the state against Union raids. He was forced to make difficult decisions regarding taking state control over crucial economic elements in Alabama, such as a factory in nearby Prattville.[44] One would expect Tichenor to provide counsel for his church member, and Watts would have sought solace in the confines of his church. Like others in the Confederacy, Tichenor would have found his resolute belief in the southern cause severely tested by the continuing course of events.

In less than a year, personal tragedy visited Tichenor. While the war spared his life, it did not spare members of his family. Just prior to the war Tichenor had married his second wife, Emily Boykin. They had two children. Not long after the birth of the second in 1864, Emily and the children were visiting her sister in Columbus when she and the infant son became ill. Tichenor was in Georgia visiting soldiers, perhaps even his old regiment, then with General Hood outside Atlanta as they prepared to move north into Tennessee, when the news arrived. He rushed to see her, but before he arrived both Emily and the child died. This was not the last personal tragedy for Tichenor. During his lifetime he was married four times but only for a total of seventeen years as each wife died suddenly and prematurely from illness or as a result of the weakness or complications resulting from childbirth. Of the seven children produced by these marriages, only four lived to adulthood.[45]

As the war dragged on and continued to turn against the South, Tichenor attempted to make other practical contributions to the war effort. He played a leading role in providing for war orphans. As chairman of the Montgomery Reserve Relief Committee, he took supplies gathered in Montgomery to the Confederate front lines as General William Tecumseh Sherman's Union army pressed Confederate forces in Georgia. Such relief efforts were not uncommon from the very beginning of the war, and efforts accelerated as Confederate forces were pushed southward. Tichenor and at least one other man took part in a Montgomery effort to carry these supplies to the besieged Confederate soldiers in Atlanta. A family tradition stated that they rode part of the way on the tender of the engine and found themselves covered with soot. When Atlanta fell, Tichenor reportedly left on the final train to Macon before Sherman's forces cut the last rail connection with the city.[46]

Tichenor's second contribution to the war effort related to Confederate prisoners of war. In late 1864 and early 1865, his church member Governor Watts became concerned about the need for warm clothing and blankets for Alabama Confederate prisoners being held in Northern prisoner camps. As a solution to this problem, Watts attempted to ship cotton through Union lines to New York. There the cotton, in great demand due to the war, would be sold and the money used to finance these purchases. President Jefferson Davis approved his request. In December the Alabama legislature authorized $5 million to purchase the cotton. Watts then enlisted Meyer Lehman, a Montgomery cotton broker, and recommended Lehman to President Davis. He also enlisted his pastor, Reverend Tichenor, to perform this vital mercy mission. In the dead of winter, Lehman and Tichenor traveled to Richmond. They communicated with Union commander General Ulysses S. Grant that their desires were humanitarian and assured him that they were not seeking the exchange of prisoners. Grant had eliminated the prisoner exchange program which, earlier in the war, had served as a way for the Confederacy to replenish its rapidly dwindling manpower. Though they submitted to any Union restrictions, Grant refused them a pass through Federal lines, stating that the established procedure for such contacts should be followed. Grant also may have rejected the proposal because reports of appalling conditions at Confederate prisoner-of-war camps in the South were coming to his attention.

Tichenor returned from Richmond, and his report on the effort became "one of the final Confederate eulogies." Testifying to his experiences in the besieged Confederate capitol, he praised Jefferson Davis and the people of Richmond, saying that their resistance was better than "submission to Abraham Lincoln and his black cohorts." The next day at FBC a meeting was held to organize the "Society of Loyal Confederates." Its members promised "to work out the independence and salvation of our country." Even as the Confederacy disintegrated, die-hards pledged allegiance to "the Cause." This type of thinking would serve as the foundation of the Lost Cause theology that developed during the Reconstruction period. It is not known if Tichenor participated in that meeting, but his earlier comments illustrate the fact that Tichenor became a die-hard Confederate. Those comments also suggest the strong racial overtones that made up Confederate rhetoric and Confederate fears about African Americans and the Republican administration as the war came to a close. Tichenor's testimony also demonstrates how important leadership from the clergy was in maintaining morale in the Confederacy's waning days. As the Confederacy's demise became inevitable, devout white southerners still expected God's intervention on the Confederacy's behalf. Even Confederate President Jefferson Davis regarded the spiritual leaders as a critical component to maintaining morale and the only hope of inspiring wearied southerners.[47] Apparently Tichenor was one minister who remained loyal to the southern cause to the bitter end.

As the war came to a close, Alabama directly experienced the destruction brought by invading Union forces. The Confederate government and justice system were collapsing. In certain regions, lawlessness was a major problem, and speculation and hoarding continued to be rampant. In Alabama a Union army captured Mobile, and General James H. Wilson launched a cavalry raid to destroy previously untouched regions of Alabama where war-making capacities still existed and supplied Confederate forces. Wilson's activities were especially devastating in the closing days of the war. Despite some resistance, Wilson moved south, capturing Montevallo on March 31, 1865, and Selma two days later. Wilson then turned toward the first capital of the Confederacy. Montgomerians, aware of what had happened recently in Columbia, South Carolina, when Sherman's army captured the capital of the first southern state to secede, shuddered with anticipation of what might come Montgomery's way as the Confederacy's first capital. Governor Watts and city officials began to organize for the anticipated attack. They appointed Tichenor and two other local ministers to a committee responsible for the confiscation and destruction of all alcoholic beverages, hoping that this might prevent the kind of alcohol-related chaos that had taken place in Columbia and other southern cities. With his concern for temperance issues, Tichenor may have seen this opportunity to dispose of liquor as the only benefit of the collapse of the Confederate cause.[48]

In the midst of crisis, Tichenor undoubtedly performed significant pastoral duties for Governor Watts. In late March, Watts and his daughter Florence received word that her husband, Colonel Daniel S. Troy, had been mortally wounded near Petersburg, Virginia. Fortunately, word came a few days later that Troy had been captured, was being treated in a Union hospital, and had miraculously survived his wounds. Tichenor, no doubt, ministered to his church member in that moment of crisis. Shortly thereafter, with Union troops closing in on Montgomery, another Watts daughter, Kate, was married to Robert M. Collins. As the family pastor, Tichenor would have performed the wedding ceremony. Likewise, Tichenor would have witnessed the entry of Union troops into Montgomery a few days later and may have even seen the U.S. flag raised again over the state capitol. For Alabama, Montgomery, and Tichenor, the war was over.[49]

In 1864 First Baptist had experienced a revival at virtually the same time revivals were sweeping the Confederate armies. This outpouring of religious sentiment was probably either a conscious or subconscious attempt by Southerners to earn divine favor at a time when Southern military fortunes were in decline. This revival greatly increased the church's membership. Nevertheless, even harder times were coming to the congregation. The end of the war and onset of Reconstruction in 1865 brought a large measure of discouragement, apathy, and economic disorder to the South and to Montgomery.[50]

Though all the achievements of the war years gave Tichenor great pride in years to come, they probably had little impact on the Confederate war effort. Taken together, they demonstrate the devotion Tichenor felt for the cause of southern independence. His granddaughter recalled that late in life "he seldom talked of his [personal] war experiences" and considered the late war "a dead issue," but those four years critically shaped his future.[51] His wartime experiences positioned him well among fellow white southerners as he rose in leadership both in the Southern Baptist Convention and in the South. His combat role at Shiloh served the purpose of verifying his legitimacy as a southerner when he advanced the ideas of the New South. The continued development of his oratorical skills aided him among a people who valued public speaking. His connections in the capital enhanced his future opportunities, his personal prestige, and his ability to enlist support for causes that he viewed as sacred. In fact, taken altogether, the war years may have been the single most critical formative period in Tichenor's life.

3
Building the New South
Tichenor as Pastor and Mining Executive, 1865–72

As Union armies swept across the Confederacy and consequently enforced Reconstruction upon the defeated South, they encountered an economic disaster unparalleled in American history. The South's socioeconomic system had been destroyed with the abolition of slavery, which caused the agricultural system to collapse. Furthermore, the region's industrial strength, never great even at its height, had been targeted for destruction by the Union war machine. All banking and government collapsed with the Confederacy's capitulation. The few industrial regions that were untouched by the Union's total war effort were decaying from neglect and overuse. The railroads and rolling stock that had not been destroyed by invading armies had been cannibalized for iron rails and spare parts. The devastation and poverty visited upon the South were incredible, and contemporary Americans cannot fully appreciate the utter demoralization and ruin that held most of the region in its grip. But at least black southerners saw the end of the war and the beginning of the Reconstruction as the promised time of "Jubilee" and celebrated freedoms they had never experienced.[1]

The devastation resulting from the war, while less severe in Alabama than in other states of the late Confederacy, was still considerable. Alabama Governor R. M. Patton, reporting one year after the war, estimated property losses at $500 million. Freed slaves comprised about forty percent of this total, but the remaining $300 million consisted primarily of devalued lands, lost livestock, and failed crops. All but one of the state's blast furnaces "were put out of production." Currency and financial investments were worthless across the state. Alabama agriculture existed in no better shape. Fields were neglected, and equipment and improvements ruined. By 1870 livestock numbers had still not reached prewar levels. The unprecedented and widespread destruction included Tichenor's Montgomery, where three steamboats, the foundry, rolling mill, and ninety-seven thousand bales of cotton were burned. The physical trauma included the human toll. It is estimated that nearly forty thousand Alabamians did not return home from the war and another thirty-five thousand were disabled. Beyond that was the emotional turmoil that resulted from the divisions that occurred in the South during and after the war. Some southerners remained loyal to the Union even after secession or became disillusioned with the war as the conflict dragged on for four years. Philosophical and theological dismay increased as the cause many white southerners considered a righteous one went down in defeat. Alabama was no exception to this.[2]

Likewise, people throughout the South feared the prospect of social disorder and upheaval that followed the end of the war. Marauding bands of outlaws roamed the countryside and mountains of the Confederate states wreaking havoc among unprotected civilians in places where government had collapsed. Crime was widespread. The months that followed Appomattox fed social uncertainty. Some parts of the South returned to prewar order somewhat quickly, and complete chaos never imperiled the South. However, crime and social disorder occurred more frequently, and the perception of seemingly worsening conditions created a culture of mistrust.[3]

Along with the tremendous economic and physical repercussions of the war, southerners also had to deal with the social and psychological implications. Prior to 1861, approximately one-half of Alabama's population was enslaved.[4] In 1865 these slaves were constitutionally free. Whites and blacks were forced to deal with the question of relations between races. Tichenor, as a pastor and leader, was obliged to deal with this serious matter. Additionally, the situation compelled him and other southern pastors and theologians to explain God's role in the defeat. Tichenor and others had maintained that God embraced the southern cause. His Fast Day sermon demonstrated the theology he developed prior to and during the war. With the war lost, Tichenor and others were pressed to deal with the theological implications of an outcome different from what they had anticipated and to explain that outcome to a white populace searching for theological answers to extremely difficult and largely unprecedented questions.

The problems of the Reconstruction era touched Tichenor and his ministry in tangible ways. One of the major concerns he and others faced was the issue of relations with former slaves. Like many of his contemporaries, he defended slavery as having been beneficial to blacks. As a representative of the Southern Baptist Convention, he attended the Northern Baptists' annual meeting and was asked to speak on the education of southern blacks. This speech led to an ugly confrontation, although his son-in-law recorded that Tichenor handled the confrontation gracefully and was later applauded for his poise. Tichenor was a messenger of "fraternal greetings" from Southern Baptists but also defended slavery as having "taken [the slaves] from their savage state." He defended the "peculiar institution" as having "brought [the slaves] into contact with Southern civilization and the true religion." Naturally, in the recent aftermath of the war's bloodbath, the crowd targeted Tichenor for immediate hostility. The participants literally hissed and shouted him from the platform, so he bowed and left the stage. Certainly, Tichenor was not alone in his viewpoint, and many southerners used this argument regularly in the following years.[5]

Although for a time Tichenor defended slavery as a good institution and never viewed African Americans as equals, he stridently claimed that Baptists in the South had an overwhelming responsibility to educate their former slaves. He chaired the SBC committee on Religious Instruction of the Colored Population that made six recommendations concerning black education. The fifth resolution was a definite anti-Northern statement:

> *Resolved,* that while we are not opposed to any right-minded man aiding in this important work, it is our decided conviction, from our knowledge of these people, and of the feelings of our citizens, that this work must be done mainly by ourselves.[6]

The sentiment expressed in this resolution indicated the feelings of many white southerners. The blue-clad troops that occupied southern cities constantly reminded southerners of defeat. White southerners resented the Freedman's Bureau, an institution that offered many possibilities for educating former slaves, as a northern intrusion into southern affairs. Many white southerners did not trust northerners working among former slaves to educate the former slaves in a fashion acceptable to antebellum racial and social standards. Many southern whites distrusted the bureau, regarded it a symbol of Confederate defeat and a source of northern occupation, and considered it an impediment to southern hopes to snatch victory from defeat and restore a type of authority similar to slavery. The SBC resolution on Baptist responsibility to blacks, written by a committee chaired by Tichenor, expressed this wariness regarding both individuals from the North and organizations such as the bureau.[7]

This resolution undoubtedly reflected Tichenor's personal ideas. He expressed a similar opinion at the meeting of the Alabama Baptist Association. He told Alabama Baptists, "If you cast them [the former slaves] off, by that act you invite them to take charge of their spiritual interests. And who will come?" Tichenor believed the answer was unscrupulous white northerners who would seek to manipulate the freedmen he regarded as impressionable because of his paternalistic attitudes. He warned that even northern missionaries might "excite the colored people to consider their former masters and real friends as their enemies, then their influence will be mischievous." He was especially concerned about ideas like "negro suffrage" and "social equality" and used a word that was dramatically alarming, "miscegenation." This led Tichenor to challenge Alabama Baptists in 1865 and Southern Baptists in 1866 to educate their former slaves before they could be "corrupted" by northern interests.[8] Obviously, white Baptists attempted to make sure that education could be used as a control mechanism to help maintain the social structure of the South while, at the same time, utilizing cheap black labor to rebuild the shattered southern economy. Certainly Christian concern motivated Tichenor, though it was expressed through the skewed perspective of paternalism. He also undoubtedly shared other southerners' desire to make sure the South was not deprived of its main source of cheap labor.

Of more immediate concern was the relationship of blacks and whites within the congregation at Montgomery's First Baptist Church. Slaves had made up a significant portion of the membership prior to the war. In fact, records indicate that the membership of FBC registered twice as many black members as white. Immediately after the war, white southerners desired that their former slaves remain affiliated with their congregations. At least some of this desire may have stemmed from their attempt to maintain some level of control over the affairs of their former slaves, in this case over spiritual matters. As demonstrated by the 1866 SBC resolution, white southerners reasoned that if freedmen separated into autonomous congregations, they would easily fall under the sway of northern missionaries. African Americans felt differently. Black Christians increasingly recognized that emancipation gave them unprecedented opportunity to chart their own spiritual course. As one social historian observes, "[B]lacks acted decisively on their own and their forebears' distinctive appropriation of Christianity. In every state of the now-defeated Confederacy they surged into separate congregations, churches, and denominations."[9]

While this development typically took place in phases, and the separation was by no means sudden, the general rapidity of the transition demonstrates that probably both black and white Christians felt the separation desirable. Tichenor wrote of FBC's experience as being representative of the transformation occurring throughout the South:[10]

> When a separation of the two bodies was deemed desirable, it was done by the colored brethren, in conference assembled, passing a resolution, couched in the kindliest terms, suggesting the wisdom of the division, and asking the concurrence of the white church in such action. The white church cordially approved the movement, and the two bodies united in erecting a suitable house of worship for the colored brethren. Until it was finished they continued to occupy jointly with the white brethren their house of worship, as they had done previous to this action. The new house was paid for in large measure by the white members of the church and individuals in the community. As soon as it was completed the colored church moved into it with its organization perfected. . . . Similar things occurred in all the states of the South.[11]

Tichenor's account here did not detail all of the events leading up to the separation as completely as does the church's history. In fact, white members of the church purchased land approximately one year before the separation took place for the purpose of constructing a building for the black congregation. Lacking funds to construct the building, Tichenor took an unsuccessful trip to the North to try and raise money. Apparently, he did raise some funds and secured a loan for the balance. A little more than a year later the FBC minutes recorded,

> Whereas, our colored brethren are erecting a house of worship and contemplate establishing an independent church, first resolved, that

whenever the colored members shall make application for these, the clerk shall issue to them a general letter of dismission for the purpose of forming a separate organization.

Second, resolved that we donate to our colored members the seats and pulpit now in the basement of the church.[12]

The minutes from the church's August business conference simply state that the transfer of six hundred letters of membership were granted. The new church was constituted as the Columbus Street Baptist Church, and the congregation ultimately became the parent congregation of all Montgomery's black Baptist churches. By 1900 some regarded it as the world's largest Baptist church with five thousand recorded members.[13]

Initially, the separation occurred at the congregational level, but ultimately it encompassed all levels of organizational structure, including, among Baptists, separate associations and conventions. Columbus Street hosted the separate occasions when the Alabama Colored Baptist State Convention and the National Baptist Convention Inc. were established.[14]

Undoubtedly, white racism contributed substantially to black efforts to establish their own congregations. On the other hand, this decision to separate actually may have been initiated by blacks themselves. Typically, those who have held to that opinion have tended to stress political reasons. However, it has been argued convincingly that while perhaps assisted and encouraged by white southerners and politically provoked by white northerners, black Christians initiated the action "acting on their own religious experience." This analysis suggests that the decision was based upon black worship patterns and, even more importantly, a desire to determine their own religious destinies. Likewise, freed slaves sincerely believed that their former masters could not or should not manage their religious interests. They desired to form their own churches, call black pastors, and educate their people through schools and colleges. While they often did receive assistance from white congregations, as in the case of Montgomery's FBC, they usually found greater assistance from northern white denominations. Ultimately, though, African-American churches found that white northerners could be almost as paternalistic and racist as white southerners. Despite this prevailing prejudice, the white northerners at least provided logistical and financial support for African Americans in their attempts to become self-governing in ecclesiastical affairs.[15] In reality, probably all these factors contributed to African-American separation into their own congregations.

Tichenor, like most white southerners, did not intend to accept black southerners as social and political equals, but he did have a sense of responsibility regarding them and their welfare. This concern seems to be genuine, however misguided it was. Indicative of this concern were the efforts he made to raise money on the Columbus Street congregation's behalf. Another indication would be his friendship with an illiterate former slave who had been a member of FBC, Jesse Goldthwaite. Many years later, Tichenor wrote of this relationship, illustrating the paternalistic attitude with which he and many southern whites viewed the former slaves. At the same time, his writing also demonstrates that Tichenor sought to help black members of the church however possible. He wrote letters for Goldthwaite and others trying to find family members from whom they had been separated by slavery. He had a high regard for Goldthwaite's genuine Christian commitment and advocated education for the former slaves.[16] It is important to note, though, that the form of education he advocated would have been considered the "right kind of education" and that "right-minded individuals" should engage in this "right kind of education."

The second problem of Reconstruction that Tichenor faced was that of finances. The budgetary problems of First Baptist Church reflected the devastated southern economy. Like many southern churches in cities, it depended upon pew rental payment for its major source of income. The depressed economy forced many members to lag behind in their payments. In turn this led to the church falling deeper into debt. The unpaid debts included the pastor's salary.[17]

The situation reached a crisis in November 1867. At a special church business conference to discuss the necessity "to raise funds now due to meet [the church's] liabilities," Tichenor resigned as meeting chair and tendered his resignation to take effect on January 1, 1868. He also addressed the meeting and urged the conference to take "immediate action." Despite this statement, the conference postponed action until the following Sunday. At that meeting the congregation appointed a committee to meet with Tichenor to "ascertain what will induce him to remain with us, or have him withdraw his offered resignation for the present." Among others, the congregation appointed his old friend Thomas Watts to the committee. Subsequently, the committee proposed a budget for 1868 and agreed upon the payments due Tichenor. Unfortunately, the church quickly fell behind in its payments. On January 12, 1868, the church minutes recorded that Tichenor "stated that necessity forced him to say he would not preach to the church again until he could receive from them the money due for the past years and also some assurance that he will be paid in the future."[18]

Five days later, in a meeting chaired by Watts, committee members discussed the full situation. They determined that the church owed Tichenor over $1,000 in back pay, including his pay thus far in 1868. In a compromise, Tichenor agreed to accept a lower annual salary for 1868 of $1,200, provided that his back pay was given immediately. The church membership agreed and subsequently passed the following resolution:

> Resolved that this church having by the stringency of the times, and the pecuniary misfortune of most of its members, been unable punctually to pay its pastor, will in the future endeavor more faithfully to comply with its obligations; and as our Pastor has shown a willingness to share in our misfortunes by agreeing to receive as a minimum the sum of $1200 as the salary for the year 1868, we pledge ourselves to pay said salary punctually, and to pay what remains due to him for past services. . . . [19]

In a second resolution, the church stated that it renewed "its assurance to its beloved pastor of its entire confidence and love, and that its failure to comply with its pecuniary engagements with him resulted from no want of appreciation of him as its minister but from the hardness of the times."[20]

Apparently, the church met its obligations, but five months later, Tichenor tendered his resignation without any explanation noted in the church minutes. He remained while the search committee began its work, and the search committee asked him for assistance. Eventually, he made his resignation effective November 1, 1868.[21]

Tichenor's role in this series of events is difficult to ascertain. Certainly, he could not have been unaware of "the hardness of the times" or the "pecuniary misfortunes of its members." Nor could he have been unaware of the strong allegiance that many of its members must have felt toward him and his family. Still, he was a man with financial obligations of his own and a family for whom he had to provide. In October 1865 he had remarried. His third wife was Lulah Boykin, sister of his second wife, Emily. While his child by Emily had died at approximately the age of five in 1867, his union with Lulah produced two more children. The first, James Boykin, died at the age of three in 1869, and the second, Emily Lulah, survived to adulthood along with the two children from his first wife. Certainly, these family crises would have been detrimental to the emotional and spiritual strength of even a strong person like Tichenor. The psychological scars of these multiple events against the backdrop of the South's social crisis may have further taxed a strained relationship with the congregation. Any assistance he may have derived from his wife's family, the prominent Boykins of Columbus, Georgia, probably suffered from the depression affecting the South. He may have felt extreme pressure to provide well for his family and maintain a lifestyle to which they had become accustomed. At least at one point, Tichenor chided a boarder for burning too much coal to warm the house "as he did not know where the next would come from."[22] Perhaps most importantly, Tichenor had developed an intense interest in material prosperity, and he had become convinced of the potential of the coal mining industry, in which he had recently invested. It could well be that this, together with a tremendous amount of personal pride and perhaps a desire for a significant change in his life and profession, was the motivating factor in his pressing the salary issue with the congregation. With one brief exception in 1871, Tichenor never served as a full-time pastor again.

President of the Montevallo Coal Mining Company

Late in 1868 and early in 1869, the country still remained in a time of transition from the late war. Southern Reconstruction was by no means complete, although the privation that immediately followed the war had been largely alleviated. Union war hero Ulysses S. Grant was elected president in 1868 with the acknowledged admonition "Let us have peace," and seven southern states, including Alabama, had been readmitted to representation in Congress. In 1869 the first transcontinental railroad was completed, linking the East Coast with the West in the most remarkable technological achievement of the nineteenth century. The taming of the West seemed inevitable. There were many reasons for optimism. At the same time, white opposition groups like the Ku Klux Klan had emerged to resist Radical Republican control of the South, and national peace was more of a political hope than a reality. The optimism generated by the completion of the transcontinental railroad was tainted by reports that had begun to surface of the worst scandal of the nineteenth century, involving construction on the transcontinental line, the Crédit Mobilier company, and bribes to congressmen. Corruption was widespread. Readmission of four southern states would not be completed for two years, and "Redeemer" candidates and governments were beginning to emerge in all southern states that would begin to unravel the fragile fabric of Reconstruction and restore white supremacy. Almost another decade would pass before the last federal troops would be withdrawn from the South. This would occur not as a result of the successful completion of their mission but as a result of a political compromise by the Republican party to maintain its control of the White House and the growing apathy and disinterest of white northerners regarding the never-ending woes of Reconstruction.

Against this background Tichenor left the pastorate at Montgomery in 1868 and moved to Shelby County, Alabama, where he bought a plantation home near Montevallo. While he continued to preach locally in churches and to involve himself in denominational affairs, Tichenor radically readjusted his career. This transformation was not sudden but had been in process for more than four years, little more than a year after he returned to the Montgomery pastorate.[23]

In January 1864 amid the Civil War and while serving as pastor in Montgomery, Tichenor—along with Governor Thomas Watts, T. J. Portis, George M. Figh, Benjamin Davis, and others—bought controlling interests in the Alabama Coal Mining Company and renamed it the Montevallo Coal Mining Company. Due to the South's prior dependence upon the North for heavy industry, Southern businessmen were especially concerned with tapping undeveloped resources in the South during the war. Coal mining in the central Alabama region went back many years. Perhaps as early as 1815, white settlers may have found and burned coal. The earliest efforts to mine coal began in the 1850s, although Alabama state geologist Michael Tuomey surveyed the Cahaba region in the 1840s and discovered extensive seams in the area. One mining historian records that the first regular underground mining took place in Alabama near Montevallo beginning in 1856 with the Alabama Coal Mining Company. The earliest coal mining endeavors actually had begun with William Phineas Browne of Montevallo approximately seven years earlier in 1849, and at least some three years earlier, in 1853, Browne was actively engaged in the coal business. Limited by difficulties in extraction and transportation, Browne's efforts never reached full potential. His efforts were further hampered by the onset of the Civil War and struggles associated with financing and maintaining the effort despite the high demand for coal. The forerunner of the Montevallo Coal Mining Company, the Alabama Coal Mining Company, began to mine coal successfully by 1859, in part through the utilization of steam technology to lift coal to the surface but especially because of its employment of Joseph Squire, a thirty-year-old English immigrant. Squire had extensive experience in the coal pits of England as a young man prior to coming to the United States and had continued in coal mining in the Midwest upon his arrival in the states. It was Squire's unceasing labor that maintained the ability of the Cahaba mines to produce coal in less than ideal circumstances. When Tichenor and his associates assumed control of the company, they recognized Squire's ability and retained his services, allowing him a number of special prerogatives. Squire remained on the job until the end of the Civil War. He used the following months for "further study of mine engineering, geology, mineralogy, coal and iron ore properties and formations."[24]

After the war and upon Squire's return from his period of study, the owners commissioned Squire to survey the Montevallo Basin and later the Cahaba Coal Field. While still residing in Montgomery, Tichenor was a main financier of this effort. During this time he formed a close friendship with the mining engineer who had rapidly become a geological and mining pioneer in Alabama. Throughout much of this time, the mining expert boarded with Tichenor in his Montgomery home and spent an extensive amount of time with him poring over survey information. Squire later kept a detailed diary during 1868 that recorded the influence of Tichenor's work as mining executive, plantation owner, and active minister. Later correspondence between the two suggests that they shared a passion for scientific discovery and mining development and that "the technical discussion and the familiar tone" demonstrates "a bond forged through years of coal mining pursuits." In 1867, while still in the pastorate, Tichenor became president of the company. Also in 1867 the company expanded its operation by purchasing mining rights to additional areas, probably upon Squire's recommendation. In 1868 Tichenor bought his home in Shelby County, and in October of that year, after Tichenor's resignation from the Montgomery pastorate, Squire "placed all of Dr. Tichenor's household goods on the steam boat at [the] Montgomery levee" and transported them by boat, rail, and wagons to the new Tichenor residence in Siluria. The Tichenor family arrived by wagons and carriages soon afterward. Tichenor's resignation from the pastorate likely had more to do with the opportunities that he believed existed in the Cahaba mining business than his dissatisfaction with the Montgomery congregation over nonpayment or slow payment of his salary. Subsequent correspondence with Squire revealed that Tichenor developed a persistent optimism that the Cahaba coal fields would make both men rich.[25]

For a time, Squire went to Pittsburgh to study mining operations there. Tichenor once again hired Squire as superintendent and mining engineer in October 1869. Squire recorded his close work with Tichenor in the preceding months and the minister's intense interest in surveying the central Alabama coal region. While still in Montgomery, Tichenor and Squire had engaged in extensive discussions of the potential of the Cahaba coal fields as well as other possible mineral deposits in the region. These discussions continued for the two years that Tichenor spent in Montevallo in 1868 and 1869. Squire left the employ of the MMC in 1870 to work for other mining companies in the area, but he and Tichenor maintained their relationship.[26]

Tichenor spent slightly more than two years in the Montevallo and Birmingham regions working as a pioneer industrialist in the area that ultimately became known as the "Pittsburgh of the South." By 1873, two years after Tichenor's presidency of the company ended, the mines produced approximately six thousand tons of coal and doubled its output a year later. By 1877 the mines produced in excess of twenty thousand tons of coal. While company president, Tichenor had inaugurated the latest steam technology and surveyed and studied the north Alabama region's geology. These surveys formed much of the basis for the region's industrialization. The business and scientific techniques learned during this time provided invaluable preparation for Tichenor's later work.[27]

Perhaps most importantly for the coal mining business in Alabama was Tichenor's close association with Squire and his decision to hire Squire, sponsor his work, and utilize his expertise. Two Alabama historians write of Squire's contributions, saying that "If Alabama were to create memorials to its industrial pioneers, Joseph Squire would merit one of the first. Squire could run coal mines with practical efficiency, but he left his most enduring mark with his exploration of the Alabama coalfields—a work that made fortunes for the capitalists who listened to him." Together with entrepreneurs like Truman Aldrich, James W. Sloss, and Henry F. DeBardeleben, Squire "laid the groundwork for the golden age of coal in the first half of the twentieth century" in Alabama. DeBardeleben also expanded into iron mining.[28]

Tichenor was part of a movement beginning to take hold among business-men, politicians, and educators in the late 1860s and 1870s. Known as the New South movement, it was led by a group of individuals who sought to transform the South from a region that was extremely reliant upon agriculture, specifically cotton, to an economy that was diversified and industrialized.[29] Squire provided essential survey information and geological studies that equipped Tichenor to lay bold claims about the economic possibilities that the Alabama mining region offered. One of the individuals at the forefront of this movement was the former Confederate general, war hero, and soon-to-be Georgia politician John B. Gordon.

In January 1868, while Tichenor still served as pastor but was already heavily involved with the Montevallo Mining Company, Gordon visited the state capital and spoke to a group at a local theater. During his brief two-evening visit, Tichenor hosted the former general. Awaiting Tichenor's arrival, Squire showed Gordon mineral specimens. Squire recorded that Gordon "approved of my work very highly." The following day Gordon returned to Squire's study and further "examined my Maps, Specimens. . . . " That evening after Gordon spoke, he, Tichenor, and Squire stayed up until the morning's early hours, discussing "the best method of operating for the future." It is unknown whether Tichenor viewed Gordon as a potential investor in the company or sought expertise from Gordon's prewar mining experience, or whether Gordon's attention to Tichenor and Squire resulted from his growing interest in issues that ultimately became nascent ideas in New South industrialization. Regardless of the reason, Tichenor probably viewed Gordon's interest in his and Squire's efforts as verification that they were headed in the right direction.[30]

Gordon was a legitimate hero of the Civil War. A businessman and politician with no military training, Gordon rose from the rank of captain to major general by the end of the war. In the waning months of the conflict, Gordon was one of Robert E. Lee's closest lieutenants and was widely known across the South. His most recent biographer states, "At war's end, he was one of the most popular men in the South." Prior to the war, he and his father had operated the Castle Rock Coal Company in northwest Georgia and northeast Alabama. After the war, he resumed a career in business but also allegedly became a leader in the early Ku Klux Klan and then a prominent southern politician in the Redeemer or Bourbon governments that reestablished white Democratic control of the southern states as Reconstruction ended. Gordon also became an outspoken advocate of the New South. He shared similar ideas and sometimes competed with fellow Georgian Benjamin H. Hill. In his landmark study *The New South Creed,* historian Paul Gaston traces the development of the concept of the "New South" to the 1860s with individuals such as J. D. B. DeBow and Daniel Harvey Hill. Gaston also suggests that the term actually originated in 1870 with Edwin DeLeon in *Putnam's Magazine.* DeLeon promoted his ideas through a series of articles in other publications. Shortly afterward, prominent Georgia politician Benjamin Harvey Hill utilized similar ideas in a speech given at the University of Georgia Alumni Association. Henry Grady, the journalistic voice of the New South movement, later credited Benjamin Hill's speech in 1871 with providing "[Grady] with the ideas and the inspiration which he carried into his crusade." Gordon's appearance in Montgomery in 1868 was apparently politically motivated, but Tichenor and Squire's contact with the former general undoubtedly encouraged them in more ways than one. This encounter with Gordon linked Tichenor to early advocates of the New South movement and to ideas that he promoted in years to come.[31] His continued interest in mining but also the increasing scope of his vision for Alabama and the South would be directly linked to this movement. In the years to come, he became fully enmeshed with the New South movement during his college presidency in Auburn.

After moving from the Montevallo area, briefly to Memphis, Tennessee, then to Auburn, Alabama, and finally to Atlanta, Georgia, Tichenor remained an investor in the mining operations and his plantation there, with Squire overseeing his investments and maintaining his interests. He continued his ventures in the region throughout his tenure at the Home Mission Board. From December 8, 1885, through the end of 1887, Tichenor wrote no fewer than forty-two letters from his office in Atlanta to Squire in Alabama concerning his Montevallo area interests.[32]

Apparently, Tichenor and Squire each had a copy of the maps that Squire had drawn of the surveys he made. The two shared their ideas regarding the Cahaba region, and Tichenor's active mind displayed the insights of a practical geologist and expert observer. In extensive correspondence, they analyzed, debated, and sometimes argued over the maps and where they supposed coal seams and basins to be. Tichenor also sought to interest Henry DeBardeleben as an investor in a company that would build a railroad to the area to remove the extracted minerals. When DeBardeleben failed to come through with the needed capital for the project, Tichenor encouraged Squire to seek out Aldrich for the needed investment capital. This was a reversal in Tichenor's attitude toward Aldrich that he had expressed in a letter to Squire on September 2, 1886. Suspicious that Aldrich was probing Squire to divulge information to which only he and Squire were privy, Tichenor called Aldrich "a shrewd Yankee and utterly unscrupulous." Tichenor's reversal of opinion probably demonstrates his desperation to maintain control of the most promising areas. He believed that these fields were "the biggest thing in Alabama, and I dislike to lose it."[33]

Ultimately, Tichenor and Squire's dreams went unrealized, but the surveys that Squire produced and that he and Tichenor analyzed, as well as the interest they stimulated, formed the basis for the development of the region. Inevitably both DeBardeleben and Aldrich became extensively involved in coal mining operations in both the Cahaba and Birmingham regions. Squire continued to assist both men as they worked to further explore and develop those regions. Ultimately, the development of the central and north Alabama coal fields and subsequent emergence of the state's iron industry led to Alabama's becoming the "fourth largest" producer of iron in the country by 1880. Likewise, records demonstrate that between 1875 and 1885 Alabama coal production grew from only about 67,000 tons to almost 2.5 million. Such advances led no less an expert than steel magnate Andrew Carnegie to declare in 1889, "the South is Pennsylvania's most formidable industrial enemy." The South's mineral production centered upon Alabama.[34]

One of the most persistent concerns of Lost Cause advocates about the New South proponents was that New South concepts fostered an attitude of materialism. They suggested that the Old South was morally superior to the North or to the New South because of the Old South's preservation of chivalry and its disdain for "Yankee materialism."[35] Certainly, some of Tichenor's correspondence with Squire during this period indicates that he had caught New South materialistic fever.

Nor did Tichenor acknowledge that there was a dark side to southern industrialization and materialism. This dark side consisted of convict labor; female and child laborers, who were paid lower wages than white male workers; African Americans who were paid lower wages or excluded; and unreasonable work hours for mill and mine workers. In some regions investors used mines "mainly as a source of revenue to help maintain their accustomed way of life, not to create a New South."[36] Tichenor's New South had a myriad of problems that exposure and development of natural resources alone could not solve.

This materialism is most reflected in a series of letters Tichenor wrote to Squire. In a letter written June 4, 1886, Tichenor enthusiastically began the letter, "'Eureka, Eureka.' I have found it." He proceeded to inform Squire that he was convinced that two geological veins were part of a larger geological vein of coal. Five days and two letters later, Tichenor proclaimed, "If I am right, there is 'millions in it.'" He then proceeded to admonish Squire, "I know how close you keep a secret and feel no necessity of charging you to keep this." While it is true as one mining historian observes, Tichenor's words seem inconsistent with "the stereotype of an otherworldly Baptist minister," it is also true that "his analysis was consistent with his interest in the development of Alabama minerals and technology as well as the acquisitive instincts of late nineteenth-century life." Unfortunately for both men, Tichenor's dreams of owning a coal-black Alabama El Dorado went unmet. He and Squire were unable at this time to acquire the needed financing from either DeBardeleben or Aldrich, and over the succeeding months, his optimism began to fade. By July of 1887, Tichenor was complaining sadly to Squire that he was "quite dispirited at the failure of our grand enterprise. . . . it ought to have made us a hundred thousand dollars apiece." Six months later he was moaning that the five thousand dollars that he and Squire each received was only ten percent of what they should have received when DeBardeleben sold to Aldrich. Tichenor believed that he and Squire were entitled to all the profits from the sale. Problems remained with "title disputes," and both Tichenor and Squire shifted their focus elsewhere. Tichenor continued to own land in Shelby County until his death. Gradually, however, his interest in mining waned as did his contact with Squire. He apparently wrote ten letters to Squire in the first six months of 1886, and then correspondence between the two slowed to a trickle. Undoubtedly, a mutual affection remained between them. In the last two letters Tichenor wrote to Squire, the latter only six months prior to Tichenor's death, the Baptist minister addressed Squire as "my dear friend."[37]

In addition to his active involvement in the affairs of the Montevallo Mining Company in the little more than two years he was in the Montevallo area, the former pastor also remained active in denominational life and virtually every week either preached or spoke at revivals. The *Christian Index* reported on the condition of churches in the Montevallo area. Tichenor's brother-in-law, T. C. Boykin, wrote:

I find that the churches in the country are more or less disorganized; and some pastorless. . . . Brother Tichenor preaches somewhere almost every Sunday, tho' he has the pastoral care of only one church. His congregations, everywhere are always highly pleased. I heard a gentleman say, the other day, "that he at first thought that brother Tichenor's coming here was a great mistake on his part, but he is now inclined to believe that he probably followed the leadings of Providence."[38]

Tichenor served as pastor of the Helena Baptist Church in 1870–71 and encouraged participation of the Shelby Association in the Alabama State Convention. Boykin held pastorates in Montevallo, Columbiana, and Helena during those years, and Tichenor preached regularly in those churches as well. In 1869 he attended the Alabama Baptist State Convention and served on a committee to revise the constitution for publication. He also spoke regarding a report on Howard College. Always an advocate of higher education and optimistic about the South's future, Tichenor

urged that in the great upheaval of society it becomes ours to lay the foundations of a new civilization, and build it up. . . . As a safeguard against the prospective mischiefs of emigration, we should preserve the distinctive principles which have made Southern Society what it is. To do this, we must educate our sons and daughters. . . . Baptists must have Howard College.[39]

Tichenor's statements about the "great upheaval of society" and the call to "lay the foundations of a new civilization" and to "educate our sons and daughters" foreshadowed concepts that would virtually obsess Tichenor in succeeding years. The foundation of the "new civilization" was the concept of a "New South" built upon the "distinctive principles that have made Southern Society what it is." His subsequent efforts at Alabama A & M and at the Home Mission Board were indicative of these words uttered in 1869. Likewise, these "distinctive principles" and the role that education and religion played "as a safeguard against the mischiefs of emigration" would be a theme to which Tichenor would return in his leadership at the Home Mission Board. It should also be added that Tichenor was not alone in his belief that religion would serve "as a safeguard against . . . mischiefs." Mine and mill companies built church buildings for their workers and both supported the churches financially and paid their pastors' salaries.[40] Not all the motivation for this support was philanthropic.

Tichenor's continued involvement in denominational matters and his bivocational work as a minister did not go unnoticed. In 1871 he decided to abandon direct involvement in the mining business and accepted the call to become pastor of the First Baptist Church of Memphis, Tennessee. While in Memphis, Tichenor served as president of the SBC Sunday Board, served on the 1871 SBC Committee on Home Evangelization, and in May addressed a Sunday school mass meeting in Memphis. His sojourn in Memphis was brief, for in 1872, at the age of forty-six, he returned to Alabama to accept the presidency of the Alabama Agricultural and Mechanical College at Auburn.[41]

The period from 1865 to 1872 was extremely significant in Tichenor's development as a major southern and Baptist leader. His concluding years in Montgomery made a definite impression that would shape his convictions that the South must change its economic approach. Increasingly, he would be drawn to the New South movement that was in its developmental years. Likewise, his understanding of racial issues was shaped by his involvement in helping African-American members of Montgomery's FBC separate into their own congregation. The years in Shelby County and in Memphis were important years in Tichenor's development as a leader. Tichenor drew upon business skills gained during this time while college president and as he led the SBC Home Mission Board. Frequently, Tichenor would draw upon the scientific knowledge acquired during these years, both while president of Alabama A & M and while corresponding secretary of the Southern Baptist Home Mission Board. Much of the inspiration for his belief in the South's potential came from the surveys that Squire had conducted during these years and the many hours Tichenor spent poring over Squire's maps. His reports to the Southern Baptist Convention were replete with examples of the South's mineral wealth. The knowledge gained would not only aid his Home Mission Board business administration but also would help him speak prophetically about the South's economic potential. He came to believe that Southern Baptists did not need financial support from their northern cohorts. They could finance adequately an entirely separate denomination if they fully recognized the South's economic potential. The year in Memphis gave him an association with the soon-to-be defunct Sunday School Board. This association would inspire Tichenor in years to come as he sought to resurrect the Sunday School Board as the SBC's publishing arm.

A less admirable side to Tichenor's persona can also be observed from these years. Certainly, his paternalistic behavior and defense of slavery at the beginning of Reconstruction was consistent with most of his white southern contemporaries. His motivation to aid the separation of the African-American members from Montgomery's FBC were questionable as were his reasons for leaving the Montgomery pastorate. Furthermore, Tichenor imbibed deeply in the materialistic spirit that captivated the Gilded Age. At times, his letters sound as if he were far more concerned with financial profit than the prospective humanitarian benefits from Alabama's economic development as he would later claim while at Auburn. Likewise, while one might argue that Tichenor desired riches to support his dreams of spreading the gospel, the tone of his correspondence indicates that he discreetly and unintentionally fell prey to the materialism that ruled the day. Increasingly, his desire for spreading the Christian faith throughout the South would be a means for defending the "southern" way against the perceived threats of immigration and social upheaval. Regardless of his motivations, Tichenor progressively invested his life in envisioning and developing a New South that he believed would elevate the "Southern Zion" into a spiritual and economic paradise.

4
Educating the New South
Tichenor as College President, 1872–82

Institutions of higher education in the United States in the republic's first one hundred years mixed diverse styles of management, finance, and organization. Prior to the War of 1812, most colleges and universities were established by Christian denominations based upon colonial patterns. However, as John S. Brubacher and Willis Rudy acknowledge, "In the United States there has been neither a national ministry of government nor a state church to impose norms of university procedure and control. The vast size of the country and the heterogeneous make-up of its population have made it difficult to establish uniformity in higher learning." In 1819 a ruling by the U.S. Supreme Court regarding Dartmouth College furthered the diversity of private education. The court's decision allowed private institutions to chart their own courses outside of legislative control thus leading to the expansion of private higher education. The trend toward a profusion of institutions of higher learning was accelerated by a populist desire in a democratic society to make education available to an increasingly broad sector of the American population. State universities began to develop primarily in the late eighteenth and early nineteenth centuries.[1]

In the 1840s and 1850s a shift began toward incorporating more utilitarian programs and scientific departments in mostly northeastern institutions. Francis Wayland, president of Brown University, led this movement and inaugurated curriculum reform in his lengthy administration there. Of the more than two hundred institutions of higher learning in the United States in 1850, Wayland complained that none of them was "designed to furnish the agriculturist, the manufacturer, the mechanic, or the merchant with the education that will prepare him for the profession to which his life is to be devoted." The populist approach that both Wayland and Tichenor took was probably influenced by their Baptist roots. Wayland's dissatisfaction ultimately led Senator Justin S. Morrill of Vermont to propose a bill that would grant federal lands to states based upon their representation in Congress. Originally introduced in 1857 but vetoed by President Buchanan, the act received a more favorable response from President Lincoln. It was not really until after the Civil War, however, that the act began to be implemented.[2]

Southern colleges built their curricula along traditional classical lines in the antebellum period. For the most part, they offered a classical education designed to equip white southern males to function as a ruling class. Educational progressives sought to disassociate scientific and technical education from manual labor in the antebellum period; they argued that graduates of southern institutions needed utilitarian educations in order to harness effectively the natural resources of the South and to free the South "from material dependence on the North." Still, industrial development and scientific education in the South lagged far behind that of the North.[3]

The Agricultural and Mechanical College of Alabama (later Auburn University) was a land-grant college created as a result of the Morrill Act of 1862.[4] Although the law did not apply to the states currently in rebellion, after the end of the war, Alabama prepared to apply for the grant of 240,000 acres of land available under the Morrill Act. Unfortunately, no substantial action toward establishing a land-grant college took place until 1871, in part because of political infighting in the state. Because the application deadline was about to expire, the legislature had to hurry. The proposed location for the college became the key issue.[5]

Several cities or regions vied for the opportunity to become the college's home. One effort sought to establish the agricultural and mechanical college as part of the University of Alabama in Tuscaloosa. Proposals were advanced for Auburn in Lee County, Florence in Morgan County, and later, for Birmingham in Jefferson County. Various legislators proposed other locations as well. Representative Sheldon Toomer of Opelika and Senator J. L. Pennington of Lee County spearheaded the proposal for Auburn. Another key issue regarded the question of higher education for blacks. The Alabama Board of Education and some legislators favored the establishment of two separate, segregated land-grant colleges. After months of wrangling and political maneuvering, the legislators agreed upon Auburn as the location of the new agricultural and mechanical college.[6]

Auburn was selected for several reasons. Perhaps foremost was the fact that the small town was already home to the East Alabama Male College. Sponsored by the Alabama Conference of the Methodist Church, the college had been chartered in 1856 and had begun classes in 1859 almost on the eve of the Civil War. The tiny college closed during the war and struggled once it reopened. In an effort to attract the land-grant college to Auburn, the trustees of the Methodist college offered its property to the state, while Auburn residents donated another one hundred acres of land. Some opponents fought the Auburn location because they were concerned that the agricultural and mechanical college might fall under "sectarian influences." After the legislature made its choice, Alabama Methodists transferred the property to the state. Also, a board of directors was selected, and monies made available through the Morrill Act were accessed.[7]

The college's directors chose Isaac Taylor Tichenor as president in their first meeting. Later that year, Tichenor started his tenure as the first president of the newly formed institution. Undoubtedly, his experience as an influential pastor in Montgomery, his regular contact with Alabama legislators and politicians, his earlier advocacy of higher education, his experience as a recognized war hero at Shiloh, and his scientific and technical experience in practical geology and mining all contributed to the decision to name him president. Apparently, Tichenor had also been considered earlier for the presidency of the University of Alabama. The *Christian Index* wrote a letter commending Tichenor to the new Auburn Board of Trustees, saying that Tichenor "possessed the highest qualifications for the Presidency" and added that "it is believed that no man can be obtained who is better posted in geology, agricultural chemistry, the mineral and coalery resources of the state . . . than he."[8] Undoubtedly, the *Index* highly valued the time Tichenor had spent as a coal mining executive in the Montevallo area as a special qualification for the job at the new university. The editors of the *Index* also respected Tichenor for the broadness of his interests and learning and his high standing in the religious community.

For ten years Tichenor served as college president. He also served as its agriculture professor and at times taught other classes as well. When he came in 1872, to use his own words, "The college was in debt, the faculty unpaid, its financial resources undetermined. We had no desks or other furniture suited to the wants of the students and no money to buy with."[9] The situation he found could not have been more bleak. Yet, Tichenor believed in the necessity and promise of agricultural and mechanical education. His emerging ideas on the role that this type of education could play and his vision for the New South spurred him to attempt innovations that would dramatically shape the college's future course and, by extension, Alabama and southern higher education.

Almost immediately, Tichenor set out to change the image of the struggling school. One of his first efforts was to give the college's constituents confidence regarding A & M's leadership. Observers recorded that he generated a positive impression. In a letter to the *Christian Index,* C. L. Thornton rendered a high opinion of the college's new leadership:

Satisfaction with Rev. Dr. I. T. Tichenor, as President of the College, begins at his chair and widens and extends to all its faculty, students, and the community, and as far as knowledge of his relation to the College is spread. . . . The working and industrial appearance of the Institution reminds one of a workshop of work, work, work. . . . These, and the sum of them make it *the College* and the *place* for our young men and boys in want and in search of education.[10]

Students from Tichenor's term as college president and Auburn residents recalled him years later in various ways. One wrote that

he was a stout, robust man of dark complexion, stood about 5 ft. 10 inches tall, weighed 180 lbs. . . . always wore a dark suit of clothes, the usual style of a preacher of those days, cut with a Prince Albert Coat.
. . . . [he] was bald, but had iron gray hair around his head.
His expression was always kind and benign, and when speaking or spoken to he was very courteous.
. . . I remember in a study on the historian Bancroft, he was so interesting one could have heard a pin drop.
His style was easy and impressive, and altogether, I think he was a distinguished looking man.[11]

A resident of Auburn remembered Tichenor as

a man of polished manners, of dignity and *presence,* reserved and *withdrawn,* as men of his type were in those days. But underneath this exterior, he had a kindly sympathetic nature. In my childhood I have seen him moved to tears of sympathy for those who suffered. He loved little children—and the lowly, white and black, and they looked up to him.[12]

She also recalled Tichenor as a "broad minded man for his time" who was "deeply interest[ed] in cultural and litery [*sic*] matters." She mentioned that he "had fine taste" and a "good library" and that he "even wrote poetry (for his friends)." She concluded that "he stood for all that was best in the Old South and his influence was far reaching in his day. He set a high standard for Auburn which has persisted to this day."[13]

Another student, J. E. D. Shipp, recalled him as a fascinating instructor in English literature and wrote, "The outstanding quality of this great teacher was his suavity of manner that enabled him to get into the full confidence of the students under his direction." Shipp added, "He was greatly beloved by all the students." Shipp recalled writing Tichenor late in 1902, expressing an interest in bringing his children to meet the aged gentleman. Shipp "desired my children should know and admire him as their father did." This opportunity was never available because Tichenor died two weeks later. Shipp remembered Tichenor as "a great Christian gentleman . . . I loved and honored him as one of the Godliest men I ever knew."[14]

An incident from Tichenor's presidency at Auburn indicates the source of such respect and admiration. Mrs. Reese Frazer of Auburn recalled the story of Bress Simmons, a young A & M student so impoverished as to become ill from want of a proper diet. Frazer remembered that Tichenor "heard of the boy's distressing condition and sent for him." After questioning Simmons for a moment, Tichenor "look[ed] hard at the boy and shook his finger in his face, and said, 'Go straight and get the finest boarding house in this town, and at the first of each month have them send the bill to me and I will pay it.'" Frazer added, "Through the years his affection for his president continued, and he always summed up his feeling, 'A grander man never lived than Isaac Taylor Tichenor.'"[15]

J. R. Rutland, longtime English professor at Auburn, wrote of Tichenor many years later. A great admirer of the much older Tichenor, Rutland recalled:

It was while at Auburn, also, that Tichenor came into the full richness of his charming literary style. His baccalaureate addresses to his graduating classes were model of choice English, and yet full of the most stimulating thought to the young men whose lives he was seeking to impress for time and eternity. He was to his pupils as a father, not only in wise council, but often in making provisions from his own purse that they might remain in college.[16]

From these remembrances one may see something of the nature of Tichenor's character and understand how he was able to garner such respect and admiration. This was to be crucial in his ability to marshal support for the struggling college. Likewise, these same character traits would be critical in his work at the Home Mission Board (HMB).

This near mythological respect resulted in part from the vast scope of the difficulties Tichenor faced upon his arrival. One of the greatest challenges he confronted in 1872 was the condition of the facilities. After reopening in 1866, the East Alabama Male College limped along barely able to meet its obligations. In 1873 only a year after opening as Alabama A & M, as it was called, a storm destroyed part of the roof and was repaired at a substantial cost equivalent to half Tichenor's annual salary. The land donated by Auburn citizens proved to be inadequate for the college's purposes. Furthermore, the college owned no farm implements, fertilizers, seeds, or laboratory equipment necessary for agricultural and mechanical pursuits. Ultimately, the repair and furnishing of the college building consumed five thousand dollars of much-needed capital.[17]

The financial problem was manifold. The land-grant monies placed in endowment from land sales proved to be inadequate for the college's needs. The state legislature refused to make appropriations to Alabama A & M, despite the fact that Tichenor regularly pleaded to the legislature and to the trustees for aid. Tichenor argued that the state awarded substantial aid to the University of Alabama, to the state mental hospital, and for the care and education of the disabled. Lack of state funding forced the small school to rely almost entirely on student tuition, gifts, and the limited funds coming from the land-grant endowment. The type of students attracted to the A & M school complicated this reliance. Many of these students lacked resources to pay tuition but sought to receive training in agricultural science to better enhance their opportunities in farming. The times themselves hampered efforts to increase enrollment and raise funds. The South generally and the state of Alabama specifically were still in the process of Reconstruction. As Paul Gaston describes the postbellum South, the region "was desperately poor, alternately despised, ridiculed or pitied and saddled with many unwelcome burdens." As Alabama was beginning to emerge from Reconstruction, the Panic of 1873 hit the country and contributed substantially to the financial distress faced by the young state college, which was already saddled with the nine thousand dollars of debt transferred from EAMC along with its building and land and approximately seven thousand dollars in debt incurred in A & M's first year of operation. Additionally, Tichenor complained in 1875 that land-grant money intended for endowment "had been misused by the state, had not been invested according to law and . . . was in great danger of being lost to the college." Fortunately, the efforts of the board restored access to these funds, and prudent investment reinstated the college's endowment.[18]

Yet another persistent problem Tichenor dealt with was the nature of the land-grant college. The very concept, emphasizing agricultural and mechanical sciences, offended critics on both extremes of society. On one hand were those in higher education who favored the traditional approach to classical training. Tichenor believed that the original purpose of the A & M colleges in the United States resulted from the desire "to benefit the Agricultural interests of the country." However, he acknowledged that "men of letters such as usually compose College Faculties rarely have any knowledge of or taste for agricultural pursuits. There is danger in every such Institution, that the agricultural department will either be strangled or starved by those who are expected to be its nurses or guardians." On the other hand were those "agriculturists" who exhibited "a strong prejudice . . . against what they call 'Book Farming.'" This suspicion led to "a misconception of the scope and design of Agricultural colleges which lead them to undervalue if not despise their advantage." Hence, Tichenor feared that the country's financial difficulty prevented some willing farmers from providing their sons a complete college education, while others who were financially able did not want their sons to become farmers. After almost four years of his presidency, Tichenor reflected further upon one reason for agriculturists' suspicion toward "book farming": "Many a farmer who has sent his son to college has been pained to find that the youthful graduate had no longer any sympathy with farm life, that all thoughts of industrial pursuits were irksome to him and that nothing but a profession would meet the requirements of his ambition." Certainly, overcoming these prejudices comprised a major portion of the task Tichenor found before him. The prejudices were not unique to Tichenor and Alabama A & M but were common in this era both in the South and throughout the nation. Tichenor's comments should be considered against the background of the rapid changes taking place both in higher education throughout the nation and in the South's economy, society, and culture.[19]

The changes then taking place were revolutionary. One historian of American higher education calls this period "The Dawning of a New Era." The new era was marked by a number of changes to traditional curriculum and to both the very context of higher education and its subsequent development. The introduction of the elective system dramatically changed higher education. Francis Wayland originally advocated the elective system as part of his attempt to reform Brown University curriculum prior to the Civil War, and Charles W. Eliot, president of Harvard University, further promoted it in the postbellum period. The elective principle allowed students greater flexibility in their studies. Another change was the promotion of professional scholarship and professional and graduate education, especially in the sciences; sometimes identified as the "German model," this approach was pioneered and best represented in the United States by Johns Hopkins University. The third change was agricultural and mechanical education with an emphasis upon experimental sciences and practical mathematics created through state colleges and land-grant institutions. This final change offered popular higher education to the broader American public and, together with the other modifications, forced most older colleges to adapt to the changing landscape of higher education.[20] All three of these alterations influenced the development of Alabama A & M.

The changes taking place in higher education were significant for the new school at Auburn, but Tichenor's personal background and the larger economic and social movement developing in the South were even more influential. In antebellum Montgomery he saw the South's commercial possibilities through utilization of transportation systems and agriculture. At the same time, he saw the devastating effects of an economy structured around a staple crop agricultural system when the crop failed to be profitable, as cotton had been during Reconstruction. While the steamboat system declined in the 1870s, Tichenor recognized that a blending of railroad transportation with both industrial and agricultural pursuits could lead to economic diversification. As an investor in the Montevallo Coal Mining Company and for four years its president, Tichenor surveyed the Cahaba region for prospective coal fields and investigated the possible use of technology to facilitate coal mining. This survey work exposed Tichenor to Alabama's and the South's potential natural resources. All these influences shaped Tichenor and made him an ideal first president for the land grant college. He already had invested a significant portion of his career in ideas associated with the New South movement. His adoption of New South concepts while at Auburn appeared in presidential reports, and his advocacy while at Auburn would rank him among the earliest proponents of the New South mentality both in higher education and the economy.

Historically, the title "The New South" has been most commonly associated with Henry W. Grady. Beginning in 1876 Grady wrote dually as a correspondent for the New York *Herald* and as a staff writer for the *Atlanta Constitution,* eventually becoming the editor of the newspaper that became the chief mouthpiece of the New South movement even as its host city became its model. Marked by boundless enthusiasm, visionary oratory, and charismatic personality, Grady became a virtual martyr for the New South cause when he died prematurely at the age of thirty-eight of an illness believed to be pneumonia that he contracted while on his extensive travels promoting the New South. Although Grady was the most well known of all promoters of the "New South" vision, he did not originate the term, nor was he the only individual to promote it. Grady first published the term "New South" in 1874, but the name had been used prior to that and was coming into more widespread usage in the South. Not really until 1886, after Grady's speech to the New England Club meeting in New York, did the concept come into popular national usage. Recounting the devastation of the Civil War and praising northern leaders such as Abraham Lincoln and General William T. Sherman, Grady moved on to describe his images of the New South. He admitted that free blacks were more valuable to the southern economy than slaves had been and lauded the idea that education should be free to all, black and white. He also stated that the Mason-Dixon Line had been eliminated. He encouraged unity and brotherhood. In similar addresses, Grady praised the agricultural South's industrial potential and promoted further diversification of its economy. His persistent efforts sought to promote both his vision and the quantitative evidence he assembled, especially regarding the impressive expansion of the southern textile industry.[21]

Gaston states that proponents of the movement identified the "New South" as a "harmonious reconciliation of sectional differences, racial peace, and a new economic and social order based on industry and scientific, diversified agriculture—all of which would lead eventually to the South's dominance in the reunited nation." While the South remained primarily a rural region, by the turn of the century, the "New South" had produced a dramatic economic and commercial transformation. Tichenor and others believed that a crucial component of the movement was the reform of higher education, especially in the areas of scientific and technical education. By promoting this reform, Tichenor sought to blend the changes taking place in higher education with the adoption of the New South ideals. His approach was not original or unique, nor was it as thorough as that taken by his successors at Auburn, but he was among those at the forefront of the changes taking place throughout the South and throughout education.[22]

New South ideals had their origins in academia in the aftermath of the Civil War. Shattered by the war, southern higher education sought to rebuild by hiring as administrators and faculty men who had served in the Confederate military or in war industries. Some of these men—Robert E. Lee, A. P. Stewart, Stephen D. Lee, and Daniel Harvey Hill—were graduates of the U.S. Military Academy at West Point prior to the war. West Point was one institution of higher education that had emphasized engineering in the antebellum period. Although engineering was primarily taught as part of military sciences, some army engineers engaged in significant civil engineering projects as well. These men brought from that background openness to technical training. They, and other Confederate veterans like them, also bore the legacy of a bitter defeat at the hands of a technologically superior North.[23]

Tichenor discussed this issue in his sixth report to the college's board of trustees on June 25, 1877. He invoked the still fresh memories of southern defeat in the recent conflict. He did not admit that the cause for which they had fought was unjust, and he praised the bravery of the enlisted southern men who had served in the war. He asserted that the South had "skilful [*sic*] generals whose nobility has won the admiration of the world" and declared that the South did not lose the war because the Confederate military had failed. Tichenor argued that the failure came because the statesmen of the South were "drivlers and incompetent when they came to grapple with the problems whose solution was demanded by that gigantic conflict." Their shortcoming resulted from education under a system which led them habitually to disregard the material interests of a country, they never comprehended that steam engines and railroads, that looms and shuttles, that plows and hoes and reapers constituted a prime element of a nation's strength upon the field of battle. They knew not how to make these fight. They did not understand how to construct a mighty bulwark of their cotton bales to break the power of the advancing foe. This was the fatal weakness of our cause. It was the mismanagement of our material resources, or rather the failure to manage them at all that caused us to be borne down in the bloody struggle.[24]

Tichenor's words, while harsh, were consistent with those of his contemporaries who placed blame for Confederate defeat upon this educational deficiency. Many southerners had been reared in a theological tradition based upon Calvinistic theology regarding predestination. They interpreted their defeat as God's will not because the republic deserved to survive or slavery deserved to die, but because God had a higher purpose. The superiority of Union scientific technology guaranteed the success of that higher purpose. This enabled Confederates to escape responsibility for their failures and to develop the Lost Cause mentality. The New South advocates perpetuated this myth and blended their progressivist educational goals with the larger agenda of the New South and the Lost Cause. Religious apologists, like Tichenor, further incorporated these ideas in a theological message that explained the South's defeat and challenged the resurrected South to both spiritual and material leadership of nation and world.[25]

Tichenor not only charged the political leaders with this deficiency but also heavily criticized the educational processes of the state's other institution of higher education, the University of Alabama. Tichenor had contended in his second report to the Board of Trustees that college faculties generally ignored the importance of scientific and mechanical education. In his fifth report, he acknowledged that the heritage and facilities of the older university were superior to that of the A & M College but also reminded them that the state had expended thousands of dollars rebuilding the university after the war. Further, the state had done so without furnishing "a single dollar" to A & M. Faculty salaries at Auburn, Tichenor complained, lagged far behind those of the University. These financial inequities came despite the fact that his college was specifically created to educate young men engaged in agricultural and mechanical pursuits that involved ninety percent of the population of the state. The inequities also existed despite the fact that by 1877, A & M enrolled more students annually than did the University. Tichenor's greatest fears were that the financial differences would make it increasingly difficult to attract quality instructors to the college.[26]

Tichenor unleashed his most scathing denunciation of the South's traditional educational system and of the University of Alabama in his sixth report. Despite the university's rich heritage, the school seemed oblivious to the fact that it stood "upon one of the richest mineral regions of the world." It was surrounded by "the great coal-field of Alabama stretching eastward and northward" that covered "an area of nearly five thousand square miles" and "the mightiest development of iron ore known on this or any other continent stands almost at its door":

> But these mighty sources of wealth and power, the very means by which England has made herself the mistress of the seas and has become the workshop of the world, have slumbered under the foundations of your University and in all its history has sent forth not one man among its graduates who know the value of and took more than a passing interest in their existence. These professors in their summer wanderings crossed the broad areas where coal beds jutted from the banks of the mountain streams and they heeded not the black diamonds that lay in such imposing masses on every side. Her students climbed the side of the Red Mountain and saw its crimson rocks jutting out in craggy grandeur from its summit but never recognized them as an ore of iron.[27]

Such a critique of the academic structure and educational goals of the state university, its faculty, and alumni would not have endeared Tichenor to those people or even to some in the legislature. His intent seems to have been to rally the support of the board for his agenda. His comments would have placed Tichenor among a group comprised of "editors, industrialists, middle-class professionals, planters, and politicians" who implored "southerners to build an industrial base, engage in diversified and scientific agriculture, and to develop the South's raw materials."[28] By unleashing such a diatribe against the University, Tichenor hoped to rally the support of Alabamians of similar belief to the objectives of Alabama A & M. One has to wonder also if the ferocity of this attack may have been prompted by the fact that he had not received the school's presidency. Certainly, some of the criticism was motivated by the favoritism legislators had shown the University.

Tichenor also appealed to a growing populist sentiment that all qualified citizens should have access to higher education. He believed that A & M stood on the movement's forefront. In his sixth report to the board, Tichenor drew upon his knowledge of history to present his opinions about higher education. He believed that the old British model for classical education imported to America and only slightly adapted was designed to educate and provide culture for the ruling class and the clergy. He appealed to patriotism, American values, and even ideas prominent in Baptist life. He argued that classical education was "born of the necessities of an established church and a hereditary nobility, suited not to the masses of the people or to interests of Republican Institutions, but to the claims and pretensions of an aristocracy." Further, he added that "it still holds in bondage to its falsities, made venerable by their antiquity and its arrogant claims strengthened by centuries of acquiesance [*sic*] almost the entire cultured intellect of the country." Rejecting this elitist view, Tichenor believed that the type of education he advocated did not eschew the value of classical learning where appropriate. He believed, however, that the "New Education" was created for the needs of the people and was consistent with the values of the republic and the possibilities benefiting the world. Clearly, Tichenor was not above appealing to patriotism in order to marshal support for his cause. He also appealed to the populism inherent in his Baptist tradition and its rejection of an established state church and its accompanying educational system.[29] This should not be misunderstood to suggest that Tichenor later embraced the Populist political movement as it became popular in the Midwest and South. With other southern white leaders, Tichenor viewed the Populist party as a threat to southern Redeemer Democrat state governments.

The background of the college at Auburn posed one of the greatest challenges to making the transition from the traditional classical model to the progressivist view of education. The East Alabama Male College had been a liberal arts college that heavily emphasized training in the classical languages, and Tichenor himself had received such an education, albeit a limited one. In adopting an agricultural and mechanical New South model of education, however, Tichenor simply grafted it onto the existing liberal arts religious college structure. He believed that teaching moral philosophy was a crucial component of any educational process and, as an ordained minister, believed that the spiritual climate of the campus contributed significantly to the academic environment. For example in his sixth report issued to the board in 1877, Tichenor lauded the "deep religious feeling" pervasive for months that had led to a large number of public conversions. He further reported that a YMCA formed "mainly of students of the college" was the chief "means of accomplishing much good." On the other hand, in his 1881 report, Tichenor lamented the establishment of secret fraternities as being detrimental to student conduct on campus and appealed to the board to prohibit the commencement "Hop" or "Ball." Apparently, good Baptist that he was, Tichenor found dancing detrimental to student morals. More likely, he believed that the criticism he received in the state due to the commencement celebration caused "serious injury to the college." Unlike some southern academics with clerical backgrounds, Tichenor did not believe that the new scientific and technological education cultivated materialism. He made frequent references to the theological motivation behind what he was attempting to do at Auburn. He believed that the scientific method of education, especially regarding agriculture but also in relationship to other areas, sought to improve people's lives. While Tichenor never clearly identified himself as a postmillenialist, he certainly made allusions in his reports that suggest that he believed that the progress a progressive education could usher in was a giant movement forward. Postmillenialism was an eschatological concept that was especially strong among some Protestants in the late nineteenth century. Postmillenialists believed that the end of history and return of Christ would be preceded by a period of peace and prosperity. Some Protestant postmillenialists believed that the global missions effort would facilitate this "ushering in" of the millenium. Some postmillenialists believed that the industrial progress witnessed at the end of the century heralded the onset of this era and would lead to moral and social advance. Tichenor repeatedly expressed sentiments consistent with this eschatological viewpoint. Certainly, his optimistic spirit, his constant emphasis upon scientific and industrial progress, and his lifelong commitment to missions were similar to other postmillenialist Protestants generally and to many educated postmillenialist Southern Baptists specifically.[30]

Tichenor also believed that even those engaged in scientific enterprise needed to have some background and training in the literary arts. He was not abandoning liberal arts education. He was attempting to reform it. In fact, Tichenor continually reported on the role of a modern languages department in higher education and occasionally taught history and literature himself, apparently demonstrating both a vast knowledge of these subjects and spellbinding lecture skills. When a new agriculture professor arrived in 1878, Tichenor requested that the board change his appointment from president and professor of agriculture to president and professor of moral philosophy. As a New South academic, he was concerned with the study of history, especially in light of new methods of studying the subject. New South educators such as William Preston Johnston and Tichenor embraced a modern scientific approach to history and considered it a necessary discipline to be adopted along with other innovative and technical studies in postbellum college curricula. Indeed, much of this perspective among southern academics came in an attempt to explain and justify the Civil War. Tichenor's biggest problem with the classical method centered upon the learning of classical languages. He believed that the requirement for Greek and Latin should be replaced for most students with increased requirements in the natural sciences. Ironically, he used his own classical training by citing examples from classical literature to argue in favor of scientific training. He also emphasized the moral necessity of utilizing scientific gifts to harness the potential of Alabama and the South to better provide for the world.[31]

Tichenor challenged the primary argument given for the instruction of ancient languages—that this study helped the student discipline his mind. Tichenor argued that natural sciences could perform the same function. As a theologian-pastor, he further argued:

> In ancient lore we have the thoughts of the sages of antiquity. In natural sciences the thoughts of the Infinite and Eternal. There may be beauty in the mental creatures of Homer and Virgil, but who will deny there is beauty whenever nature breathes, for beauty is her soul. . . .
> There may be light which still shines along the pathway trodden by the genius of the olden time, but in nature the footprints of the Creator are luminous with the glory of the Divine majesty.[32]

Tichenor believed that not only did the study of the natural sciences aid in disciplining the mind but also that it illuminated the greatness of a Creator-God. While other New South academics, including David Boyd, one of Tichenor's successors at Auburn, sometimes found themselves at odds with clerical opponents critical of contemporary scientific studies, Tichenor had no such problem. In this he had much in common with other clergymen appointed as university and college presidents in this era. These clergymen, though more conservative than their non-clerical presidential counterparts, saw no conflict between science and God or between advancing material and scientific progress while maintaining abiding religious faith and tradition.[33]

Still, Tichenor did not favor abandoning classical study completely. One of the four courses of study a student could choose in his administration was that of classical studies, called initially "a course in Letters" and later described as "Literature" or "Literary Arts." Tichenor clearly continued to believe in the necessity of a classical-style education for some disciplines and that the root of any education was a liberal arts background. Students engaged in agriculture and mechanical education were also required to enroll in the departments of English, mathematics, and moral philosophy. Despite his emphasis on scientific, technical, and professional training at A & M, he believed that any university must include liberal arts in its curriculum: "As man does not live by bread alone, but enjoys an intellectual as well as physical life, there [should] be a department purely literary, in which ancient and hidden languages, mental and moral science, philosophy in its various forms, pure mathematics should be taught which should embrace everything necessary to the wide circle of human knowledge or to direct the aspiring mind in its search after new realms of truth." In addition to teaching agriculture, he taught history, moral philosophy, and literature, and, in his last two years at Auburn, initiated "the first class in political economy" or, as it might be identified today, political science. These courses might well be considered the basis of a liberal arts or general studies curriculum. In the closing years of his administration, graduates of the literary department remained between 25 and 33 percent of the total graduating class, demonstrating that a significant portion of the students continued to prepare for careers in literary pursuits. Likewise, an 1880 survey of the occupations of 500 former students of the institution indicated that while more than 200 were engaged in agricultural pursuits and another 130 were employed in mechanical, engineering, or business occupations, approximately 60, or more than 10 percent, were involved in occupations such as ministers, attorneys, editors, and teachers that Tichenor appraised as literary pursuits.[34]

Tichenor's advocacy of reforms reached beyond these issues. One of the problems he faced at Auburn was many students' lack of educational preparation. Public education in Alabama in the Reconstruction era was woefully inadequate, so Tichenor and the faculty found themselves forced to initiate a preparatory department at Auburn that worked to address the deficiencies of entering students. Tichenor regarded the preparatory department as essential to the enterprise, not only because it raised the level of academic work for poorly prepared students before they entered formal college studies but also because its enrollment provided financial benefits. Analysis of statistics demonstrates that during Tichenor's tenure the enrollment in the preparatory department was usually between 34 and 41 percent of the entire college's enrollment. In the last three years of Tichenor's administration, total enrollment for A & M dropped more than 50 percent. The preparatory department accounted for most of the enrollment decline. While some of this decrease may have been caused by the improvement of secondary education in Alabama, it probably occurred because of the financial difficulties encountered in farming during those years, to which Tichenor referred in his last two presidential reports. The need for adequate secondary and general studies education prompted Tichenor to suggest other reforms later.[35]

Tichenor also suggested that A & M allow female students to enroll. As early as the Civil War, some southerners had recognized the need for greater educational opportunities for females, especially in the field of teaching. While some southerners believed that women did not have the learning capacity that men had, they realized that the war had created a need for female schoolteachers and thus for education for women. After the war ended, some southern progressives continued to lobby for opening higher education to women. In 1875 Tichenor reported that all but one of the faculty had approved a motion to request the board's permission for this change. Tichenor added in his report that the motion met his "hearty approval," but board members failed to act upon this recommendation. Two years later he reminded them of this suggestion and that they had failed to approve the request. It is unknown exactly whether Tichenor or a member of the faculty initiated this action. Tichenor's endorsement, however, was consistent with other New South educational progressivists who typically approved of coeducation despite the concern of some conservatives that it would lead to the demise of morals in colleges. Certainly, Tichenor as a devout Christian and ordained minister would never have endorsed any proposal that he believed would contribute to a moral decline. The motivation undoubtedly was threefold. As the father of daughters, Tichenor saw the intellectual potential that educated women offered. Like his longtime acquaintance Jabez Curry, also a New South educator, he recognized that women were capable of mastering the same academic disciplines as men. Tichenor and Curry both recognized the contributions of women during the Civil War in industrial and professional occupations and the potential of women in the New South in those occupations essential to southern business. Likewise, Tichenor recognized that many "common school," or primary and secondary school, teachers were women who needed education to prepare their students adequately for college, vocation, and life. Finally, coeducation offered his young institution the potential benefit of increased enrollment and an enlarged constituency.[36]

Yet another set of reforms dealt with methodology. Tichenor earnestly endorsed the reform of mechanical engineering by approving Colonel Robert Hardaway's work despite his and Hardaway's other differences of opinion. Hardaway, the college commandant and professor of engineering, advocated the Russian system of teaching mechanical engineering that endorsed both theoretical and practical education. Tichenor gathered the financial support necessary for the purchase of the equipment Hardaway needed to teach the Russian system.[37]

Tichenor's reform of educational processes included his active participation in the experimental farm and model farm efforts utilized at Alabama A & M that became the basis of agricultural education at the school. While there is no evidence to suggest that this method was unique among A & M colleges at that time, apparently it was impressive. Tichenor reported that J. M. Hay of Wisconsin, the government inspector of land-grant colleges, praised the concept when he visited Auburn. According to Tichenor, Hay especially commended the farm for the variety of wheat that was grown there. The experimental farm concept involved experimentation with not only wheat but also cotton, corn, cover grasses, garden crops, flowers, shrubs, fertilizers, implements, and various seeds. Chemistry classes tested and researched various soils and minerals as well. Classes conducted experiments upon recently discovered marl fields in the southern part of Alabama to determine the viability of its use as a commercial fertilizer. In 1875 Tichenor reported that an experimental farm created in the Tennessee River Valley had conducted eighty-seven experiments in corn and cotton. He could also proudly report on occasion that the cotton crop produced on the farms not only paid for itself but actually returned a profit that the college reinvested in the enterprise. The agriculture department created a flower garden on campus for not only aesthetic reasons but also to experiment with seeds, shrubs, and soils. Tichenor purchased the seeds and plants needed for this latter enterprise with his own funds.[38]

The experimental farm process became the model for other practical, scientific experimentation. Tichenor began courses of study in surveying, meteorology, telegraphy, and mining engineering—all based upon the principle of combining theoretical study with practical experience. Behind all these efforts lay underlying principles at the heart of Tichenor's progressivist views of education and the New South. He believed that providing these scientific skills would better equip the South to take advantage of the vast natural resources that were beginning to be tapped. The South's poverty and the legacy of Confederate defeat burdened Tichenor. He lamented the South's dependence upon the one-crop system and sought a way to separate southerners from their "infatuation" with cotton. He also criticized the persistent antebellum notion that manual labor was unfitting for a gentleman. Boldly, he proclaimed that "the time has come when we can no longer remit our agricultural interests to our overseers and our slaves, when we can no longer afford to buy everything we use, in clothing our persons, feeding our families, furnishing the houses, and supplying our plantations from other and distant communities. We must make all these things at home." In this attitude, Tichenor was consistent with other New South educators.[39]

Tichenor's advocacy of a specialized course of study in mining reflected his years in the mining industry and the need for qualified mining engineers in the state. His 1876 report to Alabama's governor once again lauded the natural resources available:

The resources of our State are admitted to be beyond all computation. Our mountains of iron, one thousand square miles of coal, our immense beds of marble, our splendid deposits of copper and gold, together with a great variety of other minerals less known to our people, but scarcely less valable [sic], our numberless streams furnishing sites for the factories of a nation, running idly to the sea, our varied and fertile soils all await the science and skill, that can transform them into comfort and wealth for our people.[40]

Tichenor hoped that a course of study in mining engineering would not only aid the mining interests of the state as they sought to expose and exploit these resources but also that this degree would benefit the state's manufacturing interests and aid the overall prosperity of the region.[41]

In his 1881 report to the board, Tichenor turned from essentially providing information on the college's condition to a broader proposal for educational reform throughout Alabama. In visionary fashion, Tichenor proposed an interlocking system that coordinated the efforts of the state's common schools and high schools with higher education. In fact, he proposed that the common schools that he considered "the foundation of the whole system" be "organically" linked with state colleges. Further, he introduced essentially a forerunner of the modern junior or community college system and the predecessor of an interlocked and unified state system of higher education. He argued that such a cohesive system of education would eliminate destructive competition, utilize Alabama's educational resources more effectively, and ultimately result in educational and economic prosperity for the entire state.[42]

The proposal was far-reaching. Tichenor suggested that each of Alabama's eight congressional districts establish a two-year college that would pick up the curriculum where the common schools left off. The curriculum would be "broad rather than high" and would encompass "those sciences which relate directly to human progress, to the preservation of human life and to the well being of society." This meant that the curriculum would be expanded to include diverse areas of learning. It would conclude at the end of the typical sophomore college year and would be the equivalent of a modern general studies curriculum. These colleges would also include a "normal school" for the training of common school teachers "and from them the chief supply of teachers for those schools [would] come." Tichenor further recommended that these colleges would be institutions where teachers in each district could come for assistance and training similar to what today would be called "continuing education." Each year teachers would turn to these colleges for conferences in which "methods of instruction, new text books, improvements of every kind should be brought to the attention of all and their profession be thus encouraged and facilitated." These colleges essentially would strengthen the existing common school structure by preparing and equipping better teachers, thus eliminating the need for preparatory departments at schools like A & M. They would serve as resources to continue to improve the quality of education, and they would also remove a portion of the curriculum from the university system. This experience would serve to qualify students for professional and university studies. University admission would hinge upon completion of the college course curriculum. Not only did this proposal have serious implications for educational reform, but also it may have been a subtle way to engage the idea of coeducation. Since increasingly teachers in the state were female, under this system women would have been products of these two-year schools as well as others who were moving on to the university.[43]

Above this system of colleges was the university system itself, comprised of eight departments. The university would begin with the third year of study or junior year, would last not less than three years, and would offer the prospect of "post-graduate" study. Tichenor suggested that each of these departments—law, medicine, agriculture and horticulture, chemistry, geology, natural history, engineering, and the literary department—be located in various strategic locations throughout the state. The department of medicine would be linked closely with the state health department. He modeled the agriculture and horticulture department after patterns already established at Alabama A & M, with the experimental and model farms serving as resources for the state's agriculture. Chemistry, geology, and natural history—which included botany, entomology, and zoology—would likewise have theoretical, pragmatic, and utilitarian functions. Chemistry, for example, would analyze fertilizers and samples of geological material. Natural history, in particular, would study animal sciences and determine the most suitable regions for the production of livestock and agricultural produce. The engineering department would be divided into three divisions—civil, mining, and mechanical—each to address practical engineering problems in the state. The literary department, he believed, should include the traditional liberal arts, and he insisted it was a significant component of the university system he sought to establish in Alabama.[44]

Tichenor proposed that this college system be financed through a tax placed upon the sale of commercial fertilizers, from tuition charged by the proposed schools, and from financing provided by the federal government under a proposed extension of the Morrill Act. He believed that local communities would provide buildings in the various locales for the eight proposed two-year schools. Obviously, Tichenor believed that Alabama A & M was best suited to provide the basis of such a statewide university system, though he granted that the "University at Tuscaloosa" might be involved as well, even if it meant dividing the responsibilities of this proposal or uniting the two schools under his proposition. Finally, Tichenor challenged the board:

> The worst we can do is to fail and failure in such a cause is only a little less honorable than to succeed. If we fail we will be enabled in heart and in life by the very effort we make to benefit our country and kind.

If we fail, the very fragments of our works will bear our names along the current of coming years and proud hand of future generations will gather the debris into an enduring monument for those who worked unavailingly for them.[45]

Tichenor closed his report with a reminder of the changes taking place in the South. He touted the future of the "New South," which by 1881 was becoming a more popular concept, and appealed to the board's ambition with an eloquent plea:

The New South is rapidly coming forward. If your hands shall wield these noble institutions that are to mould this nascent civilization and shape its rising power and glory, our counsels shall plan the future destiny of our state and exalt her to the highest place among the sisterhood of commonwealth, which constitute the grandest domain upon the globe; then when the hour shall come that each must take his place in the silent halls of death, we may go to our slumber in the clay as one who wraps the drapery of his couch about him and lies down to pleasant dreams.[46]

Tichenor's comprehensive plan for restructuring higher education in Alabama was certainly ambitious. It was far more grandiose than anything possible in the 1870s and 1880s, and it revealed the insight that Tichenor had developed in the ten years he served at A & M. He advocated reform because it would benefit A & M and his vision for the college. He also advocated educational reform because of his desire to see Alabama and the South attain the New South vision then developing. He incorporated the concepts of progessivist southern educators with ideas promoted by New South prophets such as Henry Grady and Richard H. Edmonds. In fact, much of Tichenor's ambitious vision for the South antedated that of Grady, Edmonds, and others who aggressively promoted such a concept. It also contested the Lost Cause religionists who criticized the New South for an education system they viewed as "utilitarian" and a morality they viewed as "materialistic."[47]

Tichenor's proposals for a statewide university system connected to a college system were similar to the junior college system that was in its infancy across America. As early as 1852, Henry Tappan, president of the University of Michigan, had suggested something like a junior college system, and in

1869 W. W. Folwell, president of the University of Minnesota, had made a similar suggestion. Their ideas revolved around the nature of the first two years of college study that they and others believed were an extension of high school. These two years would be devoted to general cultural education that served as the capstone of secondary education and the necessary groundwork for university specialization beginning in the junior year. Nothing came of their ideas. It was not until William Rainey Harper of the University of Chicago and others at Johns Hopkins University and Stanford University made similar proposals in the 1890s that the junior college movement began in earnest. These recommendations were part of the era's general educational climate including the aforementioned curricula and elective reforms Tichenor endorsed.[48] Tichenor's desire for a comprehensive university system and his request for a structure of two-year schools may have been influenced by some of these developments but in many ways demonstrates that he was visionary in his educational reforms. The precarious nature of the educational enterprise at Auburn, the poor quality of public education in Alabama, and the necessity of education for the New South's development undoubtedly prompted his proposals as well.

One year later Tichenor resigned as president of Alabama A & M to accept a position as corresponding secretary of the Home Mission Board. With the exception of one year in Memphis, he had not served in vocational ministry on a full-time basis in more than a decade. But he had not completely neglected his family or his service to Baptist life. Sadly, his third wife Lulah had died of malaria in 1868 after only three years of marriage. In 1876 he married his fourth wife, Eppie Reynolds McCraw, a widow from the Reynolds family, plantation owners in Talladega. Eppie bore him his only surviving son, Reynolds, early in 1877. Unfortunately, Eppie died a little more than a year later, leaving Tichenor a widower again with another small child for whom to care and provide. He would not remarry. In the preceding twenty-five years, he had married and buried four wives and lost three young children. Far happier occasions for Tichenor in these years were the birth of his son and the weddings of his two eldest daughters, Mary Bell to Opelika attorney C. H. Barnes in 1874 and Kate to Baptist minister Jacob S. Dill in 1882 about the time that Tichenor left Auburn to go to Atlanta. Dill had served as pastor of Auburn First Baptist Church from 1879–81, as well as churches in three other Southern states, and later in life would author two books, including a brief biography of his father-in-law.[49]

Despite his busy schedule with the college and the multitude of responsibilities that went with it and his family, Tichenor remained active in denominational activities, attending the Southern Baptist Convention and the Alabama Baptist State Convention as his schedule allowed. He effectively served as interim pastor of the Auburn Baptist Church and as lay pastor in that church during years when it was served by its pastor only one Sunday a month. No one in the Auburn church's early history directed its development as much as Tichenor did. A survey of Baptist newspapers during his Auburn presidency demonstrates that he continued to write reports of his activities in district, convention, and associational meetings and contributed editorials to these papers about particular issues. He regularly preached in churches, spoke at ministers' and deacons' meetings, took part in the Southern Baptist Theological Seminary commencement, served on committees in the Alabama Baptist State Convention, and editorialized about issues such as Sabbath desecration. He also used the *Alabama Baptist* to promote A & M.[50] During that period Tichenor was involved in two significant events that molded the future of the Home Mission Board and the SBC.

In 1879 amid talk of closing the board or merging with the Northern Baptist Home Mission Society, Tichenor rose before the convention meeting. He presented resolutions designed to strengthen the Southern Baptist Convention by defining "its territorial limits and securing the co-operation" of the Home Mission Society and thus preventing overlaps in Baptist work. Tichenor was determined to end once and for all the question of the dissolution of the convention. At the same time, he hoped to foster more cordial relations with Northern Baptists, in much the same spirit as the New South movement sought economic reconciliation. Unfortunately, some leaders misunderstood his intentions and believed he was actually encouraging the dissolution of the HMB and the SBC. When the committee Tichenor chaired reported the resolutions, John Broadus of Southern Baptist Theological Seminary moved to strike two of them, and the resulting debate raged most of the day. Finally, the convention adopted Broadus's amendment. A little less than two weeks later, the *Alabama Baptist* reported on the spirit of the Tichenor resolutions and indicated that his intentions were honorable. The misunderstanding continued long afterward, however. In 1895 convention leaders asked W. H. Whitsitt to present a historical summary of the SBC's first fifty years. In the presentation, he misinterpreted Tichenor's 1879 resolutions as an attempt to dissolve the Southern Baptist Convention. Tichenor refuted Whitsitt's error, one apparently common in the Broadus circle, in a point of order. The fact that Tichenor's intentions were misunderstood is verified by his election as corresponding secretary in 1882. If he had sought to dissolve the board and the convention in 1879, he never would have been chosen to lead the home mission effort only three years later. Rather, it appears that through focusing the attention of the convention on the plight of the Home Mission Board and the need for a spirit of conciliation between the two home mission bodies, Tichenor planted the seeds for the board's renewal. He also introduced the concept of defining geographical limits for the two competing Baptist denominations, a theme to which he would later return.[51]

The second notable event came at the Alabama State Convention meeting in 1880. At this convention, Tichenor chaired a special committee chosen to study the entire state missions program. The committee's report proved to be a decisive event in Alabama Baptist history. The report approved the district program of missions, but more importantly it laid the foundation for a cooperative missions effort for Alabama Baptists. The committee made several bold recommendations. The most significant was that all missions gifts be collected and channeled in a unified fashion through the state board.[52] This type of arrangement was remarkably similar to the arrangement used in the 1920s SBC Cooperative Program and is compellingly similar to the type of system Tichenor encouraged later as corresponding secretary of the Home Mission Board.

Perhaps this ongoing involvement and especially the redirection of the Southern Baptist Convention's Home Mission Board was too big a challenge for Tichenor to resist in 1882. When the HMB called for him to come lead it in a renewed vision, Tichenor could not turn his back upon his denomination in its hour of need. Perhaps he simply felt providentially led in this direction. He may also have missed consistent involvement in ministerial activities and may have viewed leadership of the HMB as the crowning achievement of his career. The lack of response to his reforms at Auburn and Alabama's disinterest in broader educational reforms also may have contributed to growing dissatisfaction with his situation. Apparently in the last year of his presidency, a conflict erupted between Tichenor and Colonel Hardaway, the engineering professor and commandant of the corps of cadets, that ultimately resulted in Hardaway's resignation despite the fact that Tichenor had supported him in his reforms in mechanical engineering. This conflict may have resulted from temperamental differences between the two men as well as from differences of opinion regarding discipline. Some evidence suggests that Tichenor believed the military nature of the college overemphasized, and one of Tichenor's reports to the board implied that he believed the military department was a drain on the college's slim financial resources.[53] Whatever the reasons, Tichenor resigned in 1882 to accept the position at the Home Mission Board in Atlanta.

Tichenor's presidency receives mixed evaluations. He clearly demonstrated a vision for the South's future and a belief in the prospects that mechanical and agricultural education offered the New South. He believed that the only way that Alabama and the South could recover completely from the war's devastation and be accepted into the nation's broader economic community was to marshal the state's resources and commit them to a new type of learning. This commitment would not neglect traditional learning but would intensify efforts on behalf of a new style of education represented by the A & M college and consistent with other New South progressivists. Still, he found it difficult to break with old patterns. He failed to reform the recitation method that remained the core methodology of higher education. He failed to get the board to admit female students. He divided interest in the curriculum between the classical method and the progressive method, and it remained for his successors, especially William LeRoy Broun, to continue curricular reform. He failed, like so many of his contemporaries, to deal with the problems of racial segregation. He failed in his efforts to get Alabamians to adopt a more diversified agricultural system. Ironically, not until the experimental scientific work of George Washington Carver under the leadership of Booker T. Washington at nearby Tuskegee Institute in that segregated system of higher education did Alabamians begin to diversify farming toward peanuts and other crops. Finally, Tichenor failed to put Alabama A & M's finances on the type of sound footing that he so desperately sought.[54]

His work was not all failure, of course. He successfully grafted a land-grant college onto the back of a small liberal arts denominational school and engaged in significant curricula reform. He prophetically addressed the South's economic potential and promoted the state's natural resources that he had surveyed while at Montevallo. He adopted the experimental farm method and advocated ideas that ultimately were implemented extensively at A & M. He also introduced ideas that eventually led to other educational reforms of the state's higher education system.

Likewise, the experience at Auburn benefited Tichenor significantly. In his time as college president, he exercised the organizational skills that had made him successful as a pastor and a tenacity that won him respect as an army chaplain. He also demonstrated the intuition of a visionary for his state and region. He continued to hone speaking and writing skills. He further developed business and administrative skills that were necessary in order to stabilize a struggling college. He developed an expansive vision for the South that later captured the attention of Southern Baptists. Furthermore, as college president he was exposed to those in the academic and political communities who were charting the course of what they called the New South. These political and financial connections became vitally important for him when he moved to Atlanta and attempted to apply his New South vision to the work of the Southern Baptist Home Mission Board. As college president Tichenor frequently moved among significant leaders in impressive fashion and exhibited outstanding abilities.[55] Perhaps foremost, his work at Auburn demonstrated his love for his southern homeland.

His affection for the college continued after his move to Atlanta. His son, Reynolds, attended A & M in the 1890s and is reputed to have played football while there. Tichenor returned to A & M for commencement in 1895, where some of his former students presented him with a gold-headed cane.[56] The A & M annual, the *Glomerata,* in a 1910 biographical sketch of Tichenor recalled,

> His love . . . for the college and his interest in everything about it continued until the last. Only three days before his death, upon regaining consciousness for a few minutes, he asked: "Who won the football game?" And on being told that Georgia had beaten Auburn 12 to 5, he turned to his son and said: "We don't like that a bit—do we?"—then lapsed into unconscious sleep.[57]

At the end of ten years as college president, I. T. Tichenor was ready for the momentous work of his life. At the age of fifty-six, he was respected in his state and region and an acknowledged leader in the Southern Baptist Convention. He had experience in missions, the pastorate, the military, business, and education. He had vast experience as a speaker and leader at Baptist association, state, and convention levels. He had moved among the leaders of his state and region and developed a vision that spanned not only southern religion but also the region's cultural and economic life. Yet the greatest achievements of his life lay ahead.

5

A New Mission Agency for a New South

Reinventing the Southern Baptist Home Mission Board

As 1882 began, Chester A. Arthur had been president of the United States for fewer than three months, assuming office after the assassination of James Garfield. In that year John D. Rockefeller completed the formation of the oil trust known as Standard Oil Company that since 1877 had controlled 95 percent of the oil refining capacity in the United States. Three years earlier, Thomas Edison had invented the electric lightbulb. The rapid industrialization also touched the New South that I. T. Tichenor and others had foreseen. The 1880s saw the introduction of the machine-made cigarettes that boosted the agriculture of the South by increasing tobacco sales. The decade also saw the relocation of the textile industry from the Northeast to the South, close to the source of the fiber. Redeemer governments controlled by white Democrats had been established throughout the South, overturning Reconstruction reforms instituted by Republican governments. A process was already in motion that would establish a system of racial segregation throughout the region. In the previous year, 1881, Booker T. Washington had established Tuskegee Institute to train African Americans in industrial and agricultural education in somewhat the same way that Alabama A & M sought to train white southerners in those areas.

Changes in American Christianity were also taking place. A virtual flood of European immigrants was streaming to America. Unlike many of their Protestant predecessors, these immigrants were increasingly comprised of Roman Catholic, Jewish, and Eastern Orthodox congregants. American churches were forced to deal with these new Americans as well as with the growing problems of urbanization. Northern Baptists were among those denominations that were gradually forced to reallocate missions dollars to meet the burgeoning needs of cities and immigrants.[1]

Southern Baptists were also changing. In 1882 the Southern Baptist Convention made two decisions pertaining to its Home Mission Board that altered the course of the convention's history. The first decision was to move the board from Marion, Alabama, to Atlanta, Georgia. The second was to appoint a new board and hire a new corresponding secretary. Less than two weeks later, on May 22, 1882, the recently relocated and restructured Home Mission Board met in Atlanta. After election of officers, a number of members spoke concerning the selection of a new corresponding secretary to replace the current secretary, W. T. McIntosh. Undoubtedly, they sought someone who could command the allegiance of the Old South and yet who was in tune with the ideas of the New South. They unanimously elected Isaac Taylor Tichenor, president of the Alabama Agricultural and Mechanical College. They identified him as a man known for a rich variety of antebellum and postbellum experiences, a lifelong support of missions, excellent leadership and speaking abilities, and a high profile among both southerners generally and Southern Baptists in particular. His salary was set at $2,500 per year. Recording Secretary H. H. Cabaniss telegraphed Tichenor concerning his election and requested his attendance in Atlanta the next day.[2]

The board's and convention's situations called for almost desperate measures. As the Committee on the Condition of the Home Board had reported at the convention, there was "a want of enthusiasm on the part of the denomination in the work of this Board." In 1879 there had been serious talk of the convention's reuniting with the Home Mission Society of the North, and at times it had seemed that the dissolution of the convention was inevitable. Baptists in states such as Arkansas, Texas, Georgia, and Florida had various working agreements with the northern society rather than exclusive or joint relations with the Southern Baptist board. In the 1879–80 convention year, church contributions to the board were less than twenty thousand dollars, and only seven of the twenty-one conventions and general associations that were represented in the Southern Baptist Convention allied themselves with the HMB.[3] The picture could not have been much more bleak. Into this breach stepped Tichenor. His rich variety of experience, as well as his boldness, energy, and persuasive power, were essentials for the job that lay ahead.

The Revival of the Home Mission Board

Tichenor came to the position of corresponding secretary of the Home Mission Board with an acute awareness of the problems facing the board and the Southern Baptist Convention. As an active participant in SBC life, he had advocated a more cooperative system of collecting and channeling funds to SBC mission agencies. Thus, he was well prepared to address the concerns most prevalent at the time.

The day after he was hired Tichenor appeared before the Home Mission Board in Atlanta. His reaction indicates that representatives of the board had previously approached him about his receptiveness to such a proposal. The minutes of the meeting show that Tichenor gave a dynamic and earnest message stressing the great significance of HMB work. In this address he listed the board's priorities as church planting and support in New Orleans and among the Chinese in California, and evangelism and education among southern blacks.[4]

Tichenor closed out his work in Auburn and moved his family to Atlanta. In his first meeting with the Home Mission Board in July, board members resolved that his immediate priority was to establish communications with each one of the state conventions and general associations. Consequently, the Board commissioned him to visit each Southern Baptist state mission board and each state's HMB vice president in their home states. W. H. McIntosh continued to manage the office in Atlanta while Tichenor engaged in this activity. According to the Home Mission Board report of 1883, Tichenor subsequently visited the state conventions of Mississippi, Alabama, Texas, Missouri, Tennessee, North Carolina, South Carolina, and Florida, as well as state associations in Virginia, Kentucky, Alabama, and the Indian Territory. He reported more than twenty thousand dollars in commitments in several of the state conventions.[5]

Tichenor immediately realized that he could revitalize the board only if he rejected the traditional method of written pleas for participation and left the confines of his office. This hands-on approach offered just the impression that was needed at this time.[6] These visits gave Tichenor an opportunity to hear the concerns of Baptists in those states and to express his vision for the work of the board and issue a challenge for unity around the work of *Southern* Baptists. It helped Baptists in those regions to identify a person with the name that they would frequently hear.

Tichenor faced significant barriers. The board's lack of effectiveness contributed to the tendency of the state mission boards to look toward Northern Baptists for assistance. The limited financial resources of the HMB further exacerbated the situation. In the late nineteenth century some Southern Baptists still greatly mistrusted concentrations of denominational wealth and power. Some Baptist ministers continued to resent educated and "big city" ministers and felt as if they were on the outside of denominational structures looking in. Denominational centralization also seemed to compromise with "Yankee materialism" or "commercialism" and for some was reminiscent of the rise of the mission agencies that had provoked earlier opposition from Primitive Baptists, Landmarkism, and the Churches of Christ. Still others believed that denominational centralization "reeked" of Roman Catholicism.[7] The rugged individualism and independent nature of the frontier that so contributed to the growth of Baptists in the South further contributed to a suspicion of centralized missions.

At the same time, developments were taking place throughout the United States during the Gilded Age that has been called the "Incorporation of America." Increasingly, American businesses were developing a more highly organized society with new systems of authority. Business increased its influence substantially throughout the United States, and a modern corporate model of business was emerging. Dramatically improved transportation and communication enhanced this emerging model through vastly extended railroad networks and an expanded telegraph system. Later, the telephone system further augmented this communication.[8] As demonstrated by both his work in mining and his college presidency at A & M, Tichenor embraced the business progress occurring in the United States. He benefited from the enhanced transportation and communication that enabled him to communicate more rapidly and to have greater mobility in traveling between the concentrations of Southern Baptists. This gave him the opportunity to establish a stronger connection with these Baptists and, in some cases at least, to exercise greater control. He sought to establish sound business practices as well as modernize the work of the Home Mission Board. These methods included use of strict accounting techniques, utilization of the South's transportation system, and increased promotion among the board's constituency of its work. He was careful, however, to make sure that Southern Baptists knew that use of traditional correspondence methods as well as preservation of southern values and Baptist beliefs would temper the utilization of such technology and modernization. He adopted "northern" business methods and technology without jettisoning his inherent southernness.

Immediately, Tichenor's work resulted in three important effects. He defined the focus of the Home Mission Board in two geographical areas, New Orleans and the crucial frontier state of Texas. This focus on New Orleans and Texas illustrates how Tichenor targeted areas to achieve early success in the work of the board. He had demonstrated interest in both areas previously. He realized that it was crucial for the languishing agency to experience initial triumphs in his administration. Also, Tichenor recommended that the board make no appointments east of the Mississippi River except in consultation with the individual state mission boards. This decision demonstrates how Tichenor sought to foster good relations between the independent state mission boards and the HMB. He realized that the previous operations of these organizations were fragmentary and possibly competitive. Thus, to encourage cooperation he sought coordination of efforts. He also recognized that some of these state mission boards and associations were already in relationships with the Home Mission Society and might be lost if he did not establish a positive working relationship between them and the HMB. He displayed this characteristic in several ways during the years that he served the HMB. Tichenor received a warm reception to his correspondence and visits, demonstrating both his personal charisma and the confidence Southern Baptists had in him. Southern Baptists clearly had made a wise choice in bridging the gap between those who still considered themselves loyal to the Old South and the proponents of the New South mentality. Very few changes in Southern Baptist history have created such an amazing reversal as did Tichenor's appointment. Described as "tall, forceful, commanding in voice and in presence," Tichenor had the "well-developed social and political skills and mesmerizing platform abilities" needed to reinvigorate the sluggish HMB.[9]

Tichenor also sought to manage more responsibly the financial affairs of the HMB. In the September board meeting, members presented a proposed budget with estimated receipts at $22,500, a figure based upon state conventions' and associations' pledges received during Tichenor's travels. The budget revealed HMB priorities as being Texas, Chinese missions, Indian missions, and New Orleans, with other items receiving less funding. The Home Mission Board gave and the appropriate committees the authority to make appointments and pay funds. The board especially increased its reliance upon committee recommendations concerning expenditures.[10]

The results of the transformation to this vigorous type of leadership were remarkable. From the 1881–82 year to the 1883–84 year, the total number of missionaries affiliated with the HMB jumped from 36 to 144. This resulted directly from the close alliance between the HMB and the various state mission boards. Gradually, all Baptist home missionaries in the South came under the umbrella of the Home Mission Board rather than the Home Mission Society of the North or the respective state convention mission boards. Tichenor's report a decade later summarized the success of these efforts. Giving a brief record of the totals of the previous ten years, the corresponding secretary reported more than $1.3 million in receipts and almost 2,300 churches constituted as a result of board work. By Tichenor's final report as HMB chief executive officer in 1899, the board's annual receipts had risen to more than $65,000 for the specific work of the HMB and to more than $50,000 for the Church Building Fund. The total number of missionaries employed by the board increased from 36 in 1882 to 653 in 1899.[11]

Three factors must be credited for the resurgence. Certainly, Tichenor, the HMB, and the Southern Baptist Convention profited from the renewal of the South's economy in the final two decades of the century. Uniformly in these years southern industrial growth regularly outperformed national averages, and the value of its production kept pace with similar nineteenth-century economies in industrializing nations. Surprisingly in this era, southern industrial output grew more rapidly than New England's industrial output had in its earlier period of rapid industrialization. This growth was exactly what Tichenor had sought while serving as president of the Montevallo Coal Mining Company and what he foretold while serving as president at Auburn. Unfortunately, all too often this growth was in industries where southerners faced less competition and in businesses that were notorious for "low wages and absentee owners."[12] Still, Tichenor's efforts would have been enhanced by contributions from an economically advancing South.

Tichenor also brought sound business practices to the board. His predecessor had been essentially a pastor serving as a business administrator. Tichenor's business experience as a mining executive and as college president provided crucial background for the successful administrative operation of the HMB. Tichenor modernized the HMB's business methods without affecting the basic mission enterprise or enthusiasm for it. The relocation of the board to Atlanta, the business and psychological center of the New South, made this transition possible. These modifications probably enabled the convention's survival. Tichenor realized that one way to stretch the limited resources of the HMB in the early 1880s was to be more responsible in managing those resources. Sound business practices, tighter organization, and strict accounting limited unnecessary waste and stretched scanty income and personnel so that the most pressing needs might be met.[13] Undoubtedly, Tichenor's pastoral experience helped him recognize that most Southern Baptist church members prized local church autonomy and that a strong suspicion of mission boards remained from the influence of Restorationist and Landmark movements. Such people would want a solid system of accountability before they entrusted their meager financial resources to the HMB.

The 1888 formation of the Women's Missionary Union, an auxiliary of the SBC, assisted Tichenor in his efforts to revive the board. Part of the explosive growth of missions support groups among the female Protestants of this era, the members of the Women's Missionary Union (WMU) became some of the most supportive of all Southern Baptists of Tichenor's efforts. More than a decade earlier, Northern Baptist women as well as other denominational women's groups had organized women's missionary societies. Between 1880 and 1900 the number of these societies doubled, with hundreds of thousands of women joining. These burgeoning groups might be regarded as one extension of the larger women's rights crusades. Certainly, with many doors closed to them in Southern Baptist life—women messengers had been rejected beginning in 1885, for example—Southern Baptist women found the support of the mission endeavor one way to express their role in denominational life. By doing so, they made an outstanding and lasting contribution to the development and support of the missions enterprise. Without the WMU's creation, substantial progress in Southern Baptist missions probably would not have occurred. The powerful women's organization regarded the missions enterprise as Southern Baptists' most important function.[14]

Tichenor developed a close alliance with the WMU, one of the many alliances he formed in order to promote the cause of home missions. It is not known whether he supported giving women a more active role in Southern Baptist life or whether he was one of the men who hoped that involvement in the missions organization would satisfy women's needs for leadership positions. However, it should be noted that he had unsuccessfully supported making Alabama A & M a coeducational institution while president, and he praised and promoted the work of the WMU on numerous occasions. He and WMU Corresponding Secretary Annie Armstrong consulted on many matters, and he found her a loyal supporter of the causes of the HMB, so much so in fact that critics sometimes charged that she favored the Home Board at the expense of the Foreign Mission Board. In these years Armstrong became the foremost leader of the Women's Missionary Union, and through the years her contributions and those of the WMU have been of incalculable value to the SBC. Tichenor and Armstrong's close relationship contributed to that support. The WMU created efforts to supply home missionaries on the frontier with special offerings of clothing and other items, and Tichenor lent his enthusiastic advocacy of this endeavor. Armstrong and the WMU also supported Tichenor's later efforts in Cuba. He, in turn, met with the WMU's leadership, corresponded frequently with Armstrong, and, in contrast to Armstrong's perception of one of his contemporaries at the Foreign Mission Board, held the WMU's work in high regard. In fact, in 1895 with the Home Mission Board experiencing great difficulty in the aftermath of the Panic of 1893, Tichenor turned to Armstrong and the WMU for financial assistance that greatly alleviated the board's indebtedness. The week of self-denial the women used to raise more than five thousand dollars became the basis for Southern Baptists' later adoption of a week of prayer and offerings for home missions.[15]

Armstrong's fondness and esteem for Tichenor grew over the years, and she considered him an important counselor and friend. She sought Tichenor's advice occasionally, and both she and the WMU solicited his help to settle disputes as they arose within the WMU, including a disagreement between the national WMU and Georgia WMU leadership. Armstrong consulted with Tichenor when she began correspondence with the equally legendary black Baptist leader Nannie Helen Burroughs, who founded a similar women's organization in the National Baptist Convention, the African-American Baptist convention formed in 1895. Along with Richard Willingham and James Frost, Tichenor was called upon to mediate a dispute that arose between Armstrong and WMU president Fannie Heck. Tichenor, meanwhile, relied upon Armstrong's support. She was approximately the same age as his eldest daughter, and he and Armstrong shared the same passion for missions. In many ways the partnership between Tichenor and Armstrong became equally important for both the HMB and the WMU.[16]

Finally, Tichenor's aggressive leadership and optimistic spirit also were important. His grandiose manner and style of leadership sometimes clashed with other strong-willed individuals or with those whose interests conflicted with his, but Tichenor's energy was just what the lethargic Home Mission Board needed.

Tichenor and Texas

No one knows exactly when Baptist work in Texas began. As Baptist historian H. Leon McBeth writes, "Only God knows for sure when Baptists first set foot in Texas; the lesser authorities disagree among themselves." The earliest verifiable Baptist preacher came to Texas in 1820, and some early Baptists followed later in the decade. Baptist work began in earnest in the early 1830s with the emergence of individuals such as Z. N. Morrell, Daniel Parker, R. E. B. Baylor, and Noah Byars. The first Baptist home missionaries appeared in Texas in 1840, Baylor College was founded in 1845, and the Baptist State Convention of Texas was organized in 1848.[17] Tichenor spent a brief sojourn on a preaching mission in Texas in 1850.

Perhaps nowhere was Tichenor's influence felt more strongly or more quickly than in his efforts to bring Texas back into the fold as Southern Baptist territory in the 1880s. Texas, like the rest of the South, suffered greatly in the postbellum period. Though little actual fighting had taken place on Texas soil, the war and Reconstruction disrupted the state's economy severely, the state government faced challenges regarding relations with hostile Native Americans, and even in the late 1870s and early 1880s, Texas state government consistently faced crippling financial problems. The years immediately following the war depleted wealthy plantation owners' fortunes and small landowners' and farmers' resources.[18]

Baptists were not isolated from these struggles. Many Baptists came from poorer stock, and the social and economic struggles of the day affected many of them directly. Some churches failed to retain pastors due to monetary difficulties, even as Tichenor had left Montgomery's FBC for that reason. Most Texas Baptist pastors supported themselves and their families with secular employment. Baptist associations and state conventions, suffering drastically in this financial situation, were unable to appoint missionaries or organize churches even in key communities that the railroad serviced. Frequently, Baptist organizations found themselves weeks or even months behind in the scanty support they paid to missionaries.[19]

Texas's problems were not unlike those of the remainder of the home mission field that Tichenor surveyed in 1882. Tichenor did, however, recognize the vast potential the frontier state held for the work of Baptists and for the expansion of Southern Baptist territory. Many Texas residents were transplanted southerners, and Texas had quickly seceded after the election of Lincoln in 1860 despite the efforts of its governor, Sam Houston, to keep Texas in the Union. In 1865, Texas was the last Confederate state to surrender to Union troops. All these events demonstrated to Baptist observers the southernness of the state. Tichenor hoped to capitalize upon this "southernness" and saw the vast potential the state held for the New South and for Baptist work there. Writing in the early twentieth century, Texas Baptist historian and preacher J. M. Carroll recalls that

> Tichenor had great and accurate visions of Texas and her Baptist possibilities. He was always a loyal friend of Texas. His great vision of Baptist possibilities in this State and his ability to make the Home Board see and feel as he did, enabled him to secure help for Texas somewhat commensurate with her tremendous needs, and it was due to Dr. Tichenor as to no other man out of Texas, the saving of Texas to the Home Board. . . . [20]

Thus Carroll, whose older brother Benajah H. Carroll was a Confederate veteran and prominent Texas pastor who formed a critical alliance with Tichenor, obviously recognized the substantial contribution the corresponding secretary made to preserving ties with the SBC and the Home Mission Board. Basically, Tichenor "outbid Northern Baptists for Texas affiliation."[21] He did so through an aggressive plan of visits, correspondence, and pledges of financial assistance that urged Texas Baptists to unite and to cooperate with the southern Home Mission Board. Undoubtedly, he played upon sentiments remaining from the Civil War that considered Texas a southern state. Thus, it was only logical in his mind, as well as those of his listeners, that Texas Baptists be affiliated with the SBC.

When Tichenor became the board's corresponding secretary in 1882, four of the five competing associations or conventions in Texas were affiliated with the Home Mission Society. Three of the bodies were regionally situated in Texas. Two were statewide and competed directly with one another as well as with the regionally located groups. As McBeth writes in his history of Texas Baptists, "Like a jigsaw puzzle with its pieces scattered, Baptist structures in

Texas were badly fragmented during this period." There were competing colleges, mission unions, Sunday school agencies, and newspapers. This competition divided district associations and churches. Further, there were remnants of anti-missions Baptists, especially in east Texas, who were unaffiliated with any of the organizations and who rejected any form of missions cooperation. The result was "internal fragmentation of the Baptist witness, with a bewildering array of organizations, each pursuing worthy goals no doubt, but confusing the churches by the plentitude of financial agents bumping into each other as each tried to get to the churches first to raise money for his particular cause." The situation was little short of ecclesiastical chaos.[22]

One of HMB's first actions regarding Texas was to authorize Tichenor "to secure, whenever practicable, title to lots in the frontier and new towns in Texas, for the purpose of establishing Baptist churches." Shortly thereafter, the Baptist General Association of Texas, under the leadership of R. C. Buckner, appealed through Waco pastor B. H. Carroll concerning the "[spiritual] destitution of Texas," and the BGA made overtures to the board for a cooperative effort in fund-raising for home missions. These efforts culminated in the August 1, 1882, meeting of the HMB, when the Board noted that it had received many communications from the various state mission boards regarding cooperative efforts and set Texas aside for special action. The Committee on Texas reported that "from Texas [came] two conditions precedent to cooperation." The committee regarded Texas a vital state and advised that the board spend between six and eight thousand dollars that fiscal year in matching funds to provide for the work there. The report also stated, "If we meet in a fraternal spirit, the conditions proposed, we can hold that large and rapidly growing population in sympathy and cooperation with your Board; and your Committee are clearly of the opinion that the requests of the brethren in Texas are just and wise, and that we should give them at an early day, explicit assurance of our acceptance of the terms indicated."[23]

After this communication with the more vibrant Baptist General Association, Tichenor strengthened ties with the older Baptist State Convention of Texas. At the end of September, he traveled to the convention meeting in Belton, Texas, and proposed to assist the convention in its work with $3,000 of HMB money to be matched by $1,500 from the state convention. The Baptist State Convention approved this proposal and agreed to the partnership arrangement. Tichenor also offered a similar agreement to the Baptist General Association with $3,000 of board money to be spent in Texas and matched with $3,000 from the more financially secure general association. The HMB approved both proposals, which together fell within the $6,000 budget for Texas earlier approved. In 1885 the HMB borrowed $2,000 to aid the Baptist General Association in constructing churches and to match the association funds designated for this purpose as long as the proposed churches remained affiliated with the Baptist General Association. Well into the 1890s, the HMB continued to support the work in Texas. In 1893 for example, the board voted to appropriate $4,000 out of its funds and up to another $2,000 from funds raised by Texas Baptists for the board for the extension of Southern Baptist work in Texas.[24]

These actions were important for several reasons. They demonstrate the lengths to which Tichenor and the HMB were willing to go to secure Texas to the SBC. The high priority given Texas by the HMB reaped huge benefits for the board and the Southern Baptist Convention in the years to come. These actions also demonstrate how the HMB trusted Tichenor, within certain guidelines, to initiate agreements that expanded its work. At its September meeting, the board authorized Tichenor "to offer to the State Convention of Texas, and the General Association of Texas, such sums for mission work in that state, as he thinks best." This broad statement gave the corresponding secretary the ability to act decisively and quickly, and he did so. These proposals were a bold challenge to Texas Baptists for cooperation. Simultaneously, internal events were taking place in Texas that culminated in the consolidation of the multiple conventions and associations. Within five years, the divided conventions and associations merged, and the Texas field counted 130 Southern Baptist missionaries. While the merger involved a number of factors, the efforts of Tichenor and the HMB to urge cooperation and consolidation may well have contributed. J. M. Carroll wrote that these initial proposals were "a long step forward" for mission work in Texas. Texas Baptists began work among the state's African Americans through the influence of Tichenor, who told them that if they commissioned a man to establish Minister's Institutes among blacks, the Home Mission Board would pay his salary. The general association agreed and appointed Reverend W. H. Parks.[25]

In years to come, Tichenor stayed involved with the situation in Texas. He visited the Baptist State Convention of Texas in 1883 and 1884 and the Baptist General Association in 1883 and 1885. Tichenor was asked to address the general association at its 1883 meeting. The minutes record that he did so "in his immitable [*sic*] style which thrilled the hearts of the Association and gave us large ideas of the great work our Lord Jesus has left us to do."²⁶ Conflict, however, arose between the HMB and the Texas Baptist State Convention in 1885, after O. C. Pope, corresponding secretary of the state convention mission board, reported a pastor's salary paid by his congregation as mission funds. This affected the total of the matching fund arrangement and was contrary to HMB policies. An editorial of the *Texas Baptist Herald,* the publishing arm of the state convention, criticized HMB management. Tichenor reported to the board concerning this editorial, and the board voted to respond directly to the state convention mission board. The board also may have looked unfavorably upon the state convention's continued strong ties with the American Baptist Home Mission Society. Subsequent events in the Indian Territory show that the HMB disapproved of joint relationships between the two organizations. The conflict ended when Pope left the employ of the Baptist State Convention and the merger between the state convention and the general association occurred.²⁷

J. M. Carroll recorded that during these years Texans loved Tichenor so much they almost regarded him a native Texan, perhaps because during these years he continued to participate in the annual meetings of the Baptist General Convention of Texas. Convention minutes record Tichenor's presence in the 1887, 1889, 1891, 1894, and 1895 meetings of the unified state convention. Carroll credited Tichenor as the one "who first discovered the ability" of Texas leaders such as Carroll's older brother, Waco pastor Benajah Harvey Carroll. The younger Carroll added that Tichenor's selection of B. H. Carroll to speak at the 1888 convention on behalf of the HMB catapulted the Waco pastor to prominence in the Southern Baptist Convention. B. H. Carroll became the foremost Southern Baptist leader west of the Mississippi River, and, after the turn of the century, founded Southwestern Baptist Theological Seminary. B. H. Carroll's most recent biographer suggests that the 1888 speech "was perhaps his most famous speech before the Convention."²⁸

Carroll's address on the board's behalf was a masterpiece of persuasiveness. While admitting that "the dangers which threaten the Home Board are not at present so imminent and formidable as in the past," Carroll made a stirring appeal for the sustained support of the HMB and continued assistance to Texas. He drew extensively upon historical allusions and imagery that linked the defense of the Home Mission Board with the defense of southern territory during the Civil War. Rising to the height of his rhetoric, Carroll pleaded,

On what mountain, in what valley of the South has not the Texan died? The soil all around your Home Board at Atlanta is fertile with their blood.

Shiloh, Vicksburg, and Chickamauga preserve their memory. Their battle yells yet echo in the mountains of Tennessee and Kentucky.

Because therefore Texas made common cause with you in your hour of peril, make it with us now in our time of need.[29]

Carroll utilized language nearly identical to the type of language that Tichenor and others used in attempting to rally Southern Baptists to the defense of their territory. Throughout the address Carroll employed battlefield imagery that reminded the listeners of the Civil War. Images invoking the late war and the defense of Southern Baptist territory resonated strongly with his audience. The power of his plea persuaded those who had previously opposed HMB support to swing to its favor or at least keep silent. Likewise, Carroll's support of the HMB and the SBC remained substantial. The significance of Tichenor's role in recognizing the abilities of the Texas Baptist giant and in enlisting his support and participation should also not be underestimated.[30]

Similarly, Tichenor displayed a great deal of pride in the accomplishments of the Home Mission Board in Texas. He believed that the HMB was more responsible than any other agency for the rapid growth of Baptists within Texas borders. The aid the board provided was crucial for the support of Texas Baptists; in fact, he believed it "the very backbone of her mission work." The HMB supported the construction of more than six hundred churches in seven years. Without data for the previous three years, Tichenor estimated that approximately nine hundred churches had been constructed in ten years with HMB support.[31]

These statistics verify that Tichenor's time investment and the board's financial commitment had borne fruit. While faulty record-keeping makes it difficult to ascertain accurately the number of Southern Baptist churches in Texas in 1882 when Tichenor assumed HMB leadership, obviously Texas quickly established itself as a Southern Baptist bastion. The 1894 report of the Committee on Home Missions spoke these glowing words about the potential of Texas:

In Texas there are three frontiers of magnificent distances, and splendid possibilities, East Texas, South Texas and West Texas, including the contiguous territory of New Mexico. . . . These vast regions are being settled. . . . He who has an ear to hear can already hear the tramp of the oncoming millions. The wisdom of this generation bids us preoccupy the ground. Our missionary should not wait to ride on the cowcatcher of the first engine of the new railroad, but should already be on the ground ready to welcome the engineer and his passengers, preaching the gospel to them, and baptizing them as fast as they believe.[32]

The committee also lauded HMB work in the state. Declaring that "Home Missions are the foundation of Foreign Missions," the committee asserted that the board had planted the strongest churches in Texas and provided support for Baptist pastors and congregations throughout the state. The committee acknowledged that while the HMB had done everything it possibly could for the Lone Star state, the board's work was only beginning. To stay at the forefront of the state's progress, the board needed to act aggressively during Texas' "formative period." The combined efforts of the HMB and Texas Baptists harvested substantial fruit. By 1894 J. M. Carroll recorded that Baptist churches numbered over 2,500 and counted more than 150,000 members.[33] Obviously, the convention realized Tichenor's vision for Texas and the Southwest, and Texas Baptists capitalized on the financial support and verbal affirmation they received to begin to build a Texas Baptist empire.

Texas Baptists also capitalized upon an improved economy. Between 1875 and 1890, Texas experienced an overall prosperity and a phenomenal increase in personal and corporate wealth. In some important economic areas Texas wealth either doubled or tripled. While the effective development of the state's oil resources did not come until the twentieth century, the state's economy benefited from population growth, railroad expansion, new technology, an increasing transition from subsistence-level farming and cattle-raising to commercial agriculture and ranching, and the development of lumber and mining industries. For example, between 1870 and 1890, Texas's population almost tripled from 818,579 to 2,235,527. The corresponding growth in the economy in the aforementioned areas and other economic developments greatly strengthened the state's finances.[34] Texas Baptists' resources multiplied as the state's economy developed. These developments also fit well into concepts consistent with Tichenor's New South ideals.

Tichenor's personal and vigorous approach in Texas is noteworthy for three reasons. It demonstrates the type of leadership that he provided throughout the convention. No longer was the HMB a distant overseer requesting money and deciding arbitrarily who would and would not get support. The corresponding secretary was now someone who took personal interest in each state and whom Baptists recognized as one of their own. It illustrates the perceptive powers of insight he had. He predicted the potential strength of Southern Baptists in the Southwest and planned and planted to harvest that potential. It also consolidated Southern Baptist control of the growing American Southwest and solidified southern values and relationships in this frontier region.

Texas became a model for what Tichenor sought to do in other states during his administration of the HMB. He helped Texas Baptists identify themselves further as southerners and helped Baptists outside Texas to see them in the same light. Texas became a centerpiece of the renaissance of the Southern Baptist Convention and the Home Mission Board, and Tichenor played a significant role in helping others see the vast potential of Texas. Perhaps most important for many Southern Baptists, the various mission agencies and boards in Texas no longer entertained notions of unification with Northern Baptists. No doubt, it was these reasons that led J. M. Carroll to write of Tichenor, "No man out of Texas who has ever lived holds a warmer place in the memory of Texas Baptists than . . . Dr. I. T. Tichenor."[35]

Tichenor and New Orleans

A second priority for HMB work was the mission effort in the strategic city of New Orleans. Baptist work in New Orleans had begun as early as 1816 with the appointment of the first Baptist missionary there, James A. Raynoldson. Baptist work progressed slowly, however, until around 1843 when the First Baptist Church in New Orleans constituted, subsequently called Isaac T. Hinton as pastor in 1845, and joined the Mississippi River Association the same year.[36]

Southern Baptist missionaries struggled in the Crescent City throughout the antebellum period, Civil War, and Reconstruction. Baptists perceived the city as a Roman Catholic stronghold because of the heavy influence of French and Spanish cultures. By 1882 the HMB had established New Orleans, the largest city in the South with its population in excess of two hundred thousand, as a priority. Nevertheless, only two struggling white Baptist churches existed. One of these, First Baptist, had no permanent building of its own and drew its support mainly from the Mississippi Baptist Convention. The Home

Mission Board supported the other church, Coliseum Place, which faced a significant debt on its building.[37]

Tichenor initially reaffirmed the priority of mission work in New Orleans. In 1854 while pastor of Montgomery's First Baptist, he had participated in the constitution of the Coliseum Place Church as a mission of the First Baptist Church of New Orleans. So it was not unusual that in his first meeting with the board after his election, he placed the work in New Orleans among the most significant items to be promoted in the home mission effort.[38]

In the months and years that followed, Tichenor retained an active interest in the work in New Orleans. In one of his first reports, he recommended that the board help the Coliseum Place Church pay off its indebtedness. The Home Mission Board followed through on this request, for in his 1883 report to the Southern Baptist Convention, Tichenor noted that with the help of the HMB the church reduced this debt to about four thousand dollars. He also reported that with the church's excellent location and solid growth, the denomination should no longer be concerned about the remaining debt. In early 1884, Tichenor coordinated efforts between Coliseum Place Church and the Home Mission Board for the complete payment of that debt, with the board contributing five hundred dollars.[39]

The corresponding secretary also labored to strengthen First Baptist of New Orleans and to help the church secure a permanent meeting place. In his 1883 report, he noted that while the church presently counted approximately 190 members, it still owned no sanctuary and only had half the funds it needed to purchase a meeting place. Subsequently, this issue became an important one for Tichenor. It was a frequent topic of HMB discussions, and in response to his pleas at the 1883 convention, the HMB authorized him to go to New Orleans and investigate a purchase on behalf of the church. The church purchased a building, and the board supported First Baptist with financial aid throughout 1884.[40]

Local leaders of the mission work in Louisiana also encouraged the extension of the work in New Orleans. The first extension was a mission congregation on Valence Street. Tichenor agreed with this endeavor and encouraged the board to support this new work. Baptists established the Valence Street church and by 1886 had erected a building. In 1887 Tichenor called the overall status of work in New Orleans "promising" and appealed for two new pastors to start churches in the Locust Street and Carrollton locations in the city.[41]

In the years that followed, as the total work of the board increasingly absorbed Tichenor's attention and as the Baptist situation in New Orleans stabilized, he did not emphasize board work there to such an extent. He did continue, however, to recognize New Orleans as a key strategic point in his overall plan to preserve and extend the Southern Baptist Convention. In years to come, he focused crucial board attention on strengthening the work in "weak states" and in extending Southern Baptist work to growing southern cities. The work in Louisiana and New Orleans remained a significant part of this plan.

Weak States

Near the end of his tenure as corresponding secretary, Tichenor wrote a pamphlet entitled *Phases of Home Board Work*. In the pamphlet he identified three southern states where Southern Baptist work had been weak and progress had been slow. He compared the spiritual "destitution" of these three states. Because the denomination in Arkansas, Florida, and Louisiana remained both numerically and financially too feeble to meet the huge demands of the missions endeavors in those states, Tichenor pleaded for Southern Baptists to reinforce the work there. Although Arkansas had only about 72,000 white Baptists among a rapidly growing population of approximately 1.5 million, he believed that it had the potential to become strong Baptist territory.[42]

Florida had a population of about 500,000. White Baptists comprised only approximately 1 percent of this population. Still the Home Mission Board aided Baptist churches in Jacksonville, St. Augustine, Tampa, Pensacola, and many other smaller towns and locations throughout the state. Tichenor believed that Florida, like Arkansas, also had strong potential for Southern Baptist growth.[43]

Tichenor reserved his strongest comments for Louisiana and New Orleans. Tichenor wrote, "Louisiana with a population of a million and a half" had only about one white Baptist in fifty. He added, "New Orleans, the largest city on our seacoast south of Baltimore, has but three white Baptist churches, and only one of these is able fully to sustain a pastor." This echoed his report to the 1898 SBC meeting, where he said, "The state of Louisiana is at present undergoing a wonderful development." His New South mentality ever aware of business and technical developments, Tichenor regarded Louisiana's economic development as a result of railroad extension through that state. However, he warned

In this state the Baptists are but a feeble folk. They must have aid NOW to possess and hold the vantage ground thrown open to them. One brother of another state . . . has publicly declared that the Home Mission Board might wisely expend its entire income in Louisiana.[44]

Tichenor saw New Orleans and Louisiana, as well as other southern states where Southern Baptist work was weak, as fitting within a larger plan of strengthening and extending the Southern Baptist empire. He realized that if Southern Baptists could not enlarge their influence in their "own territory," they could never expect to expand to other areas.

Cities

Work in New Orleans was one component of a larger plan to occupy the growing southern cities for the Southern Baptist Convention. Southern promoters had long hoped for urbanization in the antebellum South. Despite the efforts of some to promote the growth of urban areas, manufacturing, which drove the growth of such areas in the North, lagged far behind in the South in the antebellum period. Consequently, southern cities built their economies around commercial enterprises most often connected with the export of cotton and the import of manufactured goods. In the postbellum era, however, new cities like Atlanta and Birmingham emerged. Some older important southern cities such as New Orleans and Richmond increased in population anywhere from 70 to 100 percent in the period between 1870 and 1900, but other cities such as Atlanta, Nashville, Norfolk, and Memphis tripled, quadrupled, and quintupled in size. These cities based their explosive growth upon both commerce and manufacturing. The importance of the railroads in connecting these cities with rivers and ports and serving as a nexus for trade and migration cannot be underestimated. The problems associated with such rapid growth also concerned New South promoters. Sanitation, law enforcement, annexation of adjacent land, and newcomers flooding these cities either as migrants from depressed rural areas or immigrants coming to the United States posed serious problems for urban officials. Southern businessmen became the vanguard of efforts to establish a new economic direction and to seek social improvements.[45] Likewise, churches already established in southern cities found themselves overwhelmed with the growing urban population and the needs associated with it. Tichenor sought to establish a cohesive plan to address those concerns.

The new urban southern population also provided a major challenge for Southern Baptists who desired to expand their influence. Tichenor, as HMB leader, addressed this challenge and in his 1892 report before the convention laid out his vision for the urban South:

> While our denomination is the most numerous one in the Southern States our strength lies largely in the rural districts. A glance at the religious condition of our chief cities will show how weak we are relatively in many of these centers of population. Take Baltimore and Washington, Richmond and Norfolk, Raleigh and Wilmington, Charleston and Columbia, Atlanta and Savannah, Montgomery and Mobile, . . . Louisville and Lexington, Nashville and Memphis, and see in how few of them our Baptist churches are equal in numbers, intelligence and wealth and social position to those of other denominations.[46]

Obviously, Tichenor had taken careful stock of the religious situation. Historically, Southern Baptists found themselves strongest in rural areas or small towns. Prior to the Civil War and Reconstruction, the larger part of the denomination's constituency came from those regions. Baptist mission work found its financial support in those areas. The fact that the Home Mission Board had originally been based in Marion, Alabama, was evidence of this. Typically, Southern Baptists found themselves weakest in cities like New Orleans, Baltimore, and Mobile, where the Roman Catholic influence was strongest, and in cities like Nashville and Richmond, where more socially prominent denominations like Episcopalians, Presbyterians, and even Methodists flourished. Tichenor recognized that Southern Baptists had to reach into these urban centers and thrive if they were to continue to grow and prosper.

> These are the centers of greatest influence. They are the depositories of the wealth of our country. They are the seats of industrial activity and enterprise. From them in proportion to membership come larger contributions to support our Mission Boards, endow our colleges and help forward all our denominational interest. In many of them is found a wide field for our Board. . . .
> . . . Persuaded that much of the future welfare of our denomination depends upon the position of our churches in such cities, the Board believes that the most earnest endeavors should be made to firmly estab-

lish our cause in every growing city in the South. While we must not neglect the needs of our wide rural districts, we must in order to hold them, strengthen our cause in every one of these potential centres [sic].[47]

His 1894 report to the convention made a similar plea, focusing especially upon Baltimore, New Orleans, Washington, D.C., and St. Louis. He listed six additional major cities, including Atlanta, where the HMB was located, as places where the small number of Baptist churches was painfully obvious. He issued a challenge to organize and build, if the means could be provided, one or more new churches in the coming year in more than one hundred southern cities.[48] While the challenge went unanswered, it does indicate the level of his concern for board work in southern cities.

Tichenor's dream fit well into the New South vision for the urban South. It was no coincidence that the Home Mission Board's location was in the prototypical New South city, Atlanta. Atlanta was the home of Henry Grady and represented what many other southern urban centers hoped to become. Atlanta's growth in the Reconstruction and post-Reconstruction era was nothing short of spectacular. The Civil War had proven critical to the city's development, as Atlanta became an important industrial and railway center. Despite its destruction in Sherman's attack on the Deep South, the city quickly rebounded. Prior to the war, Atlanta's population had been fewer than 10,000. By 1880 its population more than tripled, and by 1910 it was more than 150,000, second only to New Orleans. No other single city better symbolized the emergence of the New South. Promoters like Grady insisted that Atlanta become industrialized. An entire class of prominent businessmen with interests in real estate, textiles, railroads, mining, and even new enterprises like Coca-Cola, emerged to make Atlanta the role model for the New South. An aggressive Chamber of Commerce promoted Atlanta as this role model. Bold endeavors such as the expositions of 1881, 1887, and 1895 attracted the attention of national observers and excited the locals with the possibility of Henry Grady's "Atlanta Spirit." The first of these "international expositions" modeled what the New South hoped to accomplish and initiated the New South movement. It served as a public relations vehicle and as an investment tool to promote southern potential to both southern and outside investors. The exposition also established Atlanta at the forefront of the New South. In subsequent years other southern cities and states held similar expositions that imitated the 1881 exposition and became stereotypical New South celebrations.[49] This event may very well have encouraged the SBC to relocate the HMB to Atlanta a year later.

Tichenor was captivated by what he saw taking place around him in Atlanta. It confirmed to him predictions he had made in Auburn of a brilliant future for the South. Surrounded as he was every day by the "Atlanta Spirit," he believed that it was the future of the South. After living in Atlanta for more than a decade, he challenged his denomination with a grandiose design for Baptist occupation of some of the South's key cities.

> These are all great centers of wealth, industry and material power. Baltimore is the port which receives a larger immigration than any other, with [a] single exception. . . . It will probably long remain the greatest importing and exporting city within the territory of our Convention.
>
> Washington, as the political capital of the nation, should strongly represent to the world what the world so much needs to know, the great fundamental principles of our faith—the king-ship of Christ, whose churches are composed only of regenerate men and women and the right of all men to worship God according to the dictates of their own consciences.
>
> The doctrine of religious liberty, which is the only contribution American statesmanship has made to the science of government, for which our Baptist people in the centuries past have suffered and died, ought to be made prominent in the capital [sic] of this great nation.[50]

Having outlined Baptist prospects along the East Coast and mentioned the treasured concept of religious liberty, Tichenor turned his comments to the West and South, once again focusing upon urban need. Two strategic locations he reported were St. Louis and New Orleans, places where Roman Catholicism was historically strong:

> St. Louis is seated in the very heart of the great Mississippi Valley, the most important agricultural region on the globe. The rapid increase of our population, which at the close of the first decade of the coming century will not be less than one hundred millions [sic], will then have made that city the center of an internal commerce never equaled in the history of the world. . . .
>
> New Orleans, sitting at the gateway where thirty thousand miles of

navigable waters meet and mingle with the ocean waves . . . furnishing an outlet to the products of the . . . region inhabited by the most intelligent and enterprising people of the earth, must be a seat of power measured in its far reaching influence only by the outspreading of our race.[51]

One must note that Tichenor was arguing for the support of mission work in these two strategic cities because of their commercial significance. But he also lauded a spirit of triumphalism that built upon racial concepts, American patriotism, and Protestant superiority that were popular at the time in segments of the American public. He believed it crucial that Baptists in those locations be mobilized to fulfill the mission he envisioned for them. He challenged Baptists in these cities to plant ever-increasing numbers of congregations and other Baptist institutions in them. He believed these churches and institutions would "shape . . . opinions and control . . . activities." He cautioned that if the challenge went unmet in his generation it would "be lost forever."[52]

These reports reveal several ideas inherent in Tichenor's thinking and methodology. Prophetically, he saw that the future of Southern Baptists lay in planting churches in the rapidly growing cities, especially those equipped strategically for growth. He knew that Southern Baptists could not remain primarily a rural people. To do so was to stagnate and, eventually, to die. As always, his philosophy was to expand in order to build a larger basis of support for mission endeavors. Tichenor recognized the financial future of the South lay not in the agricultural regions and the old plantations. He witnessed the entrepreneurial endeavors of Atlanta businessmen, the tremendous profits that were being made, and he wanted to position Southern Baptists to be able to tap into those potentially vast financial resources. His years in the mining business and the presidency at Alabama A & M demonstrated to him the South's potential and the ways that education could better equip southern people to develop its resources. Tichenor encouraged Southern Baptists to address urban problems with his challenging words and optimistic phrases.

Tichenor and Work among Language Groups

Tichenor's vision for urban areas was also shaped by his concern about work among ethnic minorities, typically identified by Southern Baptists in those days as "language groups." In his 1883 convention report, Tichenor made note of the fact that "In Covington and Newport, Ky., in Louisville, St. Louis, Memphis, New Orleans and in parts of Texas" large immigrant populations existed to whom Southern Baptists failed to minister. He believed these immigrants had been previously brainwashed to oppose evangelical religion and comprised a growing danger to American civilization. Work among the so-called language groups was seen as much as a defensive measure and means of social control as it was an opportunity for evangelism.[53]

This work sometimes encompassed Native Americans in its description, but initially the special focus was upon the Chinese of California and German-speaking citizens in the South. Later, Tichenor also mentioned work among French-speaking citizens in Missouri and Louisiana and among Spanish-speaking citizens of Texas and New Mexico.[54]

One of Tichenor's early priorities was to establish mission work among California's Chinese. The origins of work among the Chinese grew out of HMB's entry into the area in the years following the California gold rush of the late 1840s. The SBC began work in this area in earnest in the 1850s. The peak of the California mission came in 1859 with a total of seven Southern Baptist missionaries operating in the state, including two to the Chinese. This support abruptly ended with the beginning of the Civil War but began again in the years following Reconstruction. Mission work among the Chinese re-emerged as an HMB priority in the years after the war despite the acknowledgement that the San Francisco mission was extremely expensive and required the employment of a Chinese-speaking assistant.[55]

In December 1882, the HMB attempted to support J. B. Hartwell, the board missionary in San Francisco, in the rental and renovation of property for a place of worship. This effort proved difficult because of the board's limited resources at that time; nevertheless, the board prepared plans to that end and provided for the employment of a Chinese assistant for Hartwell.[56]

By 1884, however, Tichenor was forced to report to the convention that the board had ended its work with California Chinese. Part of the reason was cost-cutting as the board made "retrenchments," but Tichenor also mentioned the expense of furnishing the mission, estimated at twenty thousand dollars. That was more than three times what the HMB expended annually upon the entire state of Texas, for example. This total also would have exceeded the cost of sustaining a similar effort in Shanghai or Canton. The mission struggled with what Tichenor termed "adverse influences," which he listed as "the migratory character of the [Chinese], from the absence of family ties and home restraints," and he admitted that one barrier to overcome came "from the continual persecutions of the white people." Tichenor also admitted that California "lay beyond the bounds of the Southern Baptist Convention, and in the territory of a sister organization" which had the financial resources to support its mission efforts. Undoubtedly, Tichenor was referring to the American Baptist Home Mission Society. Finally, he admitted that despite the "dilligent [*sic*] and faithful" efforts of the missionaries for five years, only "six members of the church could be found." All these reasons justified discontinuing the Southern Baptist missions effort in San Francisco. Even missionary J. B. Hartwell agreed with the decision. He replied to the board's inquiries by stating that "if the financial condition of the Board demanded that any important one of its Missions should be discontinued, this one from its character, and location, and surroundings is probably the one *we* should have deemed it wise to surrender."[57]

This situation demonstrated that the Home Mission Board was intensely concerned with territorial issues and was willing to cede mission opportunities as part of those territorial concerns. The need to provide adequately for board work at a time when its resources were limited burdened Tichenor. He willingly sacrificed mission opportunities across the continent when limited HMB resources could better be used close to home. He was willing to rely upon Northern Baptists to carry on unproductive mission efforts to Chinese in San Francisco so that he could strengthen work in places most important to the SBC, such as Texas and New Orleans. Ironically, he was concerned about white "persecutions" of Chinese in California at a time when African Americans were being increasingly mistreated by southern whites in the aftermath of Reconstruction. Finally, establishing the board's fiscal responsibility especially concerned him.

The failure of Southern Baptist work among California Chinese did not end HMB efforts among language groups. HMB mission work among other language groups continued during the remainder of Tichenor's tenure as corresponding secretary.

Work among Other Language Groups

In 1890 the Committee on Missions to Foreign Populations reported to the Southern Baptist Convention that

Rationalists and Socialists and Anarchists, and other heathens, who pollute by mere contact of association are pouring into our Southland from materialistic Europe by thousands every year; Asiatic Budhism [*sic*] already numbers its swarms of blinded votaries in the United States and its hundreds in the South. . . . The Home Board cannot ignore the large foreign element within our territory, in Maryland, Missouri, Louisiana, Texas, and elsewhere.[58]

Clearly, once again, the words used by the SBC demonstrated that missions and evangelism represented methods of social control. In fact, this committee invoked historical military terminology and mixed it with theological language:

That portion of North America occupied by the United States appears to be the divinely appointed center from which evangelizing influences will radiate in every direction, all over the earth—the commanding point from which the true *Crusaders* of the nineteenth and twentieth centuries will march forth to redeem . . . and conquer the world for Christ.[59]

Then the committee placed the immigrant challenge before the convention. Stating that "a large majority of American Baptists dwell in the South" and touting the doctrinal orthodoxy of Southern Baptists, the committee waxed eloquent in its report:

The greatest breadth and depth of the divinely opened fountain seems to lie this way [the South]. Can it be kept pure with the turbid streams of corruption pouring into it from Europe and Asia? In one way it can. In only one way, so far as we can see, is it possible to supply the spiritual carbonate necessary to precipitate the poisonous filth to the bottom and keep the waters limpid and sweet. By the foreign mission work of the Home Mission Board![60]

These words, while written and spoken by a specific committee, certainly represented Tichenor's sentiments. The report reflected fear of foreign invaders and theorized that the only defense against perceived spiritual, social, and political infections carried by them was the board's aggressive evangelistic antibiotic. These immigrants had to be Christianized so that they could also be Americanized. The committee even used the word "Mongolians" in identifying those "swarming to our shores," imagery that invoked the "Mongol hordes" of Genghis Khan that swept across Asia and to the outskirts of Europe in medieval times. Alarmed by the tides of immigrants flooding the United States in the latter decades, the committee recognized that the U.S. served as a haven for "every discontented foreigner on the planet." In a triumphalist spirit the committee boldly stated that if the U.S. were the center to which these immigrants gravitated, then "upon the assumption that the Baptists hold the true doctrines of the Bible in their greatest purity, the South, with its large majority of Baptists is the center of that center."[61]

Once again, sentiments representative of Tichenor and his ambitions for the Home Mission Board reverberate throughout this report. It identified the HMB as the conservator not only of Baptist beliefs but also the standard bearer of orthodox Christianity in the United States. While Tichenor would have never agreed with Landmark theology, elements of Landmark beliefs that he combated earlier in his career echo in this report. Missions to the "Foreign Populations including Indians and Cubans" were at the forefront of the battle for the soul of the United States, and Baptist beliefs led the way in the confrontation. The defensive measures of this action are seen clearly in the charge that "Agnosticism, Materialism, Infidelism, in general and in particular, modern Judaism, Budhism, [sic] and every form of spiritual error, must be stamped out here." Believing that older immigrants were less receptive to Christian influence, the board suggested concentrating upon immigrant children. Fearing that the influx of large bodies of "foreign atheists and infidels" would "contaminate" Americans, the HMB stressed that "proper correction be applied." The board's solution was the home missionary and the home board was "the proper agency upon which to rely to place missionaries in the midst of those teeming communities, seething in wickedness and reeking with sin."[62] Clearly, the SBC, the HMB, and Tichenor believed the board's work essential not only in defending the southern way of life but also in defending American and Christian ways of life. Without knowing it, Tichenor utilized evangelism and Christianity as a means of social control.[63] Tichenor's son-in-law, Jacob S. Dill, echoed a similar sentiment in 1894 by alerting his readers to the social problems fostered by recent immigrants to the United States. Warning Southern Baptists of "problems ranging from Russian nihilism and German beer to French, Irish, and Italian Catholicism,"

Dill sounded much like his father-in-law and the Home Mission Board. Evangelism and assimilation were clearly linked. He believed foreign immigration threatened temperance, democracy, and capitalism. Effective evangelism could counter dangerous immigrant ideology and practices by Christianizing and Americanizing the immigrants.[64] An unspoken or unacknowledged emphasis upon social control in Tichenor's work was a theme repeatedly demonstrated throughout his HMB career.

As early as 1888, the HMB recognized the need among the Missouri Germans and allotted one thousand dollars of its funds for that purpose. By 1892 Tichenor's HMB report answered that the Home Mission Board and Texas Baptists had collaborated to work among Germans and Mexicans. The HMB also supported a German missionary in Louisville, Kentucky, and German missionaries in St. Louis, Kansas City, and other Missouri locations where there were large concentrations of German immigrants.[65]

In his 1894 report, Tichenor spoke with equal pride of the work the HMB had begun among the Germans in Baltimore and its ongoing work among the French of Missouri and Louisiana and the Mexicans of Texas. His 1898 pamphlet, *Phases of Home Board Work,* indicated continued growth. St. Louis's First German Baptist Church became self-sustaining by 1898, the work in Baltimore continued to grow, and the board had started a new German work in Washington, D.C., and an Italian mission in Baltimore.[66]

While the main flood tide of immigration occurred in the North during these years and ultimately influenced the course of relationships between Northern and Southern Baptists, Tichenor recognized the potential importance of this change in the ethnic and religious structure of the United States. As the financial condition of the HMB and the SBC improved during the mid-1880s, Tichenor looked for opportunities to enlarge the scope of home mission work beyond the traditional areas of the West, weaker states, the Native American and African American populations, the southern cities, and the Deep South. This movement evolved in partial response to the urban problems arising in the South and the emergence of new language groups. These priorities became only a portion of the newly emerging HMB agenda. As board work in Texas and New Orleans grew, as Southern Baptist domestic missions unified under the umbrella of the HMB, and as Tichenor looked outward to consider new arenas of Baptist work, social control became an increasingly obvious aspect of HMB efforts. Tichenor also expanded his New South vision of Baptist missions into areas that previously would never have been imagined. As this work broadened, the scope of his vision also enlarged, and he found himself and the body he represented drawn into new challenges and conflicts. As old obligations were met and work in those areas strengthened, new priorities emerged that taxed Tichenor's visions to their limits and, ultimately, expanded his vision and that of Southern Baptists. As it did, Tichenor would be forced to continue to defend SBC territory, envision new ways to spread a particular Southern Baptist brand of the gospel, and seek out means by which he could financially enlarge the scope of that work.

First Baptist Church, Montgomery, Alabama, the sanctuary constructed during Tichenor's first pastorate there. Photo c. 1874. Courtesy Lee N. Allen.

Thomas Hill Watts, Alabama governor 1863–65, Confederate attorney general 1862–63, and Tichenor's deacon, commanding officer, business partner, and friend. Courtesy of Alabama Department of Archives and History.

"Old Main Hall," built in 1856 by the East Alabama Male College and transferred to Alabama A & M in 1872. During Tichenor's tenure it was the main administration and classroom building. Courtesy of Auburn University Libraries.

Albert J. Diaz, Baptist missionary to Cuba. Courtesy of Southern Baptist Historical Library and Archives, Nashville, Tennessee.

E. L. Compere, Southern
Baptist missionary to the
Indian Territory. Courtesy of
Southern Baptist Historical
Library and Archives, Nashville,
Tennessee.

Henry L. Morehouse,
Tichenor's counterpart and
sometime adversary at the
American Baptist Home
Mission Society. Courtesy of
Southern Baptist Historical
Library and Archives, Nash-
ville, Tennessee.

6

Expanding the Vision

From the Tropics to the Mountains

After ten years of serving as HMB's chief executive, Tichenor could look back on the decade with a great deal of pride in his and the board's accomplishments. As demonstrated in his 1892 report to the Southern Baptist Convention, the HMB had reclaimed the home field. During the years 1882 to 1887, the board had begun 300 new churches compared to more than 1,800 in the years from 1887 and 1892. By 1892 the board was employing 365 missionaries compared to only 95 in 1883. Total receipts of the board had grown from about $28,000 in 1882 to more than $80,000 in 1892. Clearly the work had multiplied, and Tichenor had succeeded in unifying support for the Home Mission Board.[1]

With this growth came new resources and also a new set of emerging priorities. Board work continued to focus upon former slaves, Texas, New Orleans, and other southern cities but also branched out into new areas. Two emerging priorities to which Tichenor sought to apply his Midas touch for missions were the island of Cuba and the Appalachian Mountains. He incorporated the philosophies that he developed as leader of the Home Mission Board and synthesized those ideas with concepts that were currently popular in the "Christian America" movement. Adopting and adapting cultural, diplomatic, and economic imperialism and, to a certain extent, unintentionally advocating social Darwinism, Tichenor sought to expand the domain of the HMB and the SBC into territory previously unrecognized by Southern Baptists. By doing so, he reflected a mindset that increasingly moved toward a triumphalism inherent in southern religious and cultural life in the last years of the nineteenth century and throughout much of the century that followed.

Tichenor and Cuba

Nowhere were the emerging Home Mission Board priorities more evident than in Cuba. The mission to Cuba originated in a church begun in Key West, Florida. In 1885 Key West had a Cuban population of almost five thousand, mostly refugees driven from their homeland by mounting internal political tensions. The Florida Baptist State Mission Board recognized this ministry as an important priority and appealed for help from the HMB, who sent a missionary there. Almost immediately the missionary to Key West, W. F. Wood, received a request to visit Havana and aid A. J. Diaz, a young Baptist preacher. In December 1885, the Key West church ordained Diaz and in January of the following year constituted a church in Havana.[2]

In 1886 Tichenor included the Cuban mission in his report for the first time. The Florida mission board had appealed to the Foreign Mission Board for aid in this endeavor, and, rejected by the foreign board, turned to Tichenor for help. Wood, as a representative of the HMB, began working closely with the Cuban mission effort, and the committee on Cuban missions recommended that this effort be entrusted to the HMB. This recommendation triggered such controversy—regarding whether the mission was in Home Mission Board or Foreign Mission Board jurisdiction—that the convention tabled it until the next day. After considerable discussion, the motion finally carried, and the Home Mission Board assumed responsibility for the Cuban mission.[3]

This decision was driven by several considerations. The work logically extended that of the HMB mission to Key West and the work of the board in Florida with the growing Cuban population of that state. Another factor may have been that the FMB was preoccupied with foreign missions in more exotic locations such as China. The FMB may have been concerned that arousing foreign missions interest among Southern Baptists for a work only ninety miles off the coast would consume crucial energies that could best be directed elsewhere. Perhaps most importantly, some Americans, many of them southerners and Southern Baptists, had always been interested in Cuba. In the antebellum period, imperialistic southerners hoping to expand potential slave territory sought to annex Cuba. Ardent American expansionists in the decade that followed the Civil War modified the older concept of manifest destiny to include places in Latin America like Cuba and the Dominican Republic. By 1886 they modified this desire to an understanding that Cuba was potentially part of the home field. They based their understanding on a crumbling Spanish hold upon Cuba that eventually culminated in revolution and, subsequently, the Spanish-American War. Writing forty years later, Una Roberts Lawrence, HMB writer and wife of the HMB president, recorded that in 1886 many in the U.S., especially among Southern Baptists, believed that Cuba eventually would become part of the United States and thus be home mission territory.[4]

The corresponding secretary took a great personal interest in the work in Cuba. He saw it as an opportunity for Southern Baptists to move into the territory of Latin American Catholicism and thus devoted much time and energy to selecting a permanent meeting place for the Havana church. Tichenor plunged into support of the Cuban mission with typical ardor. Years after his death his granddaughter recalled that especially during the 1890s, the Cuban mission in Havana was one of "his enthusiams [sic]." He invited Wood and Diaz to the July 1886 HMB meeting, where the two men reported on the efforts made in Havana and the needs there. In the following years these efforts and Tichenor's support grew. In May 1887, the corresponding secretary reported to the convention that the church in Havana had increased to three hundred members and had established two other congregations. He added that "a house of worship" was "greatly needed in Havana" but that the "whole island is open to us and thousands are ready to abandon the system of superstition in which they have been reared and embrace the truth as it is in Jesus."[5]

In accordance with HMB wishes, Tichenor and A. D. Adair visited Cuba early in 1888. After their visit, they reported to the board on February 6, 1888, a list of priorities for the mission. They ascertained that the most pressing need was a large "house of worship in Havana capable of holding 1500 or 2000 people" as well as a church building for Baptists in Matanzas. Additionally, because the Roman Catholic cemeteries were closed to Baptists and other non-Catholics, both churches needed land for cemeteries. Subsequently, the Home Mission Board agreed to this priority and approved giving Diaz power of attorney for the board in Cuba. Later, the HMB approved an additional $2,500 budgeted for Cuban work out of a total of $10,000 being appropriated at that time. This support demonstrated the level of commitment the board felt for the work. Diaz initiated the purchase for the Havana house of worship, and the board authorized the first payment early in 1889. The building was a theater occupying a corner lot 120 by 150 feet and costing $65,000. Tichenor also appealed to Southern Baptists through state newspapers such as the *Alabama Baptist* to support the work.[6]

The work in Cuba progressed rapidly for the first few years, due in no small part to Tichenor's support. He and other board members traveled to Cuba periodically to observe the progress made by Diaz and the mission. Diaz and Tichenor corresponded regularly with denominational papers, and Tichenor spoke at congregations including his former pastorate at Montgomery, reporting on Cuba and soliciting support. In 1889 some criticized Tichenor, saying that he neglected other board work in order to promote Cuban missions. The corresponding secretary resoundingly denied the charges in a letter to the *Alabama Baptist*. He stated that the money expended in Cuba was not excessive and was proportionate to other board expenditures. He contended that money raised specifically for Cuba did not interfere with other fund-raising efforts and that one other key project of the HMB, the Valence Street Church in New Orleans, had received more aid than all of the Cuban missions. In 1892 HMB members committed to pay off the debt of the Havana church, and each member, including Tichenor, personally guaranteed a portion of the indebtedness. This commitment indicates the high priority HMB gave the Cuban mission and the lengths to which board members and Tichenor were willing to go to continue its support. The 1893 home board report could proudly state, with some exaggeration, that "our work among the Cubans has been pronounced by one who has seen it and studied it upon the ground, one whose knowledge and experience entitles his judgment to the highest respect, considering time and means expended as the greatest work of modern missions." By 1893 five Baptist churches and seventeen preaching points had been established in Havana and surrounding areas.[7]

The mission to Cuba was not planted without extreme difficulties. The periodic political turmoil that ultimately resulted in the Cuban revolution erupted again in 1895, and Diaz reported to Tichenor and the Southern Baptist Convention that the "jails, castles, and military headquarters are full with Cubans imprisoned." Diaz found himself in danger at times from the fighting. Tichenor requested protection for missionaries and missionary property from the U.S. State Department and communicated with President Grover Cleveland regarding this need. Cuban Baptists urgently requested Tichenor's presence in Cuba in January 1896. Subsequently, as he prepared to go, Tichenor also found Cuban officials had imprisoned Diaz. When he received word of

Diaz's arrest, he contacted the State Department on the board's behalf and quickly notified Baptists around the United States through denominational papers of Diaz's incarceration. Requests flooded the State Department pleading for intervention on Diaz's behalf, and within one week the pastor was freed.[8]

The renewal of the Cuban revolution and the subsequent Spanish-American War interrupted the Southern Baptist mission to Cuba. When war erupted in 1898, most Americans greeted it with enthusiasm, despite disputes regarding the future status of a liberated Cuba. One might safely assume that many Southern Baptists were enthusiastic as well. Despite this enthusiasm for the Cuban cause, the war disrupted Cuban missions. Tichenor wrote that most of the churches were left pastorless, church members fled Havana, and the missionaries were forced to move to Key West and Tampa. When the war ended, however, the work once again blossomed. In his 1899 and final SBC report, Tichenor spoke glowingly of the Cuban mission. A new mission had begun in Santiago, two churches had started, and 150 converts had been baptized. Diaz, who during the war had come to the United States and worked briefly for the American Baptist Publication Society, returned to Cuba and HMB employment. Former missionaries were restored to their locations, and new work began in Cuba's western regions. After the war, the HMB and the American Baptist Home Mission Society agreed that Cuba would be divided into eastern and western domains so that their work would not conflict. Ultimately, this compromise did not last, and territorial disputes arose between the two mission organizations.[9]

While Tichenor made no statements regarding U.S. imperial involvement in the Philippines, the context of his subsequent remarks regarding Cuba and Puerto Rico indicated that he favored U.S. intervention and its imperialistic tenor. With typical optimism he reported,

> Recently new conditions have arisen in the Island, and it has assumed new relations to our own country and to the nations of the earth. . . . There is every probability that union with this country will be the ultimate political destiny of this people. If so, then it becomes us to see that when Cuba enters our Union, she shall not come to swell the ranks of the vicious and the ignorant, or to add to the number of those who obey Papal power.

Cuba is now free. The restrictions imposed by the Spanish government upon the preaching of the gospel have been removed. A great and effectual door has been opened. Everything invites us to enter and possess the land. . . .

Cuba evangelized will become the light bearer to the whole Spanish speaking people of this Western world and a continent inhabited by a . . . people [who] will be open to her entrance with the truth of God.

Such facts ought not to be overlooked in our estimate of the importance of her evangelization, nor in the measurement of our efforts to accomplish this result.[10]

This quotation reveals a number of facts about Tichenor's viewpoints regarding Cuba and American imperialism. He stated that "Cuba is now free," a false assumption, and boldly suggested that freedom from Spanish rule meant that religious freedom would logically follow. Like earlier Americans as well as some of his contemporaries, Tichenor assumed that someday Cuba would become a part of the United States. In reality Cuba had been freed from Spanish rule but found itself increasingly under U.S. political and economic control. The "probability" of U.S. annexation explains why Tichenor had so vehemently defended Cuba as home board rather than foreign board territory. His position was not based exclusively on the fact that the work was begun by the Florida State Mission Board, or the proximity of Cuba to Florida, or a fear of potential neglect by the Foreign Mission Board. It was because he believed Cuba would eventually become an official part of the United States and thus HMB territory. When Tichenor stated, "Everything invites us to enter and possess the land," he used a biblical analogy reminiscent of the ancient Israelites who were given the command to do so with Canaan. The analogy also illustrates the point that Tichenor and other Southern Baptists saw themselves as the spiritual heirs of the Israelites, God's chosen people.

Tichenor's use of anti-Catholic rhetoric also indicated the imperialistic nature of evangelical work. While Tichenor did not cite the ideas of individuals like Josiah Strong and John Fiske, he agreed with their sentiments. Fiske, a well-liked historian and lecturer, published a popular pamphlet entitled *Manifest Destiny.* Based upon the ideas of an earlier generation convinced of the United States' inevitable progress, Fiske's pamphlet promoted his ideas that "America's special genius lay in a unique combination of racial and cultural inheritance, on one hand, and acquired political aptitude, on the other." Fiske has been described as "an ardent Anglo-Saxonist" who believed "that the American branch of the family had developed" the skills of "governing broad territories and large numbers of people more fully" than other Anglo-Saxons. He believed that America's secret was how the U.S. had adapted "representative democracy" and "federalism." Fiske taught that "bursting with this vitality, Americans would extend their influence and institutions across the globe."[11]

Josiah Strong served as the general secretary of the Evangelical Alliance of the United States, a loose collection of Protestant churches formed in 1867 to cooperate in a number of mutual enterprises and demonstrate evangelical unity. A forerunner of the Federal Council of Churches, the alliance received new energy when the Congregationalist pastor assumed its leadership. The author of the controversial and highly influential *Our Country: Its Possible Future and Its Present Crisis* in 1885, Strong warned Americans of the dangers of Mormonism, Catholicism, immigration, intemperance, and urbanization, among other dangers. Strong believed with Fiske that the Anglo-Saxon race would triumph over these dangers. To Fiske's Anglo-Saxonism, Strong added the superiority of Protestant Christianity, especially as manifested in the United States. According to Strong, the superiority of American Protestantism was demonstrated not only through its spiritual purity in the United States but also through the challenge to American Christians to export this alleged purer form of Christianity to other parts of the world. His ideas further became the impetus behind the Social Gospel movement that developed in the United States in the late nineteenth century. Strong was proudly Protestant, unapologetically imperialistic, and sophisticatedly racist.[12]

Tichenor did not adopt Strong's ideas regarding the Social Gospel, and he stated that southern Christianity, especially the Southern Baptist variety, was Christianity's purest form. He also saw the disestablishment of the Roman Catholic Church in Cuba as an opportunity to spread Baptist ideals. His 1896 report indicated that he fully expected a revolution to occur in Cuba. Toppling Spanish rule would lead to a corresponding demise in Roman Catholicism and a sparkling opportunity for Southern Baptist missions. Undoubtedly, he agreed with both Fiske's and Strong's ideas on Anglo-Saxon superiority and on the need for imperialism; both men's ideas obviously colored Tichenor's perspectives on Cuba and HMB work there. One can see the consistency of Fiske's and Strong's ideas with those expressed by Tichenor in his HMB reports and with SBC committee reports. Clearly, he believed home missions could be a method of defending Southern Baptist territory from the invasion of threatening or heretical ideas from the outside and a method of exporting Christian, American, and southern values elsewhere. Cuba, as "the Queen of the Antilles," was a key component of Southern Baptists' efforts to export their brand of the gospel into other parts of the hemisphere. If it were to become part of the United States someday, it must be purified by the work of Southern Baptists. If it did not become U.S. territory, a thoroughly evangelized Cuba might become a base of operations for Baptist missions to Latin America. Likewise, Tichenor's position on Cuba was consistent with his other views regarding race questions in the South. Tichenor paternalistically believed that Cubans, like African Americans, needed to be cared for by the Home Mission Board. As Texas Baptist leader James F. Love stated, white southerners believed that "The South remained the place where 'Anglo-Saxon aspirations' had 'their fullest expression and opportunity.'"[13]

Tichenor and Diaz

Since the onset of Home Mission Board work in Cuba, A. J. Diaz had served as the chief board missionary and representative. For the most part, this relationship had been a healthy one, primarily because of a close working relationship between Tichenor and Diaz. The relationship between the board and Diaz, however, had not been without controversy. On at least one occasion, Diaz incurred significant debt on behalf of the HMB without prior board approval. A committee formed to investigate this action excused this instance, and the mission transferred the property to the Home Mission Board.[14] This action, however, established a dangerous precedent. Diaz appeared resentful of HMB control, and the board bristled over his apparent disregard of its authority.

The issue of authority emerged again in 1898 in at least four separate matters. HMB advisement and control of Cuban mission finances concerned Diaz. The board also required approval of guest speakers in Diaz's church. Other issues included the HMB-appointed English-speaking pastor in Havana and the board appointment of an overseeing agent for its work in Cuba.[15]

The board's policy undoubtedly paralleled that of U.S. economic and military domination of Cuba in the aftermath of the Spanish-American War. Immediately after the war, the U.S. Army established military occupation, and the political and educational system were reestablished under U.S. control and modeled after the U.S. system. Within two years, American business quickly gained control over Cuban railways, sugar and tobacco industries, and large portions of the most fertile Cuban land. The Platt Amendment, passed by the U.S. Senate in 1901, established an American protectorate over Cuba, despite the protests of many Cubans and at least some Americans. Many Americans believed that American capitalism, democracy, and society served as a perfect model for limitless imitation by other nations. Hence, following the sentiments of individuals such as Strong and Fiske, Tichenor and the HMB sought to impose their beliefs and systems upon the Cubans in apparent disregard for Cuban indigenous control.[16] At the very least, these Southern Baptists, who normally so prized local church autonomy, apparently were not as concerned about this issue in Cuba and were more concerned with control over the Cuban Baptists. This was consistent with the approach that Tichenor took regarding board work in the Indian Territory, and it was typical of FMB policy around the world. His position on Cuba further demonstrates another form of paternalism comparable to that of the board toward African Americans. While the Cubans were different from Native Americans or African Americans, they still needed the HMB's "supervision." At the same time, the board would have defended its actions as being evidence of good stewardship and accountability to Southern Baptists who supported their mission efforts. If the Cuban mission were going to receive its financial assistance, it needed also to accept board supervision.

Diaz responded belligerently to all four of these issues. He resented the board's control of speakers, even though it permitted a Methodist minister to speak at his church. With respect to the board's appointment of an English-speaking pastor in Havana, Diaz answered that "we have been taught that [with regards to] Pastors, only the Church could appoint them." Certainly, Diaz's understanding remained consistent with normal Baptist polity. Diaz agreed that the HMB needed an agent to act on its behalf but argued that the agent's work should be solely administrative and should not interfere with individual churches. He wrote, "This authority to the agent will destroy the moral influence of our Pastors, because the people will look [at] these pastors as men who can't be trust[ed]. This agent represent[s] a kind of bishop."[17] Diaz's response revealed the depth of his distress regarding the current situation in Cuba and his growing resentment over board control. It may reflect increasing indigenous Cuban animosity regarding U.S. control over every aspect of their fledgling nation's life as later symbolized by the Platt Amendment. Diaz and other Cuban Baptists may well have expected their Christian brethren to be different from other U.S. citizens by allowing them control over their own internal affairs. If that were the case, then they were sorely disappointed.

By this time in Tichenor's tenure, he suffered periodic illnesses. In his absence, J. William Jones, Tichenor's longtime associate, responded bluntly to Diaz's charges. He reminded Diaz of his own support and of Tichenor's friendship and support. He defended HMB actions. He wrote, "it seems to me *the Board is perfectly right in every regulation and instruction they have issued.*" He added,

> Every Baptist church is, of course, free and independent, and if your church chooses to declare itself independent of the authority of the Home Mission Board at Atlanta, it has a perfect right to do so. *But in doing so they cut themselves off entirely from all support from the Home Mission Board,* which is the agent of Southern Baptists acting for them and by their authority and responsible only to the Southern Baptist Convention. Inasmuch as you are the Missionary of the Home Mission Board, and your church a Mission Station of the Home Mission Board, you are amenable to such rules and regulations as they may see fit to adopt. If you decline to acknowledge their authority or obey their instructions you have no right to use in any way their property. . . . Neither the Board nor anybody else has thought of denying you or your church this right, [to meet elsewhere] but only insists that if you exercise this right *you must not use their property, or interfere with their rights.* This is the simple issue, and I have not a shadow of a doubt that the overwhelming voice of the Baptists of the South will stand by and sustain the Board in its contention.[18]

Jones closed his letter by pleading with Diaz "to see the truth." The crisis passed when Tichenor recovered his health and worked out a compromise with Diaz that restored peace.[19]

This exchange is fascinating for a number of reasons. Seldom has a U.S. agency made a stronger case for cultural imperialism. Essentially, Jones, on behalf of the HMB, insisted that Cuban Baptists do what the Home Mission Board dictated. Jones told Diaz that if he and the church refused to comply with their instructions and with the board's oversight, funding would be eliminated. While this was consistent with the approach that Tichenor had taken in earlier attempts to exercise authority over Indian Territory missionary J. S. Murrow, normally the board would have avoided any interference in local church matters. While Jones may have been correct "that the overwhelming voice of the Baptists of the South will stand by and sustain the Board in its contention," if the board had attempted such interference with a southern Anglo congregation, the outcry would have been deafening. Undoubtedly, Jones had acted on Tichenor's behalf on other occasions. Therefore, his opinions are indicative of the kind of authority that Tichenor believed the HMB held over its missionaries. Clearly, Diaz was free to act on behalf of the Cuban mission as long as his actions were consistent with board policies. If he did not maintain this consistency, then he would be ordered to comply. In this instance, Tichenor, though a confrontational person at some points in his life, reconciled differences once he became personally involved. Apparently, at least in this instance, he served as an intermediary between the missionary in the field and the board itself. His friendship with Diaz and support for him in earlier days provided him the needed credibility to arrange a compromise. Still, Tichenor's involvement and complicity in the utilization of the HMB's control over Cuban affairs does not cast him or the board in a positive light. Throughout the 1890s American Protestant missionaries mounted a cultural invasion simultaneous with U.S. economic imperialism. Spurred by a postmillenialist eschatological urge to reach every nation with American Protestant Christianity in their generation, those missionaries became fervent apostles of American life. They provided the first significant exposure that many indigenous people had to the United States. Though racial prejudice tainted their work and cultural supremacy permeated their thought, these missionaries passionately believed their social values were desired by other peoples and were transmissible. Christian missions all too often became intricately involved with American economics. They faced missiological and theological problems associated with forcing an American form of Christianity upon the indigenous peoples and also came to rely increasingly upon wealthy U.S. businessmen. This growing complicity linked American missions with "dollar diplomacy" and with the diplomatic and financial support of U.S. government and business.[20]

The problem of Diaz's relationship to the HMB reemerged after Tichenor became secretary emeritus. Board representatives charged that Diaz and the Havana church had used the church building for political meetings. A committee—consisting of Porter King, chairman of the Cuban committee; F. H. Kerfoot, the new corresponding secretary; E. L. Connally of the Cuban committee; and Tichenor—was appointed to investigate. On April 22, 1901, the committee wrote Diaz a lengthy letter reminding him that "our especial business in Cuba is a matter of religion of the Lord Jesus Christ, and in no sense whatever a matter of politics":

> One of the greatest achievements that the Baptists have ever made in this country and in all their history, has been their work in securing in the United States an absolute separation between Church and State. Our aim has been . . . to keep all political matters, as far as possible, out of our own Churches, and separate from our Church relations.
>
> . . . We have felt that it would not be amiss, in the trying ordeal through which the brethren in Cuba are passing, for us to call attention to this fact of the complete separation between church and state. . . . We recognize the fullest right and liberty of every man to hold his own peculiar political views, and to govern himself as a citizen in his own political action. We sincerely trust . . . that our brethren in Cuba will see their way clear to plant themselves unmistakably upon this vital Baptist principle, of an entire separation between religion and matters which are purely political . . . to keep all strictly political matters entirely out of the churches with which they are connected.[21]

The key words in this letter were "an entire separation between religion and matters which are *purely political*" and "to keep all *strictly political matters* entirely out of the churches."[22] Baptists had not historically withdrawn from society or from taking an active role in government. They did not advocate "disconnection of religion and government" but did demand religious liberty and scrutinized churches that mixed religion and politics too closely. Baptists also traditionally valued the privileges and protections of civil laws. This communication conveyed the sense of this historical belief.[23]

Subsequent to this communication, Diaz wrote Tichenor offering to resign as HMB missionary. Tichenor communicated this offer to the Committee on Cuban Missions but asked permission to withhold it from the board. He attempted to placate Diaz. Communication between the two continued, and Diaz withdrew his resignation. The major issues, however, remained unresolved. Part of the reason for the delay and for Tichenor's continued involvement in the issue was the sudden death of Porter King and the long illness and ensuing death of F. H. Kerfoot. Tichenor diligently hoped that tensions might be reduced and Diaz would continue in the employ of the board. In the end, Tichenor wrote Diaz that it was in Diaz's best interest and the best interest of the Home Mission Board that he resign. On September 9, 1901, the Home Mission Board approved Diaz's resignation as superintendent and missionary for the Province of Havana and Pinar del Rio. In spite of Diaz's resignation, the work of the board continued in Cuba, and Diaz and Tichenor continued correspondence with one another until Tichenor's death in late 1902.[24]

Tichenor's support of the beginnings of Baptist missions in Cuba and his continued interest in that work was a consuming passion during the latter part of his tenure as HMB corresponding secretary. He rabidly defended Cuba as Southern Baptist territory. He constantly encouraged the Southern Baptist Convention to support this new work, and he devoted significant portions of his time to correspondence and travel related to Cuba. While Tichenor was intensely concerned with defending traditional Southern Baptist territory from incursions by Northern Baptists, he was equally concerned with expanding the influence of Southern Baptists into new areas once resources were available to do so. In the mid-1880s and the 1890s, Southern Baptists saw Cuba as a ripe mission field. Tichenor was willing to make tremendous sacrifices to establish Southern Baptist work there and, once established, to defend that territory as well. A picture of Tichenor as a conciliator emerges in the tensions between the Home Mission Board and Diaz also. Though Tichenor was sometimes perceived as "bombastic" or confrontational, in the case of Diaz he worked to bring about reconciliation. Clearly, however, he demanded loyalty to the HMB and its policies. Also, he was obviously a product of his culture in his attitudes regarding cultural imperialism. He attempted to export American culture generally and southern culture specifically into Cuba. He made it very clear that Cuban Baptists should adhere to HMB and U.S. authority. Regardless of how proper or improper his motivations and how prejudicial his methods, Tichenor's efforts were so great on behalf of Cuban missions that F. C. McConnell, in his 1903 memoriam of Tichenor at the Southern Baptist Convention, referred to him as "The Father of Cuban Missions."[25]

Tichenor and the Mountain Regions

During the latter half of Tichenor's administration, HMB mission work to the Appalachian Mountain region emerged as a priority. As early as his 1885 report, Tichenor mentioned the importance of this region: "Its people, long shut in by their mountain ranges, find their country by the construction of railways thrown open to the great world without. Sources of wealth never dreamed of start into existence about them." He defined the Appalachian region as "extending from Virginia to Alabama, and embracing parts of these States, as well as portions of Georgia, Tennessee, North Carolina, Kentucky, and West Virginia." He added, "It is filled with Baptists. But they are for the most part poor. . . . Our duty to them as brethren, and our interest, looking to the future of our denomination, alike require that we should extend to them a helping hand."[26]

By 1892 Tichenor had established the 112,000 square mile region as an HMB priority equivalent to Cuba, the work in the cities, and work among the Native Americans of the Indian Territory and African Americans. In 1893 he reported that work had begun in this area but was not nearly the proportion that was needed. F. C. McConnell in Virginia devoted significant energy to teaching pastors, two board missionaries worked in West Virginia, and the Home Mission Board added agreements coordinating their efforts with the Western North Carolina Board and the Kentucky State Board.[27]

Many Americans held little interest in the Appalachian mountain region throughout the antebellum period and noted little difference between the southern "Highlands" and other southern territory. The aftermath of the war changed that perception. Most of the residents of the mountain regions had resisted efforts to incorporate them into the Confederacy, and during the war both sides identified this region as a Unionist stronghold. Many mountaineers remained loyal to the Union or were indifferent to the cause of southern independence.[28] Certainly, there were socioeconomic differences between the rugged individualists of the mountains and the low country planters and farmers. As historian Henry Shapiro writes, during the 1870s "[t]he progress of civilization in America and Americans' self-consciousness of their progress, was such that the apparent persistence of pioneer conditions among the mountain people made Appalachia seem a strange land inhabited by a peculiar people." Popular writers from the 1870s contributed to this mystique regarding the Appalachian region. Gradually at first and then rapidly in the

1880s, southerners as well as other Americans began to classify the mountain people as different from other groups. An entire mindset emerged that identified Appalachian people as isolated and backward and as fertile soil for both benevolent and missionary work. Mostly ignoring local churches that provided a strong, independent flavor to religious beliefs, missionary agencies both North and South identified the region as largely "unchurched." Certain denominations were not represented in the region, and denominations such as Baptists who were represented there had little connection with the broader denominational work. Of all the denominations present in Appalachia, Baptists were the strongest, but the type of Baptist work represented was that of "Old School Baptists." Old School Baptists were divided between missionary Baptists who supported cooperative missions efforts and the anti-missions Baptists who had adopted extreme Calvinist views that rejected mission boards as unbiblical and who also remained suspicious of educated ministers.

In his pamphlet *Home Missions,* Tichenor summarized the need for work in the mountain regions:

There is a wonderful field for the board in the mountain region of the South. This section of country so abundant in its varied resources, the development of which must one day make it the work-shop of the continent, is filled with Baptists. They are numerically greater than all other denominations combined, but they are in sore need of development. They need all those appliances which lift men and women above the narrow views which ignorance always begets, and the enlargement of mind and heart which will fit them for the highest efficiency in the Master's work.[29]

While acknowledging the historic strength of Baptists in the region, Tichenor emphasized Appalachian backwardness, independence, and ignorance. Undoubtedly, he traced these conditions to the earlier days of the anti-missions movement. Led by rugged and individualistic frontier Baptist preachers such as John Taylor and Daniel Parker, this movement challenged the biblical nature of mission organizations, typically resented the financial efforts required for the promotion of cooperative missions and educated clergymen, and were concerned that missions organizations would threaten local church autonomy. This movement tended to be strongest along the frontier, and many Baptists in the mountain regions still held tightly to these anti-mission views. Tichenor believed that church planting and church building loans would create churches that were loyal to Southern Baptist missions. One should remember that Tichenor's home region in Kentucky dealt with these questions in his youth, and he struggled against these same sentiments in his missions work as a young representative of the Indian Mission Board and in his Alabama pastorate.[30]

Tichenor's emphasis upon the mountain region was more than just an attempt to expand Southern Baptist influence. To a certain extent, he promoted Appalachian missions as yet another form of social control. He and others feared, no doubt, that northern home missionaries might tap into preexisting Unionist sentiments there to expand their influence into the South. He directed this defense of SBC interests against not only other Baptists but also against other denominations and Mormons.[31]

Perhaps foremost among the reasons for Tichenor's intense interest in the potential of the mountain regions was the realization of Appalachia's vast mineral resources, especially coal. Tichenor's earlier expertise in geology had familiarized him with this potential, and his 1885 and 1892 reports to the SBC stressed the mineral resources of the region. He believed the area would develop vast amounts of material wealth inconceivable to most Southern Baptists. This interest in exploiting the region's vast coal and timber resources constituted one element of the growing interest in the region as a mission field.[32]

As a former mining executive, Tichenor recognized the importance of a reliable labor source in such industries as coal mining and timber. From Tichenor's perspective, improving the mountain folk's social lot and establishing churches as vehicles for peaceful and godly distractions would have contributed to the region's economic health and social order. Poor Appalachian farmers initially found coal mining an attractive option, especially at a time of declining opportunities in farming during the period. Coal mining offered a potentially steady though meager income despite the considerable physical risk involved. Likewise, these farmers provided a cheap labor source for the coal mines. Tichenor's goal of improving the lot of these poor people was consistent with characteristics he demonstrated while at Alabama A & M. Certainly, also, genuine Christian concern motivated Tichenor, as he demonstrated in numerous other cases. Baptist evangelical zeal merged with a strong sense of family to build institutions that benefited numerous local communities. Churches and schools assumed primacy in this movement. Tichenor also would have agreed with the need to Americanize these mountain people as other Protestants sought to do. However, Tichenor saw the opportunity also to "southernize" the white southerners of the region who were viewed as different from other southerners. All these necessities combined to make the Appalachian Mountains and the people living there an HMB priority during Tichenor's tenure and afterward. Finally, the Christian America movement of this era cultivated a distinct image of Appalachian Christianity that colored his perspective.[33]

Like other Protestants engaged in Appalachian ministries, Tichenor directed considerable resources toward benevolence, education, and efforts to incorporate religious groups then existing in Appalachia into the denominational mainstream. He also promoted Southern Baptist work so that other Christian denominations would not achieve a head start in the region. Denominational competition contributed significantly to American missions efforts in Appalachia.[34]

Home missionaries also attempted to spread Christianity into the Appalachians as a way "to modernize" the area. Social historian Deborah McCauley writes that in this era "to modernize" meant "to uplift, to uplift was to Christianize, to Christianize was to Americanize." For Tichenor, despite his opposition to Landmark Baptist ideas, the ultimate expression "to Christianize" would have been to "Baptize" them as well. McCauley further states that "[m]odernization went hand in hand with the task of creating a unified, homogeneous Christian nation, a Christian America. The strategy for achieving a Christian America was to integrate 'unassimilated' populations into what was perceived to be the mainstream of American life."[35] The philosophy behind this effort was similar to the ideas of Josiah Strong toward foreign regions and peoples.

Systematic Southern Baptist attempts to "uplift" the people of Appalachia originated during Tichenor's tenure at the board. Demonstrating his lifelong interest in education, Tichenor expressed a desire to build schools in Appalachia. This interest was part of Southern Baptists' social awakening but also linked SBC educational efforts in Appalachia with the "New South economic boosterism," which Tichenor ardently advocated.[36]

Tichenor's vision of a southern Zion sought to incorporate all southerners into the effort to mobilize the potential population and natural resources of the region. He often reminded the SBC of the vast potential that the Appalachian region held and worried about how little Southern Baptists were doing to incorporate the region effectively within the Baptist Zion. Genuine concern motivated his efforts. Tichenor envisioned many new facets of work that not only included education but also hospitals, orphanages, and residences for the elderly and disabled.[37] Nowhere would these types of institutions have been needed more than in the Appalachian Mountains, and Tichenor frequently demonstrated his desire to better the living conditions of the South's people.

Tichenor's advocacy of expanded efforts into Cuba and Appalachia reflected a growing confidence that he, the board, Southern Baptists, and southerners as a whole felt as the economic recovery of the South continued and as the dream of a New South spread. He and others considered both locations part of the southern Zion that offered not only potential for growth but also tremendous resources that would fill the coffers of Southern Baptist mission boards.

Tichenor's approach to the board's work in Cuba and the Appalachian Mountains denotes a great deal about his leadership style and philosophy. He continued to inspire enthusiasm for the board's projects, but he also demanded intense southern loyalty and adherence to sound business practices. He "southernized" and "baptized" American cultural, economic, and religious imperialism for Home Mission Board use as he expanded its vision to encompass regions previously untapped by the SBC.

7
"Our Southland"

Tichenor Defines Southern Baptist Territory

In his study *At Ease in Zion,* social historian Rufus Spain asks several provocative questions. Spain wonders whether Southern Baptists of the late nineteenth century thought of themselves primarily as Baptists or southerners and whether they were shaped more deeply by southern attitudes and culture than by their environment. In the case of I. T. Tichenor, it appears that to be "Baptist" and "Southern" were synonymous. While not a proponent of the Landmark Baptist movement, Tichenor may have been shaped by Landmark influences nonetheless. Tichenor did have a distinct vision that both the South and Baptists were appointed for a special mission to the world. He and his contemporaries frequently referred to the South as the Baptist "Zion" or "Canaan."[1] No doubt Tichenor believed that his "Beloved Southland" was the promised land for Baptists, and the new ideas that he "southernized" and "baptized" were tools that enabled him to define more accurately that Southland.

As the chief executive and operating officer of the SBC's Home Mission Board, Tichenor played a primary role in developing a denominational identity for the body that was to become the largest Protestant denomination in the United States. Faced with a crisis of catastrophic proportions, the possible collapse of the Home Mission Board, which threatened the very life of the Southern Baptist Convention, Tichenor responded by calling Southern Baptists to define the convention's territory and then defending this territory against incursions from Northern Baptists. As demonstrated, Tichenor clarified the mission of the Home Mission Board and expanded that mission as opportunity and resources allowed. As he did so, and as his tenure as corresponding secretary continued, his definition of who Southern Baptists were was modified.

Tichenor was firmly convinced of the necessity of preserving the Home Mission Board. He was even more convinced of the necessity of maintaining a separate and strong Southern Baptist Convention and of not reuniting with Northern Baptists. To Tichenor these two goals were closely linked. Immediately, he set about his task of persuasion. For Tichenor, it was imperative that Southern Baptists reclaim the South for *Southern* Baptists. He saw efforts by the American Baptist Home Mission Society to consolidate and extend their work in the South as a direct attack on southern autonomy. Repeatedly, the annual reports of the Home Mission Society called for denominational reunion. The Home Mission Society had poured thousands of dollars in church building loans into the South during Reconstruction, and because of this support, many conventions and associations across the region had moved or were moving into affiliation with the society. Furthermore, the Home Mission Society had almost complete control over Baptist mission work in the West. As Tichenor later said about the situation, "A survey of the field indicated a great defeat and a lost cause."[2]

A rapid transformation took place in the outlook of Southern Baptists and the Home Mission Board between 1882 and 1890. How were Tichenor and his colleagues able to achieve such a metamorphosis? In accomplishing this, did Tichenor and his fellow Southern Baptists also foster a spirit of sectionalism and encourage attitudes that were already pervasive in southern life? By doing so, did he also promote the triumphalism and provincialism that became key characteristics of southerners generally and Southern Baptists specifically in the years that followed? Regardless of the outcomes, Tichenor defined and defended Southern Baptist Convention territory in the years between 1882 and 1899 and thus saved the convention from dissolution by giving Southern Baptists a denominational identity. By saving the "home field" exclusively for Southern Baptist mission efforts, in essence he saved the convention and dispelled permanently talk of reunification with Northern Baptists. In his history of the Southern Baptist Convention Sunday School Board, denominational historian Walter Shurden writes of Tichenor,

> He used every gift God had given him to call Southern Baptists to their potential in poverty stricken days. Southern Baptists responded and ral-

lied! And they did so because Tichenor instilled a denominational consciousness in them.

He made them proud of being *Southern* Baptists.[3]

In the most recent history of the SBC, Jesse Fletcher writes of Tichenor that he "was especially adroit in stirring the denominational consciousness to which . . . convention-type polity . . . lent itself. Tichenor made it clear that the Home Mission Board and the Southern Baptist Convention were one entity. If a person was for one, he was for the other." Fletcher adds, "His role in revitalizing the Home Mission Board is matched by his success in heightening denominational pride and commitment." Tichenor has been identified as one of the key leaders who developed ideas both of "denominational connectionalism" and "denominational consciousness" in the years from 1882 to 1894. Some historians also have suggested that more than any other he "defined what was 'southern' about the Southern Baptist Convention."[4] How he accomplished this is an important story in Christian sectionalism and denominational identity.

One of the most significant ways Tichenor defined and defended SBC territory was through numerous speeches and reports. While still a pastor in Montgomery during the Civil War, he indicated his vision for the South in his Fast Day sermon delivered before a joint session of the Alabama legislature on August 21, 1863. In it he stated, "God in his own way will save our Southland." He also declared that "it may be that God has for the South a world mission, and that by these sufferings [the Civil War] he is preparing them for the trust."[5] Tichenor never lost sight of this vision for the South and, long after the war ended, often repeated these sentiments to Southern Baptists.

Tichenor was a powerful speaker in a denomination that highly valued inspiring rhetoric. Many have overlooked the fact that Southern Baptists widely recognized him as one of the finest preachers of the nineteenth century. Southern Baptist historian Robert Baker stated that Tichenor was probably one of the top two or three Southern Baptist preachers of his day. This evaluation would place Tichenor among the top pulpiteers of this era, an era known as the golden age of American denominationalism and a period ruled by the "princes of the pulpit." Unfortunately, few of Tichenor's sermons are available for study. From those that do remain, from observations of his preaching style made by his contemporaries, and from other addresses that he made, the modern observer can derive several conclusions about the relationship his outstanding skill had to his ability to rally the SBC behind the home missions effort.[6] Much in the same way that Winston Churchill is said to have mobilized even the English language and marched it to war, Tichenor mobilized the Baptist pulpit and marched it into a war defining and defending Southern Baptist territory.

J. B. Hawthorne, a leading Southern Baptist minister who had occasion to hear Tichenor preach often while he was pastor in Montgomery, noted that Tichenor's preaching was both thoughtful and forceful. He recalled that Tichenor's preaching was "topical" with "brief" and "simple" analysis. Hawthorne observed that Tichenor "gave . . . but little attention to modern textbooks on homiletics but was a careful student of rhetoric."[7] The emphasis on the study of rhetoric would have been consistent with Tichenor's classical education in his adolescence.

Two years before Tichenor assumed the mantle at the HMB, John R. Sampey, then seventeen years old but later president of the Southern Baptist Theological Seminary, heard Tichenor preach to the Alabama Baptist State Convention. The sermon made such an impression on Sampey that many years later he recalled the occasion in his memoirs:

> There I heard a most impressive address by Dr. I. T. Tichenor. . . . As he moved into his peroration on the moral dignity and high value of the missionary enterprise, I could hardly keep my seat. If anyone near me had risen, I would have risen beside him. My soul had never before been so transported with the vision of the nations accepting Jesus as Saviour and Lord.[8]

Another Baptist who often heard Tichenor preach in the 1890s, W. O. Carver, professor of comparative religion and missions at Southern Seminary, recalled in 1950 that Tichenor rarely spoke longer than thirty minutes but compared favorably with the great orators of the twentieth century. Carver commented that he often thought of Tichenor when he heard Churchill, arguably the greatest orator of the English language in the twentieth century. Regarding Tichenor's eloquence, Carver remarked, "I sometimes wondered if Doctor Tichenor didn't dream eloquently."[9]

Tichenor frequently painted lengthy word pictures and utilized language laden with vivid imagery. Yet another Baptist who heard Tichenor speak often was W. B. Crumpton, for twenty-eight years executive secretary of the Alabama Baptist State Convention. Crumpton mentioned one such word picture in his own memoirs as he recalled Tichenor years later. He wrote,

> [Tichenor] was every inch a great man, in heart, in brain, in spirit. I came to regard him as the greatest orator I ever heard. . . . Could a passage of his speech before the Convention at Atlanta be reproduced and published, it would be prized as an oratorical gem. He pictured an iceberg, breaking loose from its icy fastnesses in the far North and drifting Southward in its grandeur, endangering shipping on its journey, until the tropical sunshine and warming currents, gradually melted away its jagged sides and brought down its towering peaks and mingled them with the waters of the Southern Seas. . . . [10]

As Hawthorne mentioned, Tichenor's preaching was generally topical. Typically, he chose a subject and then referenced it with scripture, using the force of his speaking voice and rhetoric as well as illustrations from classical literature to support his arguments. His granddaughter recalled him as an "avid reader and great student." He drew vivid illustrations from his experiences as a mining executive, as president of Alabama A & M, and in battle at Shiloh.[11]

Tichenor's preaching represented the moderate Calvinism of Baptist life in his day. His topical sermons focused on the common themes of salvation, grace, and God's sovereignty. He balanced God's sovereignty in the world against a need for human response. His theology of mission was that the Christian's primary call was to spread the gospel. He believed that although God ultimately controlled all situations, it was still necessary for humans to answer God's call for change. As might be expected, missiological themes played a significant role in Tichenor's preaching, both before coming to the Home Mission Board and especially afterward. An ardent student of eschatology, Tichenor linked the success of the missions enterprise with the return of Jesus Christ.[12]

Listeners observed that in the pulpit Tichenor radiated "an air of distinction" centered on his "erect posture" and "dignified manner." With penetrating "deep, blue eyes," "fair complexion," and neatly trimmed beard that became gray and silver with age, Tichenor also exuded an attractive and confident air. Like many of the "princes of the pulpit," Tichenor emanated energy while expounding the gospel. His granddaughter recalled that his preaching was "emotional at times," punctuated by the stamping of his left foot at moments of "earnest." After preaching "he would often stay awake all night reading because he couldn't sleep." While not speaking rapidly, Tichenor seems to have "never hesitated for a word." Although a bout with the measles damaged his speaking voice, Tichenor overcame this malady by vigorous use of his diaphragm when preaching. Apparently, the only lasting effect of the illness was a need to clear his voice regularly, especially as he grew older. Tichenor said that as he aged, his voice lost the "flexibility" of his earlier years. In his memorial of Tichenor, Hawthorne said,

> Those who never heard Dr. Tichenor before his voice was impaired by bronchial troubles, can scarcely conceive of its original flexibility, compass, clearness, strength, and sweetness. It was remarkable for his range and variety of tones. When he was rallying his congregation . . . it was like the blast of a brazen trumpet; but when lamenting misfortune or commiserating suffering, it was as tender and as plantive as the notes of a funeral chant.[13]

Hawthorne also quoted the firebrand secessionist of the Civil War era and one of the most highly regarded of southern orators, Alabamian William L. Yancey, regarding Tichenor's speaking ability. Hawthorne reported that Yancey "declared that [Tichenor] was one of the most instructive, impressive, and irresistible of living preachers."[14]

Tichenor's HMB reports challenged and inspired SBC meetings. His 1885 report before the convention in Augusta, Georgia, upon the occasion of the fortieth anniversary of the SBC's creation is only one example of his powerful summons to missions. Drawing upon deep veins of Southern Baptist triumphalism, he issued a call for Southern Baptists to save themselves and their denomination, country, and world with a Baptist version of the gospel. Reminding the body of the fortieth anniversary of the creation of the SBC and the HMB, he called the messengers and indeed all Southern Baptists to be "liberalized by the proper conception of His grand design, and elevated into sympathy with His purpose to save humanity from the ignorance and poverty, as well as from the guilt which sin has entailed" and to "rise to loftier heights of duty." He finished with a dramatic conclusion:

> The breath of the Divine Spirit can dissipate the mist of worldliness that bedim the vision of His people, and show us even now that both duty

and happiness require such consecration. A New Pentecost, with its disparted tongues of fire, may impart new life, even in our day, to His children. A few chosen men, like Carey and Judson and Luther Rice, may lift up their voices, as did John the Baptist, and be heard and answered by every church in all our broad domain. A mighty revolution, shaking as with the might of an earthquake, the sleeping Christians of our time, may break upon us as a meteor breaks through the midnight sky. The voice of the Almighty may call to this valley of dry bones, "O, ye dry bones, hear the word of the Lord," and starting from their long slumbers, they may stand up an exceeding great army prepared for the conquest of the world. God grant that the meeting of this Convention may date the hour of our resurrection to nobler views of duty and consuming activity in the work of our Lord. But, brethren, if it may not be, if our eyes shall never be gladdened by seeing the church of God going forth as an army with banners, let us, believing that it will come, labor for its accomplishment. If not here, surely one day from the further shore, we shall see the shadows lifting from this dark world, once our home, and our hearts, filled with heavenly rapture, break forth and sing as we never could before that grand old hymn: "The morning light is breaking, The darkness disappears."[15]

Sometimes called a "seer" or "visionary" by his peers, the Baptist statesman was convinced of a bright future for Christianity and for Baptists in America and the world. He used every rhetorical avenue open to him to communicate to Southern Baptists his vision, optimism, and aspirations regarding the future endeavors of the convention. More than anything else Tichenor conveyed the message that he believed in them and that God had a high purpose for the people of the South. Tichenor understood that people characteristically respond to confident and enthusiastic attitudes and typically need encouragement and hope. The confidence of Southern Baptists, shattered by the crushing defeat of the Civil War, Reconstruction, and the lethargy of the Home Mission Board, had to be rebuilt and challenged if the Southern Baptist Convention were to survive. Likewise, confidence in the Home Mission Board and its work had to be revived as well. Bluntly, Tichenor told the convention at its 1887 meeting, "The surest, speediest way to the dissolution of this Convention is to so weaken your Home Mission Board as to render it powerless to do the work committed to its hands."[16] This was a key point for Tichenor. He believed fervently in foreign missions. He recognized and promoted the essential nature of publications. To him, however, these significant enterprises would fail if Southern Baptists ignored or neglected the base of operations, the home field. Existing churches should be strengthened and new churches established if Southern Baptists were to continue to meet the region's growing needs. As this occurred, these churches could then support the growing foreign missions endeavors and publish the materials that would nurture the work of Southern Baptists.

Southern Baptists heard his pleas for support in his annual reports, in his visits with them, and in the articles and pamphlets he published, and they responded. Though the response was slower in coming and never as strong as Tichenor would have liked, his dynamic leadership and pervasive optimism were exactly what the Southern Baptist Convention needed to rouse it from its apathy toward home missions.

Defining the Territory

Tichenor consistently argued that "the field of the Home Board has been from the first the territory of our Southern Baptist Convention, embracing work among the Indians of the West, the negroes of the South, the Foreigners who have crowded into our States, and the destitute among our own native population."[17] Essentially, he meant that geographically the South consisted of the old slave states and the Indian Territory. He devoted his diligent energies to increasing Southern Baptists' hold on these areas. He infused convention members with his own viewpoint about the necessity of preserving the home field. A report by the committee on "Missions to the Native White Population" to the 1890 convention echoed his feelings:

> One thing of good importance brings this work before us. Whatever may be the means by which the work is enlarged, to the enlargement must we look for the ability to do greater things. At present, and for years to come, this field must yield the money needed for both home and foreign missions. *To neglect the base of supplies is criminal.*[18]

Tichenor's vision, however, expanded beyond traditional boundaries. In his first report before the Southern Baptist Convention, he said, "Had sufficient resources been at our disposal, we could have occupied other grounds in California, New Mexico, Arizona, and Colorado." Despite his desire to increase board influence, he believed the SBC did not require assistance from Northern Baptists. Southern Baptists, he felt, should be self-sufficient and possessed the resources to reach the masses within their sphere of ministry.[19]

As he defined Southern Baptist territory, he also demonstrated himself as a product of the culture in which he lived. Tichenor ardently defended sectionalism. During this time period Southern Baptists probably did more to promote sectionalism than they did to lessen existent tensions.[20] Certainly, Tichenor was no exception. In fact, sectionalism was one tool that Tichenor used to unify Southern Baptists. As he had done in trying to promote the need for scientific and mechanical education while president at Alabama A & M, he focused his addresses and writings to the SBC on the South's potential. He used military terminology that evoked memories of the Civil War. He built the pride of white southerners and utilized their fears of imminent change. He also used every opportunity to refer to the "Southland" as a mission base for evangelizing the world.

Sectionalism

Occasions of political sectionalism erupted most frequently in the years immediately after the war and during the elections of 1876 and 1880. Likewise, the death of Jefferson Davis late in 1889 and subsequent 1892 re-interment of his body in Richmond stirred patriotic southern convictions.[21] Reunification of the Baptist denomination might have encouraged more positive feelings between North and South had Baptists been willing to participate in it, but most Southern Baptists favored continuing exclusively southern organizations. Baptists were not alone in this failure, as the two other major southern denominations that divided prior to the war, Methodists and Presbyterians, also remained separated. As Charles Reagan Wilson's landmark study *Baptized in Blood: The Religion of the Lost Cause, 1865–1920* indicates, southern Christians developed their own particular theology that reinforced this sectionalism and dealt with Confederate defeat. Rather than experience a loss of faith or an admission of guilt over the evils of slavery, southerners rationalized the defeat by clinging to a belief that God purified his people for his ultimate purposes through the crucible of war.[22] Tichenor was among those who adopted and utilized this sectionalist theology.

Tichenor employed sectionalist sentiments as he fought to inspire Southern Baptists to support the Home Mission Board. In his 1891 report before the convention, Tichenor extolled the virtues, promise, and potential of the "Southland." He envisioned expansion of the work of southerners, and he demonstrated pride in the South.[23] Tichenor quoted an article written by another Southern Baptist leader, J. B. Gambrell, as part of his report to the 1893 Southern Baptist Convention:

> Multitudes of peoples speaking strange tongues will flow into this Southland. At first the Northern man with American ideas will come . . . followed by men from every nation under heaven. To prepare for, meet and christianize these millions is the work of the Home Board. Along the mountain fastnesses [*sic*] of the Virginias, Kentucky, . . . and the great coming cities of the South, the battles are to be fought . . . which will decide the spiritual destiny of this country a thousand years. . . . Nor is this the whole of it. The great numbers and strength of the Baptists of the South, through our Home Board, must be turned on the millions of lost souls in the North who are overbearing our Northern brethren.
>
> This is a defensive measure, since these people greatly affect our common country.[24]

His attitude was consistent with his times. Speaking to the 1890 Southern Baptist Convention meeting in Fort Worth, J. B. Hawthorne said, "Some men say they know no North, no South, no East, no West. I know and love them all. But I know best and love most the land that gave me birth, the land of the sunny South." Southerners typically romanticized the South and its heritage, culture, and climate during the post-Reconstruction era. Having suffered defeat in the war and humiliation in the Reconstruction period, white southerners responded by retreating to a mythic South that was an American paradise. Hence, the frequent references to the South as a "Southern Zion" and identification with the biblical Israelites. Southern Baptists were not alone in this latter sentiment either. As Wilson writes, southern Protestants in general tended "to identify themselves with the biblical chosen people, the Israelites."[25]

Racial Attitudes

The years of Reconstruction were difficult ones for Americans, North and South, black and white, and Baptists were no exception. African Americans were encouraged to form separate churches and associations by both southern whites, who were sometimes outnumbered by their former slaves in the churches, and by northern leaders who felt that this separation was necessary for black leadership to develop. Political motivations reinforced these desires as well, because the black churches sometimes became forums for Republican policies, and southerners spurned support of entities that sustained the ideas of Reconstruction. Further, as early as 1866, the beginning of Reconstruction, many southern churches determined that their southern denominations should remain autonomous. Thus, Southern Baptists failed to provide adequate financial and educational help for African American churches in the South.[26] The work of the Southern Baptist Convention's Home Board and the southern economy had been devastated by the war, and funds to support any institutions or churches were meager. While there were efforts by some to provide more substantial aid to southern blacks for their churches and schools, only toward the end of the century did Southern Baptists begin to provide some support. In spite of this, the Southern Baptist attitude existed that the control of black Baptist education should rest in white hands.

Therefore, the arena of race relations defined another crucial element of SBC territory. Here, as well as in his sectionalist attitudes, Tichenor both contributed to his culture and defended what he believed to be southern values. These racial attitudes were closely tied to his ideas on sectionalism and the development of the Southern Baptist Convention. Sectionalism substantially impeded closer cooperation between the SBC and the Northern Home Mission Society. A report given by the Southern Baptist committee on Religious Instruction of the Colored Population at the first SBC meeting after the Civil War indicated this spirit. Tichenor chaired this committee, and this report represented his later attitudes on the subject.[27]

While welcoming the assistance of the "right-minded," Southern Baptists were suspicious of Northern Baptist work among southern blacks. To most white Southern Baptists, "right-minded" individuals were those pledged to preserve the social structure of the South and white dominance. Furthermore, they identified defeat in the Civil War as a punishment for their sins, and many never refuted the idea of the justness of "the Cause." Tichenor originally believed that the benefits of the system outweighed the blight that slavery had inflicted upon the nation. He never completely admitted that slavery was wrong, although in his later years he probably agreed with the New South advocates who believed that slavery had retarded the region's economic development. To Tichenor slavery provided another opportunity to spread the gospel to the "pagans." He and his family had owned a few slaves. His mindset continued to reflect the general spirit of these attitudes.

During the period that Tichenor led the Home Mission Board, Southern Baptists began to get involved in social issues while at the same time maintaining their focus on evangelism. While they focused mainly upon family issues and institution building, Southern Baptists were mindful of other areas of social concern, including race. Observing Joel Williamson's models of racial attitudes in the post-Reconstruction South, social historian Keith Harper places Southern Baptists in the "conservative mentality" between the "liberal" model that sought progress for blacks and the "radical" model that wanted to force blacks from the South.

Certainly, a case could be made that all three models would, at least, describe some Southern Baptists, but the vast majority would fall in this conservative category. This mentality rejected social equality for African Americans but did not advocate forcible removal of African Americans from the South. These "conservatives" would gladly accept continued African American residency in the South if a system of segregation were implemented, and political and social control delegated to white southerners. Subsequently, the type of opportunities offered to support African-American education, especially ministerial education, reflected this attitude. Occasionally, too, when resources were limited by financial difficulties, one of the areas of support eliminated or reduced was that for blacks.[28]

Tichenor's paternalistic attitudes toward the former slaves are seen in two of his writings, "Uncle Ben's Golden Wedding" and "Jesse Goldthwaite: A Christian Slave." Both of these writings demonstrated a genuine compassion and concern for loyal blacks and attempted to pose a positive picture of southern slavery. The former depicted the most humane side of slavery. It was drawn from Tichenor's fourth wife's family life and described Tichenor's friendship with his in-laws' elderly slaves. Uncle Ben and Aunt Jenny remained residents on the family plantation after emancipation. Tichenor described in glowing terms the close bonds that remained between the aging couple and their former masters. Even the names "Uncle" and "Aunt" suggest a "family" role for the slaves, even as they indicate subtle forms of racism and paternalism. The fact that his in-laws recognized and, in fact, honored Ben and Jenny's marriage would have appealed to Tichenor since he criticized those masters who had not recognized slave marriages.[29]

The latter story depicted Tichenor's relationship with Jesse Goldthwaite, an African-American member of Tichenor's Montgomery church:

When the last years of the war came on, there was on the part of some of my colored congregation a manifest expectation of freedom. They could not disguise their anxiety for its coming. Though submissive and obedient to the will of their masters to the very last day of their bondage, they could not repress the uplifting thought that they were soon to be free. But with Jesse there was no such manifestation. It may have arisen from the consciousness that his easy task scarcely remunerated his owner for his food and raiment; but far more probably it emanated from his entire submission to the will of God. To him life was but a journey home; and it seemed to matter little whether he performed that short journey as a freeman or a slave. . . .

When the day of deliverance came, many were . . . too much absorbed in their newfound freedom to think of their connection with the church or their duty to their God. They left their homes in multitudes, and flocked by thousands to see the great armies that had set them free. They gave loose reins to every inclination, and thousands perished in the time of their great jubilee. But Jesse was the same. Freedom wrought no change in him. Whether free or slave, Christ was still his master.[30]

Each of these writings demonstrates a paternalistic and condescending attitude toward other races on the part of Tichenor and many of his contemporaries. The romanticizing of these older blacks like Goldthwaite was not uncommon in the late nineteenth century. Christian ministers especially reveled in relating stories of slave loyalty prior to or during the war, holding out these examples of loyalty or faith as models of racial order, and crediting them for the positive influences they had upon white southerners. Not only were these blacks employed as examples, but they might also be used to vindicate slavery.[31] Tichenor does not acknowledge that perhaps part of Goldthwaite's condition was that he was old and that for his entire life he had been deprived of freedom. He passes lightly over the fact that Goldthwaite was trying to locate family members from whom he had been separated, certainly one of the greatest tragedies of slavery. Tichenor's statement that many of the slaves "gave loose reins to every inclination" is an indication of one of his and other white Southerners' greatest fears—that of social, and especially, racial anarchy. By glorifying the "Christian slave," Tichenor made a social statement about the kind of behavior sought by the New South for the former slaves.

He further demonstrated this paternalistic spirit in frequent references to ministry among blacks in his SBC reports. In his 1890 report, Tichenor said, "no part of our work gives promise of better results." He added, however,

> that oral instruction is peculiarly fitted to the negro mind. He remembers what you tell him far better than what he reads from a book, and remembers it better than the average white man of the same degree of intelligence. This no doubt arises from the difference in the mental habitudes of the two races.[32]

This report related an obvious concern for work among African Americans but also revealed Tichenor's prejudice. In an attempt to compliment blacks, he, in fact, denigrated their intellectual abilities regarding their retention of written information. He refused to acknowledge that the reason for this perceived deficiency resulted from inadequate educational, social, and economic opportunities.

The 1891 Home Mission Board report on Southern Baptist work among African Americans revealed further prejudice. Tichenor stated that an easy solution to the "race problem" existed despite the fact that statesmen regarded it "the most perplexing of all questions affecting our society and our political institutions."

> Nothing is plainer to any one who knows this race than its perfect willingness to accept a subordinate place, provided there be confidence that in that position of subordination it will receive justice and kindness. That is the condition it prefers above all others, and this is the condition in which it attains the highest development of every attribute of manhood. Whenever it shall understandingly and cheerfully accept this condition, the race problem is settled forever.
>
> The only thing needed now on his part is the assurance that he may confidently rely upon the justice and kindness which such a condition always demands and should always receive.
>
> This assurance the Christian men and women of this Southern land ought to give. Not the assurance of words, simply, nor yet of resolutions passed by political or religious conventions; nor simply the enactment of laws that are just and equal, but that higher and stronger assurance which springs from a persistent course of Christian conduct that looks with kindly eye and open hand upon his physical and mental needs,

and, above all, upon his soul's necessities. It is perfectly in the power of the Baptist people of the South to do all and give all that is needed to accomplish this end.

. . . If the Baptists of the South will but open their eyes to see their opportunity and open their hearts to the stimulating influences of Christian obligation to these people, they will themselves be amazed and gratified at the ease and rapidity with which the end will be attained.[33]

Tichenor's words exude "a strange combination of genuine concern, authentic effort at ministry, and incredible paternalism, racism and misunderstanding."[34] Yet it entirely reflected Tichenor's attitudes, as well as those of many other Southern Baptists toward African Americans. He utilized home missions as an instrument of social control over African Americans much in the same way that the board used missions in Cuba to achieve political and economic control. Adequate investment in home missions to African Americans would settle the race question and thus preserve southern culture as it then existed.

His 1898 pamphlet *Work of Southern Baptists among the Negroes* reflected more of his personal racial attitudes. The first portion summarized the history of early work among blacks, including the missionary appointments of slaves "purchased or hired from his master" for the purpose of propagating the gospel among his fellow slaves. In particular, he submitted the example of Caesar McLemore, a slave whose freedom was purchased by the Alabama Association. McLemore spent his life teaching and preaching among African Americans, and the association also frequently chose him to preach to congregations composed of hundreds of white Baptist representatives to their meetings. Tichenor used examples such as this to vindicate slavery for its "positive" effects and laud an African American who was loyal to his position in society. Tichenor shared statistics that demonstrated the strength of Baptists among southern blacks. Recalling his experience as pastor of Montgomery's First Baptist Church, he stated that in fifteen years he "baptized 500 colored people into its fellowship." Furthermore, he related the amicable terms upon which the black and white congregations split after the war.[35]

In this pamphlet, Tichenor also praised the cooperative efforts of the Home Mission Board, the Home Mission Society, state mission boards across the South, and African American churches in establishing "New Era Institutes." Baptists patterned these institutes after the training schools for black ministers established during Tichenor's tenure. Theological instruction of black preachers was the primary objective of the institutes. Southern Baptists also hoped that such education would overcome perceived tendencies of black churches toward "innate emotionalism" that "resulted in" what some southern white ministers called "a false religion." Black notables such as Booker T. Washington contributed significantly toward the desire for an educated black ministry while at the same time angering some longstanding African American ministers by criticizing their lack of education and thus limiting the effectiveness of educational efforts. Tichenor found common ground with Washington in the necessity to educate black ministers. But he conditioned such support with the provision that it be done only by Southern Baptists or white southerners. Interracial tension sometimes limited cooperation between whites and blacks, and attempts to unify the efforts of white southerners and northerners sometimes suffered because of sectionalist attitudes promulgated by Tichenor and others in their attempts to maintain control over southern territory.[36]

While Tichenor held paternalistic and prejudiced attitudes toward blacks, his reports indicated no lack of concern for mission work among African Americans. As late as the conclusion of his 1898 HMB report, he requested, "that the millions of Negroes of our Southern land, to whom we owe so much, may receive our earnest and hearty co-operation in their efforts to evangelize their race." Repeatedly, he pleaded for additional support to be given to ministries among the freedmen, and he influenced the provision of theological instructors for southern blacks. His pleas were echoed by others in the convention. There are other indications that Tichenor was not merely an advocate of black religious instruction but for black education as a whole. His daughter recalled, "My father helped Booker T. Washington at Tuskegee. He would drop anything he was doing to go to help Washington as he started his school."[37] Tichenor's support of Washington's efforts was entirely consistent with that of other New South advocates who applauded the black educator's work in Tuskegee.

Booker T. Washington was born in Virginia in 1856 and educated after the Civil War. In 1881, a year before Tichenor left nearby Auburn, Washington founded the Tuskegee Institute with the support of both blacks and whites. Washington's entreaties to a practical and scientific form of industrial and agricultural education for African Americans won him broad support from northern white philanthropists and limited independence from southern whites. He corresponded with New South advocates such as Henry Grady and wielded considerable power in the southern black community. He sometimes angered African Americans who believed that he was compromising too much in his efforts to acquire white support. Other blacks embraced Washington's ideas regarding practical education because they believed it was the only option truly open to them. Washington urged blacks to make the best of the situation in which they found themselves in the South. Because of his ideas and his success at Tuskegee, Washington was asked to speak at the 1895 meeting in Atlanta of the Cotton States and International Exposition. There he made his famous speech reiterating his approach to southern economics and society, which included the famous statement, "In all things that are purely social we can be as separate as the fingers, yet one as the hand in all things essential to mutual progress." This speech catapulted Washington to national prominence and earned him the plaudits of both northern and southern whites. It especially endeared him to advocates of the New South who recognized the necessity of racial harmony if their New South dream were to be realized.[38]

Washington and his white advocates such as Tichenor found themselves trapped within the myth of the New South creed they sought to create. Washington's endorsement of segregation ignored the myriad issues already emerging within the New South that demonstrated that progress was not truly taking place throughout the region. Washington's eloquent remarks made no mention of the growing violence against African Americans in the South, the steady progress of African-American disenfranchisement, the burgeoning numbers of black sharecroppers, or segregation's institutionalization in the Jim Crow laws upheld a year later by the Supreme Court in *Plessy v. Ferguson.* Washington and the white educators and industrialists desperately needed the financial support that could be provided by northern philanthropists and investors, and thus they presented a South consistently moving forward in race relations. Some of these men probably believed what they said. However, even those who did not had to pretend that racial reconciliation was not only possible but was actually already taking place. They became trapped in their own rhetoric and became prisoners of their own propaganda.[39]

Washington's plan for African Americans meshed perfectly with Tichenor's New South vision. Tichenor and others with the paternalistic conservative mindset of New South businessmen embraced Washington's concepts regarding industrial education. This attempt to couple social progress with economic progress and urban development has been called "New Paternalism."

This concept developed from "a combination of genuine humanitarian sentiment, often grounded in religious faith, and a calculating grasp of the necessity of upgrading the South's human capital as a prerequisite to economic development."[40] Tichenor would have identified at several points with these ideas. He found similarities between Washington's approach at Tuskegee Institute and his own efforts at Alabama A & M to incorporate scientific methodology in agriculture. Tichenor undoubtedly applauded Washington's efforts to provide industrial and agricultural education for African Americans, especially because these methods helped to insure the continuance of a ready and necessary labor force for white southern industrialists and agriculturists. He welcomed the organization and structure that Washington's approach brought to African American culture, especially since it was not viewed as a threat to the institutionalization of segregation then consolidating across the South. He also saw this approach as a means to maintain control over the southern social and political situation while continuing to achieve his objectives both for Southern Baptists and for the New South.

Tichenor's reports reflected the sociological and psychological dimensions of the conflict within southern white culture at that time as discussed in Winthrop Jordan's *The White Man's Burden*. As Jordan writes,

> Within every white American who stood confronted by the Negro, there had arisen a perpetual duel between his higher and lower natures. His cultural conscience—his Christianity, his humanitarianism, his ideology of liberty and equality—demanded that he regard and treat the Negro as his brother and his countryman, as his equal. At the same moment, however, many of his most profound urges, especially his yearning to maintain the identity of his folk, his passion for domination, his sheer avarice, and his sexual desire, impelled him toward conceiving and treating the Negro as inferior to himself, as an American leper.[41]

As Jordan indicates, this conflict "appears more complex than a conflict between the best and worst in the white man's nature, for in a variety of ways the white man translated his 'worst' into his 'best.'" It must be understood, however, that while this occurred, "these translations, so necessary to the white man's peace of mind, were achieved at devastating cost to another people."[42] Southern clergymen, especially leaders such as Tichenor, were important for translating what they saw as the "worst" into the what they believed the "best" and giving southern Christians generally—and in Tichenor's case, Southern Baptists specifically—"peace of mind." They worked to help white southerners resolve obvious conflicts between scriptural mandates and the ethic they lived. While they were responsible for giving this peace of mind to whites, they remained responsible for the racial prejudice against African Americans that they encouraged. Rather than contributing to a system that encouraged diversity and unity, Tichenor built a religious system that was increasingly devoted to Southern Baptist triumphalism and correspondingly racist in its prejudices. Because of Tichenor and other leaders, white Southern Baptists were unable to break with their racist southern culture and, in fact, were encouraged to drink more deeply from its cultural cup.

Seer of the South

Southern Baptists believed that Tichenor spoke with an almost prophetic voice regarding some aspects of the South's future. He envisioned Southern Baptists on the forefront of a spiritual battle being waged for the soul of the country and the world. He saw southern whites as God's chosen ones in carrying missions forward. He wrote in his 1890 report to the SBC,

> In looking forward through coming years, the Board is profoundly impressed with the magnitude of its work and the responsibility of its position. It cannot overlook the fact that the religious destiny of the world is lodged in the hands of the English-speaking people. To the Anglo-Saxon race God seems to have committed the enterprise of the world's conversion. The aggressive forces of Christianity are limited to this race, and of this race the American people constitute a rapidly increasing majority. Of the five millions of Baptists in the world, more than three millions [*sic*] of them are in this country, and a majority of them live within the bounds of this Convention.[43]

Tichenor repeatedly returned to this theme. In the same report, he depicted the South, with its untapped material wealth and dynamic spiritual health, as a tremendous base of operations first to evangelize the country and then to redeem the world. His 1893 report reflected his belief that evangelizing the South was, of all human endeavors, "the mightiest factor in the world's redemption." The last sentence in his 1896 report echoed this sentiment: "From this land of ours shall go forth to the furthest nation the gospel's joyful tidings, and the redemption of our own country becomes the redemption of the world."[44]

This type of rhetoric was exactly what Southern Baptists wanted to hear. Tichenor's words gave them pride in being both Baptists and southerners, but Tichenor did not only define Southern Baptist territory geographically and philosophically. His contemporaries believed Tichenor a visionary with a broad understanding of the potential of Southern Baptists. In his rhetoric he combined the language of Southern Baptist theology and missiology with the language, objectives, and goals of the New South movement. Using the forums of the home missions effort and of the Baptist pulpit, Tichenor reached large numbers of Baptists with these concepts, "baptizing" and incorporating ideas that had more in common with the New South movement than with theology. The influence of the South's cultural values upon Tichenor and his part in shaping the identity of the Southern Baptist Convention through his definition of SBC territory was a particularly important contribution to both the SBC and the South.

8
Buildings, Books, and Battles
Tichenor Defends Southern Baptist Territory

While serving as a chaplain in the Confederate army at Shiloh, I. T. Tichenor wielded a Colt repeating rifle in defense of his "homeland." Later in the battle, he also used his leadership skills to rally disorganized troops and utilized his considerable oratorical gifts to inspire the troops "by preaching 'them a sermon.'"[1] This would not be the last time that Tichenor would use his vast gifts for leadership or rhetoric to protect the southern territory from "foreign" invaders.

When Tichenor began his defense of Southern Baptist territory as corresponding secretary of the Home Mission Board, the very life of the Southern Baptist Convention was at stake. Due in large part to his leadership, however, by 1887 Tichenor could proudly announce that the Board had "reclaimed the field." Five years later the situation had improved even further, and Tichenor boasted that all Baptist missionaries working with southern whites had some direct connection with the HMB. He also insisted, "the Board had demonstrated its right to live, and had won the confidence of the denomination."[2] What Tichenor did not address in 1892 was the fact that his defense of the South and revitalization of the Home Mission Board had brought him and the board into direct conflict with the American Baptist Home Mission Society and its corresponding secretary, Henry L. Morehouse.

Part of Tichenor's interest in promoting Home Mission Board work in cities and among language groups and African Americans was to defend the South and its way of life. But these elements constituted only part of the denominational edifice he had in mind. Tichenor also encouraged the creation of a church building department within the Home Mission Board. A second component was his persistent desire for the resurrection of the Southern Baptist Sunday School Board as a publishing arm for the convention. A final element was his protection of Southern Baptist geographical territory in two border regions, Missouri and the Indian Territory. As conflict resulted from this defense strategy, he used the opportunity to promote Southern Baptist control of African Americans in the South.

The first of these defensive measures, the creation of a church building department within the Home Mission Board, brought no serious conflict with Northern Baptists. The latter two precipitated serious conflict. Tichenor, as corresponding secretary of the Home Mission Board, served as strategist, for this conflict.

Tichenor and the Creation of the Church Building Department

The American Baptist Home Mission Society was established in 1832 at the insistence of American Baptists because of the pressing need to expand work in the rapidly growing West. The Baptist Triennial Convention had appointed pioneer Baptist home missionary John Mason Peck in 1817 to work in the quickly expanding Missouri Territory, and the American Baptist Home Mission Society supported him after its establishment. Northern Baptists established a Church Edifice Fund in 1850 after Southern Baptists formed the SBC in 1845, but it was not until after the Civil War that Southern Baptists utilized this source of loans and gifts.[3] The devastation wrought by the war and the inability of the Home Mission Board to assist in the rebuilding of churches destroyed and neglected, or in the construction of new churches, made the northern society's fund attractive to southern churches and became a critical factor in establishing ties between southern churches and the society. Once they established this link, these churches naturally associated more formally with the American Baptist Home Mission Society.

Between 1874 and 1881, the Church Edifice Fund experienced extreme difficulties. The Panic of 1873, combined with continued Reconstruction in the South, forced churches into financial distress and subsequently caused many of them to default on their loans. Black and white southern churches owed the society's fund more than $45,000 in 1881. As a result, the society reorganized the makeup of the fund and in the next thirteen years made more than $80,000 in loans and gifts to black, Native American, and white Baptist churches in the South. To receive the gifts, the churches had to raise twice the matching amounts in their local communities. Churches had to secure a legitimate title to the land upon which a building was to be erected and demonstrate that, without the gift, the church building could not be constructed. Usually the building would have to be free of any indebtedness and had to be insured. Perhaps most importantly, each church had to pledge annual contributions to the northern society in order to receive the loan or grant.[4]

More than anything else, this last condition that connected these churches to the Home Mission Society created HMB concern. Although Southern Baptists did not initially object to these provisions, only two years after the society launched its new initiative, the Home Mission Board started its own church edifice program in 1884.[5]

Tichenor firmly believed that home missionaries could not conduct permanent work until church buildings existed. Recognizing the tenuous nature of frontier finances, he acknowledged that most new settlers had little financial ability to construct permanent church structures. He urged that a fund be established to provide gifts or loans to build churches in "destitute" areas—areas without a significant Baptist presence. He hoped that money from the HMB would serve to "stimulate" Baptists in those areas "to successful exertions" and planned that eventually the new congregations would be self-supporting. A subsequent committee report to the convention endorsed Tichenor's proposal.[6]

After the convention accepted this report, the HMB created the new department and planned that funds "be secured in bequests and special donations." The board chose G. A. Nunnally to lead the department. For the first year he was relatively successful raising funds. In 1885, however, the board placed restrictions on how Nunnally could raise the money. Essentially, board members felt that Nunnally's work interfered with the gifts that individuals and churches supplied to the general fund of the HMB. In response, Nunnally resigned, and the department languished for a number of years without leadership.[7]

In the 1895 convention meeting, some leaders attempted to create a new "building board." The Convention voted down this proposal by an almost two-to-one margin, despite the fact that Tichenor reported that in the five previous years the HMB had spent more than seventy thousand dollars from its treasury to aid church construction. It was not until after 1903 that the board consistently aided the construction efforts of new churches. In that year, the HMB asked the Women's Missionary Union to inaugurate a Tichenor Memorial to finance the Church Building Loan Fund. The board and the WMU paid tribute to Tichenor's interest in this vital area of Southern Baptist expansion, and Southern Baptists raised more than twenty thousand dollars in the memorial's initial years.[8]

While apparently few opposed Southern Baptists' use of the Home Mission Society's fund, a letter from Southern Seminary professor Basil Manly Jr. to Tichenor in 1888 indicated that the failure of the board's fund to checkmate other denominations concerned Southern Baptist leaders. Manly believed that unless the SBC responded aggressively with its own building fund their work would be surpassed by other denominations. Manly, Tichenor, and other Southern Baptist leaders feared the financial potential of the more highly structured Methodist denomination and the huge financial resources of the Home Mission Society that drew upon the wealth of Northern Baptists such as George A. Pillsbury, the founder of a flour fortune, and John D. Rockefeller Sr. the Standard Oil multimillionaire, reputedly the richest man in America. Rockefeller's support of the Home Mission Society and his friendship with Henry L. Morehouse, chief executive of the ABHMS, was well known by this time. Increasingly in the 1880s, Rockefeller channeled most of his philanthropy through the ABHMS and later through the American Baptist Education Society. Tichenor would have become aware of these resources and believed that the board's future depended upon being able to tie the allegiance of Baptist churches in the South to the SBC. One method of doing this was to provide the necessary resources for church construction so that these churches would not turn to the ABHMS Church Edifice Fund.[9]

Tichenor and the Resurrection of the Sunday School Board

Tichenor realized from the beginning of his tenure as corresponding secretary that if Southern Baptists were to reclaim the South for the Home Mission Board, the Southern Baptist Convention must ultimately have its own publishing arm. As early as his pastorate in Montgomery, he had been concerned with literature publication and promotion. He promoted the work of the Southern Baptist Bible Board prior to the Civil War and served as an agent for the Alabama Baptist Bible Society. The first attempt to establish a Southern Baptist Sunday School Board for publishing began in the midst of the Civil War and failed miserably due to the war, the Reconstruction, and the Panic of 1873. The Sunday School Board ceased publication in 1873 and transferred the responsibility of publishing to the then Domestic Mission Board. This consolidation resulted in the Domestic and Indian Mission Boards being renamed the Home Mission Board. The board then assumed the printing of the *Kind Words* series of Sunday School literature and limited publication of books. Tichenor had been intimately involved in the Sunday School Board's early years and served as its vice president in 1866 and 1867 and as its president in 1871.[10]

In 1885 the Home Mission Board began to increase the types of literature it printed. The secretary believed the growth of Southern Baptist work required literature publication. As long as Southern Baptists used American Baptist Publication Society literature, churches might turn to the North for other aid and, in turn, support the Home Mission Society's work. Tichenor's efforts to expand the board's publishing work and to manage carefully its resources bore fruit. Undoubtedly, part of the reason for his success was the incorporation of the same sound business principles utilized in other areas of the HMB's work. By 1885 Tichenor proudly reported the *Kind Words* series was out of debt and making an annual profit of one thousand dollars. He called upon the Baptists of the South to support this publication. In the 1885 convention, he demonstrated his conviction that failure to do so would allow others to expand their influence to the detriment of Southern Baptists. He hoped to develop literature for all ages so that, as the committee on *Kind Words* stated, Southern Baptists would not look elsewhere, including the North, for Sunday School literature.[11]

One year later Tichenor reported to the convention that the HMB was expanding publication, and in 1887 a new series of literature began, using noted Southern Baptist writers such as Basil Manly Jr., F. H. Kerfoot, and J. M. Frost. Tichenor reflected that the board's success had been "truly gratifying." Southern Baptists so strongly demanded this literature that the publisher was forced to enlarge his physical facilities. Tichenor added that no effort would be spared to insure that all SBC churches were furnished with enough quality literature to meet the demand.[12]

Quite naturally, tension arose with the American Baptist Publication Society over this new development. The northern society correctly foresaw the demise of its monopoly on Baptist publications. In an effort to stop this decline, the ABPS continued to seek out prominent Southern Baptist writers who would appeal to Southern Baptist readers. The society also continued to insist that it was the publisher for all Baptists in America. Tichenor, however, would not desist on this issue.[13]

At the end of the 1880s, Tichenor found the publication leader for whom he had been looking. The man was James M. Frost, a veteran Southern Baptist pastor. Frost was originally from Kentucky and a graduate of Georgetown College, a leading Baptist school in that state. He had served as a pastor in Alabama and Virginia and had also written for the publishing arm of the Home Mission Board. Like Tichenor, Frost was convinced that Southern Baptists needed their own publishing board. Frost later wrote of Tichenor, "No one surpassed [Tichenor] as a dreamer of dreams and seer of visions in denominational needs and power of conquest, and not many equaled him in making others through his eloquence on the platform see what he saw and believe what he believed." These dreams included the publication movement. He added: "Dr. Tichenor believed in the movement profoundly, even unto conviction, and walked the heights in his vision of what these periodicals were worth for the onward movement of our cause."[14] Later events and the tremendous influence of the Baptist Sunday School Board in the twentieth century were to prove him correct.

Tichenor recruited Frost to support his efforts. He undoubtedly realized that a new board required an energetic and loyal advocate. He was approaching age seventy, and he realized that the growing needs of the Home Mission Board required his full attention. Later, Frost described Tichenor's persuasive powers:

> I recall an incident concerning him. We had attended a State Mission Board meeting at Selma, Ala., where I was then pastor. Though after midnight we stood at the gate . . . , and talked for two hours. Rather he talked and I listened. I was sympathetic, but unable to follow his sweep of thought in outlining the future, showing what Baptists of the South might accomplish, and the imperative need that a people make their own literature.[15]

Frost could not shake this conversation from his memory and after moving to Richmond to serve as pastor, became convinced that Tichenor was correct. Frost's own successful administration of the Sunday School Board indicates that Tichenor had found his man.[16]

In the 1890 Southern Baptist Convention meeting in Fort Worth, Texas,

Frost presented a series of resolutions that eventually led to the transfer of Sunday School publications from the HMB to the resurrected Sunday School Board. A committee that he chaired endorsed the majority of the resolutions. Tichenor supported the resolutions, though obviously with mixed emotions over giving up control of an enterprise he endorsed so strongly. He noted that the board held publications work in highest esteem both in its present and in its potential worth to the SBC. With pride he reported that the HMB was enthusiastic that its efforts had been so successful that the SBC deemed a separate board advisable and that the HMB pledged cooperation with the new Sunday School Board in SBC work. He added, however, that if the convention decided to continue publications under the umbrella of the board, the HMB would do its best to continue to expand publications and improve their quality. In the next meeting of the HMB, he led the board in a further endorsement of the resolutions.[17]

The Sunday School Committee met during the remainder of 1890 and early 1891 and brought its report to the Southern Baptist Convention in Birmingham. Tichenor was absent from this meeting because of illness. At this meeting Frost moved the creation of a Sunday School Board to be located in Nashville with its primary function the publication of Sunday School literature. There was some conflict within the convention due to the wording of the resolution, especially with regard to how this move might affect the autonomy of local churches. Apparently, the growing power of the convention and its boards concerned some pastors of Landmark persuasion. After John Broadus made a moving appeal for peace in the convention, the report passed and the SBC created the Sunday School Board. The board ultimately chose J. M. Frost as its first director. He served a first term of eighteen months but returned in 1896 and spent the next twenty years serving the Sunday School Board.

The early years of the resurrected Sunday School Board were tenuous. The American Baptist Publication Society provided fierce competition. Northern Baptists marketed their publications in the South and utilized recognized Southern Baptist writers to appeal to the southern audience. The ABPS was reluctant to relinquish its extensive southern market. Some Southern Baptists chose continued use of the society for their publishing needs while others criticized those choices as disloyal. In fact, Theodore P. Bell, who served as the head of the board in the three years between Frost's two tenures, often wrote that he believed the powerful ABPS sought the destruction of the board. Bell may have resigned because he felt he was perceived as too *Southern* Baptist. A. J. Rowland of the ABPS proposed changes in the SSB that would have resulted in the older and larger society's consumption of the new board. Later in Frost's second term as corresponding secretary, the tensions erupted on the floor of the SBC meeting in Wilmington, North Carolina. At the convention, ABPS representatives openly attacked the board's work. The hostile nature of the representatives' language produced a backlash that led to an endorsement of the board's continued work. Subsequently, Frost engaged in bitter correspondence with his counterpart at the society. Ultimately, Frost prevailed and the Sunday School Board survived. Frost became to the Sunday School Board what Tichenor was to the Home Mission Board, and in the twentieth century, the Sunday School Board became one of the most powerful agencies of the SBC as well as one of its most recognizable and influential institutions within evangelical denominational publishing.[18]

Tichenor's contributions to the resurrection of the Sunday School Board should not be underestimated. He believed that the Southern Baptist Convention could not expect to maintain complete allegiance from its constituency as long as Southern Baptists continued to look to the American Baptist Publication Society for its Sunday School literature. As a voracious reader, Tichenor recognized the significance of literature in shaping minds and opinions. Additionally, the production and publication of southern religious literature benefited the South and the SBC economically. With his sound mind for business, Tichenor was sensitive to the potential loss of revenue. The subsequent success of the Sunday School Board proved his intuition correct. Even though reluctant to give up control of a potentially revenue-producing and influential activity, Tichenor willingly sacrificed to further the convention's work. He would much rather have had the Sunday School Board placed under someone else's control than for the publishing needs of the SBC to be met by the American Baptist Publication Society. He inspired fellow Southern Baptists such as Frost with similar ideas. So significant were Tichenor's contributions to the Sunday School Board that it has been observed that "if Frost was the father of the Sunday School Board, Tichenor was its grandfather." Leon McBeth captures the enduring influence of this agency: "If the mission boards largely determine what Southern Baptists do, the Sunday School Board has shaped what Southern Baptists think." Perhaps no single Southern Baptist agency in the twentieth century has done more in molding the denomination.[19]

The Clash of Baptist Titans

During the 1880s Tichenor's aggressive procedures to rejuvenate the HMB and his call for loyalty to the Southern Baptist Convention led to a "war of words" with Henry Lyman Morehouse, head of the Home Mission Society. As the board strengthened its work throughout the South during the mid-1880s, the conflict deepened. But the conflict was more than one of sectional rivalries; it was also a conflict of ideologies between the society's methods and the convention's approaches to missions. Morehouse defended the society as being an "American" organization with all of North America as its territory; Tichenor and others felt that if the society continued to expand into the South, it would undermine and eventually destroy the SBC.[20]

H. L. Morehouse, like I. T. Tichenor, was a denominational giant among Baptists in America during the late nineteenth century. A former pastor, Morehouse became corresponding secretary of the American Baptist Home Mission Society in 1879, serving in that capacity until 1893. In 1893 he began service as field secretary of the society, filling this position until 1903, when he resumed service as corresponding secretary. He held this office until his death in 1917.[21]

Morehouse was an organizational genius. Like Tichenor, he was also a visionary. His view of the Home Mission Society was that the organization's mission encompassed the entire nation, and he probably hoped for eventual reunification of Baptists in America. He saw the tremendous potential of the society's resources as a mandate for continuing its work in the South. By 1880 Arkansas, Georgia, and Florida had formed partnership agreements with the society, and four of the five Texas associations and conventions had some affiliation. Several other southern associations and conventions had agreements with the HMS as well. These initiatives triggered accusations from Southern Baptists of "intrusion" into the South. In 1882 E. T. Winkler, president of the Southern Baptist Home Mission Board, launched the war of words by denouncing this northern invasion and calling on the SBC to resist. With memories of the Civil War and Reconstruction still fresh, words such as "intrusion" and "invasion" were certain to bring to mind negative images. Morehouse responded that the society "was in the South to stay." One historian of the dispute computes that from 1881 to 1894 the northern society's Church Edifice Program made gifts of more than $37,000 to churches in the South and loans of more than $43,000. Obviously, society gifts did not disappear simply because the Home Mission Board experienced a resurgence or because Winkler, Tichenor, and others protested against Northern involvement in Southern Baptist churches. In fact, in some states these funds actually increased.[22]

Considering their inherently different mission philosophies and their powerful personalities, conflict was inevitable. Once Tichenor had reclaimed the southern field by the late 1880s, this dispute shifted to the border state of Missouri and the frontier area then known as the Indian Territory [Oklahoma]. Tichenor also used these two conflicts to defend Southern Baptist work among African Americans. Each of these disputes provide insights into Tichenor's work as corresponding secretary and how he defended Southern Baptist territory and influenced the development of the Southern Baptist Convention.

In the years between 1866 and 1875, the Home Mission Society made more than seventeen thousand dollars worth of loans to Missouri Baptist churches. This amount increased even further by the 1880s. Morehouse believed that the society's expenditures of more than eighty thousand dollars in the state and additional loans of almost thirty thousand dollars to the state's churches entitled the HMS to an alliance with Missouri Baptists. Clearly, Morehouse believed that Missouri Baptists not only had a natural tie to the HMS because of this support but also were morally obligated to align themselves with Northern Baptists. The HMS injected this vital capital despite the fact that in 1865 two separate Baptist groups had organized in the aftermath of the Civil War. One of these groups drew support from the Home Mission Society while the other had definite ties with the Home Mission Board.[23] Undoubtedly, the sectional animosities remaining after the war contributed not only to this division but also to the lingering suspicion and anger that smoldered during Reconstruction. While Missouri had never formally seceded from the Union, many Missourians fought on the Confederate side and identified themselves as southerners. Other Missourians remained loyal to the Union and naturally aligned with northern denominations. Even two decades after the war, resentment lingered.

Tichenor took as active a role in promoting the Home Mission Board in Missouri as he did in other states. His predecessor, W. H. McIntosh, had not attended meetings of the Missouri Baptist General Association in any of the three previous years. Tichenor, on the other hand, appeared at four of the first five meetings of the association after he became corresponding secretary. He first visited the Missouri Baptist General Association in October 1882 as part of his original assignment with the board. The records indicate that he participated in the decisions and discussions of the association. In 1883 Tichenor supported the appointment of G. A. Lofton as pastor of Park Avenue Baptist Church in St. Louis, a new work being established in that city. The Missouri Baptist General Association and the HMB appointed Lofton as part of a cooperative agreement in which one-third of Lofton's salary would be paid by the Home Mission Board and two-thirds by Missouri Baptists. Tichenor and the board adopted similar arrangements in agreements with other states at this time.[24]

Tichenor attended the 1884 and 1885 meetings of the Missouri association. In each of these meetings, participants discussed the dual relationship of Missouri Baptists with the Home Mission Society and the Home Mission Board, and in 1884 participants mentioned the large expenditures by both bodies and the relatively small amounts contributed by Missouri Baptists to each of the organizations.[25] The nature of Baptist ecclesiology further complicated the issues. Baptists historically accepted the principle that denominations, conventions, and societies were voluntary agencies and the churches, associations, and conventions were autonomous and self-governing bodies. According to this ecclesiology, any Missouri Baptist church could align with whichever body it chose. Likewise, the general association could align itself with either national body or neither.

Tichenor intensified his efforts on the board's behalf at the same time the board was seeking to consolidate its territory in the rest of the South. Thus, the rivalry within the state and between collecting agents from the society and board grew so intense that the Missouri association passed a series of resolutions presented to both Northern and Southern Baptists. Tichenor responded:

In a series of resolutions adopted by that body, the General Association of Missouri calls attention to the fact that two sets of agents, representing the missionary organizations both North and South, are appealing to their churches for support, and in the kindest spirit asks for some relief of this double appeal. Other cases of friction between Boards of this Convention and the great coordinate Societies of our Northern brethren exist.[26]

With this in mind, Tichenor suggested that a meeting be held to settle the issue. Representatives of the Home Mission Board, the Home Mission Society, and the Missouri Baptist General Association met in December 1888. Essentially the representatives agreed to a compromise. However, as the report to the MBGA stated, while the meeting had resulted in compromise, subsequent actions reflected that no compromise had in actuality been achieved. Essentially the bodies tentatively agreed not to collect funds from churches allied with the other entity. Other nonaligned Baptist churches could be "cultivated" by either or both agencies. The HMB ratified the agreement, but the HMS rejected it claiming that "it must be privileged to appeal to 'all the churches of Missouri.'"[27]

After the Home Mission Society failed to ratify this agreement, Tichenor and board member Henry McDonald sent a stinging letter to Morehouse, arguing principles of church polity, Missouri history, and common courtesy. They wrote that the action of the HMS "asserts the right, and contemplates the act of canvassing ALL THE CHURCHES OF MISSOURI in the interest of your Society. We hold that . . . churches have voluntarily associated themselves with either of the bodies we respectfully represent, such action of the sovereign churches ought to be respected." For the society to continue to canvass and collect violated the principle of local congregational autonomy according to the two. Tichenor and McDonald also argued that, as the society knew, "very many" Missouri Baptist churches historically related to the Southern Baptist Convention. They also appealed to Christian and Baptist courtesy.

The expression of a purpose, at some time in the future to disregard this fact and the principle underlying it, is in our judgment seriously to threaten the kindly relations between your Society and the Southern Baptist Convention. We trust that a reconsideration of the question will lead your Board to conclude that the best interest of the cause of our common Master will be promoted by a strict observance of these Christian courtesies due from one great denominational body to another.[28]

Tichenor and McDonald criticized other situations as well, primarily society "interference" in the board's African-American work in Texas. To Tichenor the issue was not how much money had been spent by the Home Mission Society in Missouri or anywhere else. The issue for him was which churches had been traditionally associated with the Southern Baptist Convention and what comprised Southern Baptist territory. For him and many other white southerners, the South included the former slave states and those churches traditionally associated with the Home Mission Board. Southern Baptists believed that the SBC had historic ties with Missouri Baptists but also had racial concerns about society involvement in the South.

The war of words continued. Morehouse responded angrily on May 6, 1889, with a letter approved by the society's board. An excerpt from the letter indicates how tense the situation had become between the two bodies:

> You say: "The action of your Board, declining to accept the arrangement entered into at Richmond as a finality is in our view tantamount to its rejection." In view of the fact that the Board expressly approved and adopted the terms of the agreement and instructed its representative in Missouri to conduct his work on the lines therein indicated, this is a surprising inference and is regarded neither just nor generous to this Board. Against such inference we place the fact that we are to-day working according to the proposed plan. We shall doubtless do so indefinitely. But the arrangement is of the nature of a compromise and an experiment rather than a final, inflexible, irrevocable thing.
>
> You apprehend that this Board may terminate it at pleasure without notification to the Board you represent. We regret that you should suspect us capable of such discourteous action. Be assured that if the time shall come when this Board thinks the arrangement should be modified or terminated, your Board will be duly notified thereof.[29]

With the two denominational boards unable to resolve matters, Missouri Baptists took matters into their own hands. In October 1889, the Missouri Baptist General Association reached a decision regarding the ongoing conflict between the two bodies.

The MBGA passed three resolutions. These resolutions requested that the two boards withdraw their representatives in the state. Further, the assembly instructed the missions board for Missouri Baptists "to conduct its work in the way that will create the least possible friction." The resolutions acknowledged what Tichenor claimed was true; many Missouri Baptists preferred an alliance with the Southern Baptist Convention. Further, the MBGA instructed the state missions board to send designated missions gifts to the ap-

propriate regional organization and "to divide all [undesignated] funds" between the boards based upon a formula that was an average of the gifts to
each board in the previous five years.[30]

This "Missouri Plan," as it was called, effectively ended the collecting system in the state. E. W. Stephens, chairman of the Missouri association, communicated the plan to Morehouse in a letter on October 25, 1889, and then
answered several questions by Morehouse once the society acquiesced to this
plan. He wrote that the MBGA hoped that the churches would designate their
funds. This would alleviate much of the problem. However, in cases where
churches failed to designate their home missions gifts, he stated that the history of the church would guide the division of the gifts. He promised that
every attempt would be made to ascertain what the church's preference would
be. He added that "such cases must be left to the fairness and discretion of
the [state] board and the [corresponding] secretary." The Missouri Baptist
General Association activated the new plan on January 1, 1890.[31]

The compromise served as a temporary solution and ultimately calmed the
troubled situation in Missouri. The *Home Mission Monthly* reported that

the results have been gratifying, the plan has been approved with una-
nimity and the success has exceeded our expectations, and confidence
has been established. The Boards, North and South, have expressed their
satisfaction and the plan has been received with favor by the churches.
Sectionalism has disappeared and financial resources have not been di-
minished.[32]

The confrontation over Missouri was significant for several reasons. It
demonstrates the volatility of the competition between the two boards. The
exchange of letters between Tichenor and Morehouse clearly reveals the positions of the two Baptist titans concerning territory. Tichenor identified Southern Baptist territory as the old slave states and those churches that had traditionally been affiliated with the Southern Baptist Convention. He defended
the autonomy of the local church and its right to choose its own affiliation.
To him it mattered not who had spent the most money in Missouri. This
attitude becomes even more significant when contrasted with Tichenor's viewpoints concerning J. S. Murrow and the situation in the Indian Territory.

On the other hand, Morehouse considered the aid given to Missouri churches as the society's investment in the future of the West. No doubt, the attitudes of many Southern Baptist churches disappointed him. They benefited from the society's aid but retained their ultimate allegiance to the Home Mission Board. Morehouse may have decided to make Missouri an example and to use that state to rationalize the arguments that the society had used in modifying the 1888 agreement.[33]

Finally, the debate over the Missouri question should be considered a critical precursor to the heated confrontation that erupted between Tichenor and the Home Mission Board and one of its missionaries to the Indian Territory, J. S. Murrow. Likewise, the Missouri question serves as an important background to the Fortress Monroe agreement.

The conflict over the Indian Territory was far more complicated than the situation in Missouri because of the complexity of personalities involved. Not only were Baptist giants Tichenor and Morehouse involved but also veteran missionaries to the Indians, J. S. Murrow and E. L. Compere. Since 1857 Murrow had been a missionary of the Rehoboth Association in Georgia. He had worked with H. F. Buckner among the Creek Indians and had successful years of ministry among the Seminole, Choctaw, and Chickasaw Indians after leaving Buckner. He became an almost legendary figure among the Native Americans in the territory. Compere served as a pastor in Fort Smith, Arkansas, after 1860, spending about half of his time working in the Indian Territory. The Home Mission Board appointed him as missionary in 1878. Trouble between Murrow and Compere can be traced back to the early 1870s, and in fact, some of the rivalry may have related both to tensions originating in the Civil War and in both intra- and intertribal rivalries in the Indian Territory.[34]

Accusations between the two climaxed in 1882 with correspondence exchanged between Murrow, Compere, and Buckner shortly before Buckner's death in 1882. I. G. Vore, also a missionary in the Indian Territory, sought to have Compere appointed by the Home Mission Board as Buckner's successor. He added to his letter advice that the "Indians here want no Holts, *no more Murrows,* and *no Tuggles,* in the Creek nations, but a square honest Baptist missionary, *with clean hands* and a pure heart."[35]

Tichenor became involved when it came to his attention that Murrow desired a "neutral" or "dual-alliance" with both the Home Mission Society and the Home Mission Board. Murrow believed the board had not paid enough attention to the work among Native Americans and that his ministry would be better served receiving the support of both groups. As the controversy developed, Murrow falsely concluded that Tichenor had decided work in the Indian Territory was insignificant in the board's larger strategy.[36]

Several considerations prompted Tichenor's failure to aid Murrow significantly. Tichenor freely admitted to Compere that, despite his desire to help the missionaries in the territories, resources were lacking: "The churches don't furnish us the means to do it and we have no other resources." Tichenor and others consistently pleaded before the Southern Baptist Convention for more money to provide for home missions, but sometimes the money simply was not available. He added, though, in a letter to Compere, "They [the churches] have been slowly rallying to us—and I have no doubt they will continue to do so."[37]

Despite Tichenor's reply, Compere besieged Tichenor's office with pleas for help. His insistent and frequent pleas were pitiful. In less than six months, Compere sent seventeen letters to Tichenor. Rather than providing reports to the board of his work, most of his letters dealt with requests for funds that the board did not have.[38] Ironically, Tichenor rejected Compere's constant pleas at approximately the same time the board initiated and expanded mission work in Cuba.

Another consideration was a personality clash between two strong-willed individuals, Tichenor and Murrow. An experienced missionary, Murrow chafed under what he saw as restrictions placed upon him by administrators in faraway places. He exercised a good measure of independence when in the employ of the Rehoboth Association and performed his duties in his own way. He apparently resented his transfer to the Home Mission Board's authority. His biographer wrote:

> There can be no doubt that Murrow remained unconvinced that the work of mission could best be done through the agency of a mission board. He believed that the worker on the field would know more about the needs of that field than someone living far away and completely unfamiliar with the local situation.[39]

Furthermore, it appears that Murrow inclined strongly toward independent missions work, so much so that charges of "gospel mission" tendencies were leveled against him.[40]

To be marked with "gospel mission" sympathies was a serious charge among Southern Baptists in the late 1880s and 1890s. The so-called "Gospel-Mission Movement" originated in those years, promoted by a Southern Baptist missionary to China, Tarleton Perry Crawford. Heavily influenced by the Landmark Baptist ideas of J. R. Graves that Tichenor had combated in his pastorate at FBC of Montgomery, Crawford believed that mission boards were unbiblical. He believed churches, not convention agencies, should send missionaries. His ecclesiology was consistent with Landmark ecclesiological emphasis upon local church autonomy. Crawford also believed mission schools and social work on the foreign field should cease and missionaries should engage only in direct evangelism of the indigenous people. Crawford seethed under Foreign Mission Board supervision, and having failed to influence the FMB to change its philosophy and methodology, he resigned as a missionary in 1892. The dissension created by gospel missionism caused another eruption of Landmark controversy in the SBC.[41]

At this time in the convention's life, Tichenor may well have believed Murrow to be the domestic missions version of Crawford. He would have feared that, if Murrow was a proponent of gospel missionism, his advocacy of such an approach might prove disruptive to what Tichenor was trying to accomplish with the HMB. Tichenor sought to unify Southern Baptists' approach to missions and bring competing agencies, boards, missions, and missionaries into a systematic program. While some might have seen the issue as one of control—perhaps correctly—Tichenor also held logistical reasons for a more comprehensive approach to missions. He recognized that it was incredibly difficult to maintain budgets and expand HMB work if expenditures could not be budgeted and funds guaranteed.

All these considerations coupled with Murrow's insistence upon remaining aligned with both the Home Mission Society and the Home Mission Board brought the matter to a climax. Murrow's desires to remain dually aligned directly challenged Tichenor's desires to unify the Southern Baptist Convention and Home Mission Board under its southern banner. Tichenor also received reports of Murrow's greater allegiance to the Home Mission Society. On June 20, 1890, Compere wrote HMB assistant corresponding secretary J. William Jones,

Again his work is more with *Northern* than *Southern* Baptists. And he will ever prejudice and hinder the work of *Southern* Baptists in the Ind. Ter. His associates & coworkers are Northern men and women. Now

Bro. Jones, the Northern Baptists *are Baptists*. But why is it they cannot find a field for operations on Northern soil? Ind. Ter. Is Southern. But the Northern folks are spending a great deal of money over there.[42]

This was not the only charge Compere made against Murrow in the rest of the letter. The others are of a distinctly scandalous nature. This writer has been unable to confirm them but has perceived a real sense of jealousy between Compere and Murrow. The charges and countercharges made by these men are an indication of the heated dispute between them.

J. William Jones was an important advocate and ally for Tichenor in these disputes. Jones was a Virginia Baptist and a graduate of the University of Virginia and Southern Baptist Theological Seminary. In the Civil War, Jones served as a soldier but primarily as Confederate chaplain working with Robert E. Lee and Stonewall Jackson, both glorified in subsequent southern literature for their strong Christian commitments. Jones played a prominent role in the revivals that broke out in the Confederate army during the war and later published his account of these revivals, *Christ in the Camp; or Religion in Lee's Army*. After the war, Jones served as a pastor in Lexington, where Lee resided and served as president of tiny Washington College, and the two continued their relationship. After Lee's death in 1870, Jones became a leader of the movement that memorialized Lee and, ultimately, the Southern Lost Cause. While maintaining his ministry as an evangelist and pastor, Jones served as the secretary-treasurer of the Southern Historical Society and editor of fourteen volumes of the *Southern Historical Society Papers*. Southern historian Charles Reagan Wilson identifies Jones as "The Evangelist of the Lost Cause."[43]

Jones's considerable experience as an evangelist prior to, during, and after the war aided him as he sought to win both converts to Christianity and to the cult of southern civil religion, and he provided an important link between the two. He remained "unreconstructed," but he "understood that a separate culture, with religion at its heart, could thrive within the boundaries of the nation." More than anyone else, Jones maintained an extensive network of contacts with prominent former Confederates. He worked full-time for the Home Mission Board for ten years between 1883 and 1893 and continued his relationship with Tichenor and the board throughout the close of the century. Jones corresponded in Tichenor's behalf in significant matters for the board.[44]

While Tichenor did not agree with all the ideas presented by the Lost Cause school because of his support of New South business philosophy, he would have certainly needed this connection with the Old South and its appeal to Southern Baptists, and with Jones's help, he utilized it. Likewise, Jones also profited from Southern Baptist connections that he made through board auspices. During the final years of Tichenor's HMB tenure, Jones frequently acted on Tichenor's behalf and would have benefited from this opportunity to become more widely known throughout the South. The influence of Jones's radically pro-southern mindset upon Tichenor in these disputes should not be underestimated.

In late 1890, Jones wrote Compere concerning the ongoing dispute. He stated that he completely sympathized with Compere's views *in reference to brother Murrow's Territorial Assn or Convention . . . —that I have no sympathy whatever with its mongrel composition, and that* I shall never do or say any thing *to promote it.*" Jones insisted that he wanted good relations with Northern Baptists but added that Southern Baptists must maintain separate operations; he opposed any sort of reunification of Baptists. He argued, "we must do *our own work in our own way.*"[45]

These comments are revealing. While Jones authored the letter, the words probably reflected Tichenor's sentiments as well. Jones and Tichenor advocated Northern Baptist work as long as it was "legitimate." However, they clearly considered the Indian Territory Southern Baptist territory and believed Northern Baptist work there "illegitimate." The comment "our own work in our own way" suggests that Jones and Tichenor remained convinced of the superiority of the Southern Baptist Convention method of missions over that of the Home Mission Society approach to mission funding.

In 1891 the conflict deepened. Murrow ran articles in his publication, *The Indian Missionary,* that Tichenor, Jones, and Compere considered inflammatory. Tichenor wrote Murrow in March 1891 "a very plain letter, in which he told him that the churches of [the] Indian Territory should be in full co-operation with the Southern Baptist Convention and put him to the categorical question, 'Are you ready to enter into and promote such co-operation?'"[46]

Following an unfavorable response by Murrow, Tichenor brought charges against him before the Home Mission Board meeting. Murrow also appeared before the board. The central charge was that Murrow had refused "organic union" primarily out of concern that the Home Mission Society would withdraw its support from his work in the territory. Murrow responded to these charges in a letter to the Home Mission Board. Essentially he denied accusations that he showed favoritism toward the northern society. He acknowledged that he had received support for the HMS but argued that he was seeking to rally as much support as possible to his cause. Unwilling to comply with the request to affiliate only with the Southern Baptist Convention, Murrow tendered his resignation on July 15, 1891. The HMB accepted his resignation on August 4, 1891. Approximately one month later, the Home Mission Board appointed E. K. Branch as Murrow's replacement. Subsequently, the Home Mission Society appointed Murrow as its missionary to the Indian Territory.[47]

Tichenor and the board held the position that Murrow had violated their trust as an agent of the SBC. In response to an article written by Murrow in *The Indian Missionary,* Jones wrote Compere that Murrow hoped to mislead others to believe that the board had been exclusively guided by sectionalism and that the HMB sought "to *force* him" and Indian Territory churches into an alliance with the SBC. Jones insisted, "We have never taken any such position, but have only urged him as our missionary, supported by our funds, *to use his influence* to form an organization in the Territory of such churches as were willing to cooperate with the Southern Baptist Convention."[48]

Unfortunately, the controversy did not end there. Accusations continued to be made throughout 1892, and tensions increased. Because of this conflict, two conventions arose in the Indian Territory as they had in Missouri a decade earlier, one looking to the Home Mission Society for support and the other looking to the Home Mission Board—precisely the scenario that Tichenor had sought to avoid. The situation was not fully resolved until the twentieth century when Oklahoma Baptists voted to affiliate with the Southern Baptist Convention.[49]

Tichenor's role in this controversy is easily ascertained. For ten years, he attempted to bring all missionaries in the South into direct and sole affiliation with the Home Mission Board with the exception of the society's work among blacks. Murrow's refusal to cooperate exclusively with the Home Mission Board directly challenged this policy. In response to Murrow's resignation, Jones summarized Tichenor's views. He indicated that Tichenor did not presume "to dictate to the churches" or to the Arkansas State Convention issues of policy. But Tichenor did believe sole alignment of missionaries to be less confusing and more efficient than dual alignment. He regarded his correspondence simply "a suggestion" but may have hoped for it to carry considerable weight.[50]

Jones's assessment of Tichenor's philosophy at this point was probably correct. Tichenor was not attempting to override traditional Baptist polity. He did suggest a similar arrangement and agreement as that which had been made in Texas. He believed clearly that consolidation of competing state conventions or associations into one state board affiliated with one national board was the most effective way to guarantee efficient mission work. Tichenor defended the Indian Territory as Southern Baptist territory, and he believed Murrow, as an employee of the SBC Home Mission Board, was bound by his service to promote the interests of the SBC. Jones further summarized Tichenor's views for Compere:

> Dr. Tichenor has from time to time pressed upon Rev. J. S. Murrow the importance in the Indian Territory that would cooperate with the S.B.C., and on that account Brother Murrow has tendered his resignation, we have accepted it, and we are now seeking for another man suitable to take his place. Bro. Murrow says that the churches in [the] Indian Territory will not cooperate with the So. Bap. Con., which means . . . that *he will not use his influence to attain that end.* I have no doubt that he will now go into the employ of the Northern Board, and will carry everything that he can in that direction, but we feel that it is very important that there should be an organization in the Territory that will cooperate with the S.B.C.[51]

All attempts at reconciliation failed. The conflict is simply one indication, albeit a volatile one, of the dispute that had been raging between Northern and Southern Baptists since the early 1880s. To Tichenor and his associates, the Indian Territory belonged in the South. He was not opposed to Murrow's receiving aid from the Home Mission Society. He argued that Murrow had been appointed as a Southern Baptist missionary and worked under the auspices of the board in a "southern" territory. Therefore, Murrow should promote exclusive allegiance to the Home Mission Board. Tichenor, as he saw it, simply defended Southern Baptist territory from Northern Baptist control as part of his plan to consolidate HMB hold over all the South.

The Fortress Monroe Agreement

Disputes such as the ones in Missouri and the Indian Territory indicated a larger problem. Now that the Southern Baptist Convention and the Home Mission Board were reestablished in the South and competition with the HMS had intensified, some sort of an agreement needed to be reached. At the 1894 Southern Baptist Convention meeting in Dallas, the assembly passed a resolution requesting that a committee of five HMB representatives meet with an equal number from the HMS. The purpose of this meeting was to discuss cooperative work among African Americans in the South and to develop clear territorial boundaries between the board and the society.[52] The SBC chose Tichenor as one of the board representatives.

Practical considerations also made it necessary for the two bodies to reach some sort of agreement defining cooperation and territories. The Home Mission Board sincerely desired an increase of education work among blacks. Likewise the society's growing work in the West, the flood of immigration into primarily northern urban areas, and the start of a financial depression in the United States placed increased demand on its resources and further strained its reserves. The Home Mission Board saw that its cause could only be aided by the society's recognition of its right to exist as a separate and equal entity. Finally, perhaps the Society hoped that some form of conciliation might lead to eventual reunification of Baptists North and South.[53]

The representatives met in a spirit of accommodation at Fortress Monroe, Virginia, on September 12–13, 1894. The conference established territorial limitations and scheduled future conferences to discuss disagreements concerning territory. They agreed to coordinate efforts in working with African Americans in the South.[54]

Essentially, three major components comprised the Fortress Monroe agreement. The conference agreed that the Home Mission Society would continue to control and administer schools among African Americans but agreed to appoint a local advisory board for each. The agreement concluded that the Home Mission Board should promote the financial support of these institutions in the South and would encourage attendance of young African Americans with outstanding potential. They further agreed that the two bodies would cooperate in mission work among southern blacks through the Home Mission Board and the Home Mission Society. The details of the plan were to be worked out by the society and the board. Finally, the agreement did not set territorial limits on work among African Americans, stating that this was outside the scope the Home Mission Society had given the northern committee. It did recommend "that for the promotion of fraternal feeling and of the best interests of the Redeemer's kingdom," the two organizations should not establish competing work in the same regions. Where competing work already existed, it recommended "that all antagonisms be avoided, and that their officers and employees be instructed to co-operate in all practicable ways in the spirit of Christ." It further reminded members of the board and society that there were many places in the country where no Baptist work existed and suggested their efforts be concentrated upon those locations. In an ironic note the committee also commended the admission of the new Oregon Convention into the SBC. Oregon, due to geography and previous HMS efforts on the frontier, should have been considered Northern Baptist territory.[55]

The Home Mission Monthly recorded the report of the society's committee to the HMS annual meeting. It stated that a spirit of conciliation had dominated and that "the discussions were full, frank, and always brotherly. . . . Never was meeting held by men of equally pronounced convictions, from North and South, where there was profounder exhibition of the fact that 'we are brethren in Christ Jesus.'"[56]

In the agreement, both sides received what they desired. The Home Mission Society got a commitment from representatives of the SBC for aid in their educational and mission work among blacks. The Home Mission Board received assurance from HMS representatives that territorial limits would be respected and that competing work would not be initiated on the same field. The committee of cooperation further reported to the Home Mission Society that "the day of unity, peace, and loving co-operation . . . has come."[57]

This agreement was a major achievement for Morehouse. He hoped that the meeting would serve as a catalyst for further cooperation between the two bodies. Perhaps Morehouse was one key leader who hoped for eventual reunification of the two Baptist bodies.[58] Certainly, Morehouse's later work with the Baptist World Alliance and other ecumenical groups indicated a unifying spirit. Thus, Morehouse may have actually capitulated on key issues in an effort to be conciliatory. If he sought reunification of the two bodies into a truly "American" Baptist Convention, however, he was to be sorely disappointed.

The agreement was also a major achievement for Tichenor and the Home Mission Board. He had sought this type of agreement as early as 1879.[59] It implied recognition of the right of the HMB and the SBC to exist as separate entities. It laid a foundation of cooperation that theoretically would prevent further disagreements, like those in Missouri and the Indian Territory, from occurring in the future. Finally, it allowed society financial support of work in the South among African Americans with a measure of Southern Baptist control. The "paternalistic-conservative" viewpoint that Tichenor and SBC leadership held was exemplified in the Fortress Monroe agreements. Both sides basically achieved the goals they sought and reduced tension in Baptist life.

Unfortunately, the Fortress Monroe agreement sparked racial tensions. While black Baptists welcomed the financial assistance offered from both Southern and Northern Baptists as part of the "New Era Institutes," they resented white control of these training schools, even if the institutes made provisions for allowing black ministers to teach. Furthermore, segregationist policies prohibited African Americans from attending Southern Baptist Theological Seminary, and some whites "opposed any funding for or cooperative endeavors with African Americans." These tensions continued to haunt cooperative efforts between Southern Baptists and the black National Baptists, and Southern Baptists provided financial support under the condition that "only 'safe' missionaries be appointed and that troublesome racial issues be avoided."[60] Tichenor and others had advocated similar policies and concepts approximately thirty years earlier.

For a time, a spirit of conciliation reigned between the two bodies. The type of agreement that occurred at Fortress Monroe was not unique. There were indications in the mid- and late 1890s that the South was being reintegrated into the nation's economy and culture. Southern women participated in the broader national movement for a new role of women; in the North and South many, though not all, applauded the "Atlanta Compromise" proposed by Booker T. Washington in 1895 that seemed to suggest agreement on racial questions; and the Spanish-American War in 1898 sparked further sectional reconciliation. While these developments had their limitations, the conciliatory spirit indicated at the 1894 conference indicated a broader sentiment.[61] At the September 24, 1894, HMB meeting, the board approved the report resulting from the Fortress Monroe conference and notified the Home Mission Society of its approval. The tone of the correspondence indicated the prevailing spirit. In July 1895, Tichenor wrote Morehouse concerning the ap-

pointment of the Southern "advisory committees" as agreed at Fortress Monroe. Apparently, after receiving this letter, Morehouse listed a series of conces-
sions the society was willing to make and needed to receive regarding the
society's educational work among African Americans in the South. In October 1895, communication between the two bodies continued on the territorial question. Tichenor moved "that the President of this Board be instructed
to answer Dr. Moorehouse, [sic] that this Board would not work in localities
occupied by the Home Mission Society of New York unless instructed to do
so by the Southern Baptist Convention." In November of that year, the two
bodies planned joint work in North Carolina and Alabama.[62]

Nevertheless, these agreements did not end controversy. Tichenor and
Morehouse continued to correspond on the issue of territorial boundaries un-
til virtually the end of Tichenor's tenure as corresponding secretary. A brief
look at this continued conflict demonstrates that despite the aspirations of the
Fortress Monroe conference, Tichenor did not end his defense of Southern
Baptist territory.

Despite the efforts to cooperate in work among African Americans in the
South, by 1898 the confrontation between Tichenor and Morehouse erupted
again. Having recently returned from Cuba, Tichenor was unable to attend a
meeting between the joint committee in Washington, D.C., in November, so
he telegraphed these proposals to Morehouse,

> I proposed to give to your Society Porto [sic] Rico and the two Eastern
> Provinces of Cuba, and that Indian Territory, Oklahoma, Arizona and
> New Mexico should be ceded to us as the territory of the Southern
> Baptist Convention. I was disappointed in the result. Our Committee
> conceded Porto [sic] Rico and the Cuban Provinces and received noth-
> ing in return from your Society. I am sure this division of territory is the
> one which ought to be made between the two organizations.
>
> First, on general principles this would divide the territory of the
> United States very nearly into two equal parts. Your part of it would
> embrace about two thirds of the population and one third of the Bap-
> tists. Ours would embrace about one third of the population and two
> thirds of the Baptists in the country. Leaving out of the question the
> negro Baptists, your territory would contain two fifths and ours three
> fifths of the white Baptists of the country.

Second, this division is a natural one, and would throw those states and territories having a common climate, productions and populations together.[63]

Next, Tichenor discussed the continuing disagreement over the Indian Territory. He contended that the territory had historically been exclusively the mission field of the SBC prior to the Civil War. Erroneously, he stated that it was settled exclusively by "Southern Indians" relocated west of the Mississippi River, ignoring the fact that Native Americans from the North, such as the Shawnee or the Sauk and Fox tribes, had also been removed to the Indian Territory. He argued that the Home Mission Society's work after the Civil War occurred without SBC agreement and continued there without any later consent. He declared that the society's work in the Indian Territory constituted an invasion of territory that southern missionaries had always served. He concluded by essentially adding that this proposal represented the only possible compromise.[64]

These comments by Tichenor are enlightening. He believed that the Home Mission Board was attempting a compromise. Technically, one might argue, as Morehouse did, that the HMB was not really "giving up" anything. The territories in Cuba and Puerto Rico were already the mission fields of the HMS. Given the recent addition of these areas to U.S. control because of the Spanish-American War and uncertainty about the future political arrangements in Cuba and Puerto Rico, it was presumptuous of Tichenor and others to make assumptions about future mission work in these areas. These countries might have also rightly been considered the "territory" of either the Foreign Mission Board or the Foreign Mission Society, especially in the case of Cuba. The statement that Tichenor made, "this division is a natural one . . . ," was clearly an antagonistic sectionalist statement. He also used militaristic terminology in considering the work of the HMS in the Indian Territory to be an intrusion into an SBC dominion. He failed to acknowledge that after the Civil War and throughout Reconstruction, the resources of the Home Mission Board had been so depleted that it was virtually impossible for the SBC to promote mission work in the Indian Territory. In fact, the HMS simply stepped in to fill the void left by the decline of postbellum SBC home mission endeavors, not only in the Indian Territory but also throughout the South.

Morehouse's reply was equally heated. He believed the "proposed exchange" was "immensely in your favor." Concerning western territory, he alluded to the controversial origins of the SBC. According to Morehouse the HMS and the HMB had never agreed upon "an equal share of our western territory" that historically had been the society's field. Morehouse challenged Tichenor, "If your Board has resources for larger undertakings, we hope it will not be disrespectful for us to suggest that you take a larger share of the work for the Colored peopled [sic] of the South for whose benefit the Home Mission Society has expended over three million dollars." In response to Tichenor's statement regarding climate, Morehouse retorted, "This Society's field includes the widest variety of climate and productions from Maine to Alaska on the North to New Mexico, California and even old Mexico on the South."[65]

Morehouse argued that the society held equal commonality with the people of the territories in dispute and claimed that the historical basis of the society's claim to the Indian Territory was greater than any claim of Southern Baptists. He recounted the vast expenditures of the Home Mission Society in New Mexico, asking Tichenor, "Why should we now be asked to surrender to you a field on which we have expended fully $500,000, while your expenditures therein have only been a fraction of this sum?" He closed his arguments with another question, "Can it be seriously supposed that the American Baptist Home Mission Society will regard with favor a proposition of such a character that requires the sacrifice of everything by us and of nothing by you?"[66]

Morehouse closed his lengthy letter by essentially proposing that the disputed conventions, associations, and churches be allowed to determine their own affiliations and by making a plea for unity rather than sectional animosity. Certainly, such a proposal would have been acceptable under historic Baptist principles of self-governance and the autonomy of the local church. To Tichenor, however, traditional Baptist concerns in these areas were not reason enough to surrender his sectionalism. Since the gulf separating the two Baptist titans appeared so wide, Tichenor responded by terminating correspondence with Morehouse. This effectively concluded negotiations until after Tichenor's retirement later that year.[67]

After Tichenor's retirement in 1899 and death in 1902, the two mission agencies continued to work toward a set of "principles of comity." When New Mexico became a particular point of contention in the first decade of the twentieth century, HMS and HMB representatives held another comity conference in 1909. It was not, however, until 1912 that the two bodies finalized comity principles. The principles essentially guided Northern and Southern

Baptist cooperation until the mid-twentieth century. Tensions remained in some locations, especially border states, until as late as 1919.[68]

Throughout these sectional conflicts, Tichenor utilized his considerable gifts of personal magnetism and oratory, prestigious position as leader of the Home Mission Board, and a tenacious loyalty to Southern Baptists to define and defend denominational territory. From his definition and defense of SBC territory, several characteristics of Tichenor and the Southern Baptists whom he represented emerge.

Tichenor capitalized on the anxiety permeating the South regarding loss of identity and fear of the future, especially as it related to racial issues. He was able to achieve a transformation in the vision of Southern Baptists by appealing to sectionalist sentiments common during his day. He believed defeat and Reconstruction were not disaster but God's preparatory discipline. With emotional appeals linking southern travails with those of the biblical Israelites, he utilized the forum of the Southern Baptist Convention to rally support for the HMB and its southern banner. Sectionalist emotions were intrinsic to southern culture during the 1880s. As Wilson suggests, "Southern romanticism had never vanished, and the 1880s saw a resurgence, a reintensification of romanticism with particular importance in sentimentalizing the Confederacy."[69] Tichenor used this romanticism but was not guilty of sentimentalizing the Confederacy. Rather, he sentimentalized the geographic South, its virtues, and especially the heritage of Southern Baptist mission work.

Much in the same way that Tichenor grafted a New South model of an agricultural and mechanical college onto a small, traditional, denominational liberal arts college at Auburn, he grafted a New South vision of solid business techniques, modern American society, and cultural progress onto a strongly sectionalist and strict Baptist denominational consciousness. By imparting a denominational consciousness in Southern Baptists, he helped transform the convention from a denomination in retreat to one on the forefront of American Christianity at the turn of the century. At the same time, he further entrenched racial and social prejudices that continued to be characteristic of Southern Baptists well into the twentieth century.

Conclusion

Isaac Taylor Tichenor: The Man and His Legacy

In the final years of the century, Tichenor's health declined and the Home Mission Board replaced him as its corresponding secretary. The incident occurred with no small measure of hurt to the aged secretary. The board elected him as secretary emeritus, a position he held until his death.[1]

The 1900 Southern Baptist Convention held in Hot Springs, Arkansas, made two tributes to the elderly Baptist statesman. In a moving display, Dr. Lansing Burrows presented Tichenor with a silver victory vase carrying the inscription,

> In testimony of the efficient and blameless service through eighteen years, of Isaac Taylor Tichenor, D.D., as corresponding secretary of the Home Mission Board of the Southern Baptist Convention, from friends that have felt the inspiration of his genius and rejoiced in the triumph of his leadership.[2]

After the presentation there was "a spontaneous ovation of greeting and congratulation to Dr. Tichenor." The second tribute came in F. H. Kerfoot's Home Mission Board report:

> The name of I. T. Tichenor will always stand with those of Boyce . . . Broadus . . . Manly . . . Jeter . . . Furman . . . a galaxy of as great and good and noble men as God ever gave to any denomination of Christian people. And among all these, no man has perhaps had more to do with

the maintenance of the Southern Baptist Convention, and with shaping its policies, than has this noble man of God, the long time honored Secretary of the Home Mission Board.[3]

With these tributes, Tichenor passed into retirement at the age of 73. He remained somewhat active in the affairs of the Home Mission Board as its secretary emeritus, serving briefly as acting secretary when Kerfoot died unexpectedly. Throughout 1901 and 1902 his health continued to decline until he died peacefully on December 2, 1902. He was buried in Atlanta's West View Cemetery. Subsequently, the Women's Missionary Union established the "Tichenor Memorial of the Church Building Fund." Its purpose was to raise monuments to Tichenor "not in one spot but in thousands; on hilltops and valleys; upon crowded avenues of rapidly enlarging cities, where in the face of determined opposition a feeble band seeks to plant the banner of truth as it is in Jesus."[4]

At the 1903 Southern Baptist Convention, Corresponding Secretary F. C. McConnell began his Home Mission Board report with a "Memoriam" of the recently deceased secretary emeritus. He considered Tichenor's greatest achievements his vision of the South's and the SBC's potential and his protection of and "loyalty to what he regarded the most evangelical type of America's denominationalism." To him "more than any other man . . . is due the solidarity of the denomination."[5]

In his book *Home and Foreign Fields*, Baron Dekalb Gray, corresponding secretary of the HMB from 1903 to 1928, called Tichenor the "Father of Cooperation."[6] He earned this title not only by establishing positive communication with the state boards and SBC churches but also through consistent appeals for systematic support for all of the convention's institutions and boards, especially the HMB. As early as 1883, Tichenor challenged the messengers of the Southern Baptist Convention at its annual meeting,

What we need is some system of contribution in all our churches, by which every member will be reached and the mites of the poor, as well as the munificent offering of the rich, flow into the treasury of the Lord. That system whatever it may cost of patient thought and prayer for wisdom in its elaboration, or of men and means to secure its efficient action, we must have. Without it we shall always have a meagre [*sic*] support for our Boards; continued embarrassment of those who compose them, crying destitution on every hand, and our land filled with churches whose piety and activity are dwarfed by the want of proper training for the very work for which they were organized.

The grandest duty of the hour, the noblest work of this Convention, is to devise and make effective some plan that will elicit and combine the benevolence of our people.[7]

His proposals were remarkably similar to proposals made by a committee that he chaired in 1880 at the request of the Alabama Baptist State Convention. These proposals were based on a chain of organization through which mission contributions might be channeled. This chain led from the churches through the associations and state boards to the Southern Baptist Convention. As late as 1897, Tichenor was still lobbying for some method of systematic beneficence. His culminating statement to the Home Mission Board in a presentation made in 1897 was

in view of the great needs of methods of systematic beneficence by which our people may be reached and induced to give regularly and liberally to the work of missions, we will gladly co-operate with the various State Boards in devising and securing the adoption of such measures looking to the result as may be mutually agreeable to the Home Board and to the State Boards of each of the states within the bounds of the Southern Baptist Convention.[8]

In his memorial to Tichenor in 1903, F. C. McConnell said,

Dr. Tichenor was the apostle of co-ordination and co-operation. To his superb executive mind is due the well organized system of co-operating State Boards. Dr. Tichenor was without a superior on the platform of the Convention, or in the pulpit, in his presentation of the obligations, aims, methods and results of evangelization in our homeland.[9]

While the proposals Tichenor made were primitive by modern cooperative program methods, Tichenor had, in the words of one Sunday School Board writer, "laid the foundation for our present Co-operative Program."[10] Baptist historian Robert Baker recognized this contribution:

Farsighted denominational leaders glimpsed the weakness of the prevailing plan, especially those who had to face the dilemma of haphazard planning and giving in the execution of missionary responsibilities. Especially notable was I. T. Tichenor . . . as he regularly called for a more systematic plan of giving to home missions and indeed to all benevolences.[11]

Tichenor might well be called the grandfather of the SBC Cooperative Program, developed in the 1920s, which became one of the most effective financial systems in the history of American evangelicalism.

Tichenor's contributions have not gone unnoticed by Southern Baptist historians. W. W. Barnes called him "one of the greatest statesmen and most devoted servants the Convention has ever had." In his history of the Home Mission Board, J. B. Lawrence wrote of him, "No man ever faced a more difficult task than Dr. Tichenor when he became secretary of the Home Mission Board; no man ever triumphed more gloriously than he." Robert Baker concluded: "Perhaps he more than any other single person should be credited with saving the home field." Baptist historian John Franklin Loftis observed, "I. T. Tichenor defined what was 'southern' about the SBC." Writing most recently, Leon McBeth recorded, "Perhaps no better choice could have been made [as head of the HMB]; Tichenor brought to the work a new energy, vision, creativity, and above all a consuming commitment to the SBC."[12]

Not only did Tichenor preserve the Home Mission Board through his work, but he also profoundly extended the expanse of Southern Baptist work. By 1887 he had effectively "erased the debt of the [Home Mission] Board."[13] This movement toward fiscal responsibility begun in the early days of his administration enabled him to consider and implement plans to expand the board's work. Unfortunately, contemporary historians outside the SBC have largely ignored or passed lightly over Tichenor's role in developing sectional Christianity and southern culture in general.

Tichenor was a child of the Old South. Understanding the formative years of his life and ministry, from 1825 to 1868, is crucial to understanding both his character and the methods he used as corresponding secretary of the Home Mission Board. His allegiance to the denomination was forged in the early days of the Southern Baptist Convention. He was influenced by the pervasive optimism inherent in American life in the late 1840s and the early 1850s, and this optimism carried over into his life as a denominational and southern leader. He was heavily influenced by the tendency toward organization promi-nent in evangelical American Christianity in the nineteenth century. His Montgomery pastorate vaulted him into prominence in the Southern Baptist Convention and in the state of Alabama. The crucible of the Civil War helped to further define him as a southerner, even though later in life, unlike many of his contemporaries, he felt that the war was "a dead issue." Like all south-erners, Reconstruction aroused him to the plight of the South. He, however, responded in a different way than did many southerners. He used the occasion of Reconstruction and its aftermath to call for economic, educational, and industrial reforms that would modernize the South.

The years from 1868 to 1882 were also significant in shaping him as a religious spokesman for the vision of the New South. The years spent as a mining executive and as president of Alabama A & M were critical ones in his development and implementation his conception of modernization. His brief time as a mining executive was especially important. It helped to teach him modern business procedures that equipped him later to administer effec-tively the work of the Home Mission Board. The geological surveys that he conducted or was privy to gave him a greater comprehension of southern economic and demographic potential. As president of Alabama A & M, he pioneered progressive technical and scientific education. In both roles he fully embraced the language and the concepts of the nascent New South move-ment. At the same time, he moved in business and educational circles and networked with southern political leadership. The broad contacts he estab-lished during this time would significantly aid him in the years to come. Once he came to head the Home Mission Board his influence dramatically multi-plied.

Tichenor not only preserved the Home Mission Board but also extended its influence. He set priorities and supported them while at the same time maintaining the necessary flexibility needed in such a responsible position. He looked for every possibility with which to expand Southern Baptist work. He helped secure Texas as Southern Baptist territory. The visionary nature of his efforts there paid huge dividends as Texas continued to grow and eventually became Southern Baptists' most powerful stronghold. He expanded Southern Baptist work in New Orleans and other urban areas and in southern states where SBC work had lagged. His visionary efforts regarding the significance of urban areas became critical in the twentieth century as the denomination increasingly drew its financial and numerical strength from such places. He continued and extended work among language groups and enthusiastically promoted Southern Baptist work in Cuba. While the efforts in Cuba did not bear significant long-term results, the growing diversity of Southern Baptist work among different language and ethnic groups in the latter part of the twentieth century once again proved Tichenor prophetic. He enlarged mission work in the Appalachian Mountain regions. His sound financial policies strengthened the credibility of the Home Mission Board and made possible all this expansion. Tichenor's contagious enthusiasm and visionary hopes for Southern Baptists renewed the confidence of the convention's people and perhaps, at the same time, other southerners as well.

In another extremely significant effort, he promoted the establishment of the publishing arm of Southern Baptist life, the Sunday School Board. Tichenor's role in the resurrection of this entity created one of his lasting legacies and did as much as anything else in forging Southern Baptist identity in the twentieth century. He defined slightly more progressive Southern Baptist attitudes on racial questions, despite the fact that he continued to be captive to the culture in which he lived. Sectionalism figured most prominently in Tichenor's methods in rallying Southern Baptists to the cause of the Home Mission Board. He romanticized southern culture as a means of strengthening the Home Mission Board's work. He did not allow, however, this romanticist viewpoint to stand in the way of his reformative hopes for the New South. He worked to wed the staid traditions of the Old South with the vision of his New South contemporaries. Despite his progressive views in many areas, like so many other white southern leaders, he could never move completely beyond the concept of racial paternalism and white superiority. While much of his rhetoric was admittedly defensive in nature, especially with regard to his sectionalism and racial attitudes, Tichenor moved beyond defensive sectionalism to a promotion of the mission enterprise in order to spread the Southern Baptist version of Christianity beyond traditional southern boundaries.

Finally, his promotion of cooperation among Southern Baptists was foundational in the development of the main means of twentieth-century financial support for Southern Baptist missions. Beginning in 1925 with the "Seventy Five Million Campaign" almost three decades after Tichenor's death, Southern Baptists adopted a systematic approach eventually called the Cooperative Program whereby churches were encouraged to give a regular percentage of their offerings each month to support the denomination's seminaries, agencies, and boards. Tichenor was among the first to call for such a systematic approach for funding Baptist mission endeavors. His efforts to establish collaborative efforts between the HMB and various state mission boards also contributed to this development. While he may never have envisioned the scope that the modern day Cooperative Program encompassed and the similar approaches adopted by Baptist state conventions, his promotion of these ideas became the answer to many of the questions that he raised, especially during his tenure as a denominational leader.

Not all of his influence was positive. He created a spirit of competition with Northern Baptists that contributed to ongoing conflict between the two bodies. He did little to alleviate racial tensions existent in his day. He largely ignored the working conditions for laborers in the mills and mines of the New South, frequently emphasizing evangelism and church-building over attacking the social issues created by the growth of New South urban areas and industries. He contributed negatively to an internal spirit of competition between the Home and Foreign Mission Boards, especially regarding Cuba. He also contributed to the spirit of triumphalism among Southern Baptists that was persistent throughout the twentieth century. Tichenor and those like him promoted a sectarian spirit that was enhanced not only by its theological and religious background but also by its sectionalist sentiments. He was an intensely spiritual individual concerned with the intricacies of the metaphysical. Yet the materialism of the "Gilded Age" captured him, and he became obsessed with financial and material progression both in his personal and professional life. This obsession with profit and materialism became a subtle characteristic of much Southern Baptist life in the subsequent century.

Tichenor looms as one of the most significant figures in Southern Baptist history and in the history of southern Christianity. Despite the fact that his throat was irreparably damaged as a youth, he mesmerized and inspired masses with his speaking abilities. He was highly opinionated, aggressive, and outspoken, yet in two different churches he unified divided factions after a period of schism. He was essentially a self-taught man of little formal education who had tremendous mental abilities and was involved in the founding of Southern Baptist Theological Seminary in South Carolina and its reestablishment in Kentucky and in early support of Howard College in Alabama. Despite this limited formal education, all of which was classically based, he made key decisions and laid critical groundwork that established what eventually became Auburn University. In doing so, he grafted a modern agricultural and mechanical college that was part of his New South vision onto a classical education model. He published little, but one of his greatest concerns was with publication; he was a practical businessman who utilized techniques that were ahead of his time, yet he was a dreamer and a visionary. He knew personal tragedy in its most severe fashions and yet maintained an optimistic spirit. Tichenor embodies both the best and the worst of the staid tradition of the Old South and the progressive vision for the New South, even though the New South remained largely an illusion for many southerners.

In an article written in 1981, Baptist historian Walter Shurden develops a thesis suggesting that the Southern Baptist Convention is comprised of a synthesis of four distinct Southern Baptist traditions. Shurden identifies these as the "order" of the "Charleston Tradition," the "ardor" of the "Sandy Creek Tradition," the "cultural" and "denominational" identity of the "Georgia Tradition," and the "ecclesiological" identity of the "Tennessee Tradition." In an article published ten years later, Baptist historian Leon McBeth expanded this thesis to recognize a fifth tradition, the "conservative, evangelistic, independent" nature of the "Texas Tradition." Shurden's article included the vital role I. T. Tichenor played in forming this synthesis and suggests that Tichenor heightened "ideas of sectionalism and denominationalism."[14] But Tichenor did more than merely heighten ideas. By using his charismatic personality, tremendous leadership and organizational skills, rich diversity of experience, and intense loyalty to the South and to the Southern Baptist Convention, I. T. Tichenor rallied Southern Baptists to define and defend the territory of the Southern Baptist Convention. These actions saved the Home Mission Board and thereby preserved the Southern Baptist Convention as a separate entity. As church historian Martin Marty writes in his work *Righteous Empire,* after the Civil War "recovery of pride was essential" for the South.[15] Through restoring a pride in ideals treasured by Southern Baptists, uniting the Southern Baptist Convention around the banner of the Home Mission Board, "baptizing" a New South vision and promoting his own vision for the work of Southern Baptists in the nation and around the world, Tichenor played not only a significant role but *the* major role in forging a Southern Baptist synthesis. He laid the groundwork for the formation of the Sunday School Board and the Cooperative Program, which together did more to solidify the Southern Baptist Convention than any other institutions. If the mid- to late-nineteenth century is to be considered the era in which the Baptists of the South became "Southern Baptists," then Tichenor should be considered the primary figure of late nineteenth-century Southern Baptist life. Herein lies his major contribution to the Southern Baptist Convention and to American Christianity. In the life and work of Isaac Taylor Tichenor, one may see a microcosm of the Southern Baptist Convention. By looking at his life, one may see a picture of the Southern Baptist Convention itself. As the convention has left a legacy to this nation's and the world's religious heritage, so too has Isaac Taylor Tichenor left a legacy of cooperation, optimism, and mission to the Southern Baptist Convention and to the world. As the epitaph on his gravestone says, "He had understanding of the times, to know what Israel ought to do." For better or worse, this entitles him to the appellations "Seer of the South" and "Creator of a Baptist Empire in the New South."

Notes

Introduction

1. Jacob Smilser Dill, *Isaac Taylor Tichenor: Home Mission Board Statesman* (Nashville: Sunday School Board, 1908), 10–11.

2. Sydney Ahlstrom, *A Religious History of the American People* (New Haven, CT: Yale University Press, 1972), 436, 462; Winthrop Hudson and John Corrigan, *Religion in America: An Historical Account of the Development of American Religious Life,* 5th ed. (New York: MacMillan Publishing Company, 1992), 144ff.

3. H. Leon McBeth, *The Baptist Heritage: Four Centuries of Baptist Witness* (Nashville: Broadman Press, 1987), 344–66.

4. Ahlstrom, *Religious History,* 541.

5. Ibid., 763–84.

6. Hudson, *Religion in America,* 267.

7. Jesse Fletcher, *The Southern Baptist Convention: A Sesquicentennial History* (Nashville: Broadman & Holman, 1994), 89–91, 105–6.

8. McBeth, *Baptist Heritage,* 425; Robert A. Baker, *The Southern Baptist Convention and Its People, 1607–1972* (Nashville: Broadman Press, 1974), 204.

9. *Proceedings of the Southern Baptist Convention, 1880,* 72, hereafter cited as *Annual, SBC;* W. W. Barnes, *The Southern Baptist Convention, 1845–1953* (Nashville: Broadman Press, 1954), 77–78; and *Annual, SBC, 1892,* X.

10. *Annual, SBC, 1882,* 29.

11. The Indian Mission Association later merged with the Southern Baptist Domestic Mission Board to become the Home Mission Board.

12. Martin Marty, "The Protestant Experience and Perspectives," in *American Religious Values and the Future of America,* ed. Rodger van Allen, (Philadelphia: Fortress, 1978), 40, as cited in Bill Leonard, *God's Last and Only Hope* (Grand Rapids: Eerdmans Publishing, 1990), 3; Walter B. Shurden, "The Southern Baptist Synthesis: Is It Cracking?" *The Baptist History and Heritage* 16, no. 2 (April 1981): 6–7; McBeth, *Baptist Heritage,* 428–29; Baker, *Southern Baptist Convention and Its People,* 264; John Franklin Loftis,

"Factors in Southern Baptist Identity as Reflected by Ministerial Role Models, 1750–1925" (Ph.D. diss., Southern Baptist Theological Seminary, 1987), 138; Barnes, *Southern Baptist Convention,* 69–70, 78; and Joe W. Burton, *Epochs of Home Missions, Southern Baptist Convention, 1845–1945* (Atlanta: Home Missions Board, 1945), 77.

Chapter 1

1. "I. T. Tichenor, Record of Ancestry," Una Roberts Lawrence Papers, Southern Baptist Historical Commission Archives, box 10, file 33, hereafter cited as Lawrence papers; Kate Ellen Gruver, "Interview with Annie Kate Barnes, granddaughter of I. T. Tichenor, 18 November 1970," Lawrence papers, box 15a, file 52; Dill, *Tichenor,* 9; Harold A. Tichenor, *Tichenor Families in America* (Napton, MO: privately printed, 1988), 202, 438–42; Kenneth W. Noe, "The Fighting Chaplain of Shiloh: Isaac Tichenor's Civil War and the Roles of Confederate Ministers," unpublished manuscript adapted from presentation at Society of Military Historians Conference, 5 April 2002, note 4; and E-mails between the author and W. B. Tichenor, June–July 2003.

2. "Dictation from Dr. I. T. Tichenor," copy in Lawrence papers, box 10, file 33; Dill, *Tichenor,* 10; Tichenor, *Tichenor Families,* 438; Lee Norcross Allen, *The First 150 Years: Montgomery's First Baptist Church, 1829–1979* (Birmingham, AL: Oxmoor Press, 1979), 50; and John Henderson Spencer, *A History of Kentucky Baptists* (Cincinnati: privately printed, 1886), 1:75.

3. Dill, *Tichenor,* 10–11.

4. Spencer, *Kentucky Baptists,* 1:215–16.

5. Dill, *Tichenor,* 12, 13; Spencer, *Kentucky Baptists,* 1:216, 219.

6. The Bloomfield church was a member of the Salem Association, one of the earliest associations organized in the Mississippi Valley region and one of the strongest associations in Kentucky. Later it had a leading role in the Nelson Association of Kentucky Baptists. See Spencer, *Kentucky Baptists,* 2:44–45 for more detail on the Salem Association.

7. Taylorsville is in Spencer County and is about forty-five miles due west of Lexington and about twenty miles southeast of Louisville, in the north central part of Kentucky.

8. Joe W. Burton, "Interview with Mrs. J. S. Dill, daughter of I. T. Tichenor," 31 May 1944, Lawrence papers, box 10, file 34, 6; and Dill, *Tichenor,* 11–13. See also Donald G. Mathews, *Religion in the Old South* (Chicago: University of Chicago Press, 1977), 85.

9. Dill, *Tichenor,* 14–15; Spencer, *Kentucky Baptists,* 1:679–80.

10. Dill, *Tichenor,* 15. See also I. T. Tichenor, "Joseph Islands, Apostle to the Indians," in Dill, *Tichenor,* 159–68.

11. *Minutes of the Annual Meeting of the Mississippi Baptist Convention, 1847,* 3, 12, hereafter cited as *Minutes, MBC.*

12. Dill, *Tichenor,* 18–20; Emily Tichenor Whitner, paper read before the Jackson Hill Baptist Church Ladies Missionary Society, n.d., Kimball Johnson papers, Whitner Collection, Auburn University Archives. Johnson papers hereafter cited as KJ papers.

13. Dill, *Tichenor,* 18–20; *Minutes, MBC, 1848,* 3, 4, and appendix M.

14. C. C. Goen, *Broken Churches, Broken Nation: Denominational Schism and the Coming of the Civil War* (Macon, GA: Mercer University Press, 1985), 90–98; Fletcher,

Southern Baptist Convention, 44–52; and Robert G. Gardner, *Decade of Debate and Division: Georgia Baptists and the Formation of the Southern Baptist Convention* (Macon, GA: Mercer University Press, 1995), 33–44, 60.

15. Dill, *Tichenor*, 19–20; *Annual, SBC, 1849*, 30, 32. The convention meeting was an adjourned meeting with small representation. The earlier meeting in Nashville had adjourned to Charleston because of the outbreak of a cholera epidemic in the former city.

16. Matilda James to Mrs. Wilkinson, 25 June 1849, copy in Lawrence papers, box 10, file 33.

17. *Minutes, MBC, 1849*, 7–9, 12; Dill, *Tichenor*, 20.

18. *South Western Baptist*, 4 December 1850, 2; Dill, *Tichenor*, 20; and *South Western Baptist*, 23 July 1851, 2.

19. Diary of I. T. Tichenor, 1, entry undated, 9, 3, entry dated 22 November 1850. Southern Baptist Historical Archives and Library, item 127, microfilm copy at Southwestern Baptist Theological Seminary; Keith Harper, *The Quality of Mercy: Southern Baptists and Social Christianity, 1890–1920* (Tuscaloosa: University of Alabama Press, 1996), 38.

20. Tichenor diary, 11 November 1850; Harper, *Quality of Mercy*, 38–40.

21. Dill, *Tichenor*, 21; Allen, *First 150 Years*, 51, 52, 54.

22. W. W. Rogers and others, *Alabama: The History of a Deep South State* (Tuscaloosa: University of Alabama Press, 1994), 95, 121, 133, 191; W. W. Rogers Jr., *Confederate Home Front: Montgomery During the Civil War* (Tuscaloosa: University of Alabama Press, 1999), 3–4, 5; and Allen, *First 150 Years*, 52.

23. E. Brooks Holifield, *The Gentlemen Theologians* (Durham, NC: Duke University Press, 1978), 17, 18, 39, 40, 43–44; Mathews, *Old South*, 82ff.

24. J. Wayne Flynt, *Alabama Baptists: Southern Baptists in the Heart of Dixie* (Tuscaloosa: University of Alabama Press, 1998), 83; B. F. Riley, *A Memorial History of the Baptists of Alabama*, (Philadelphia: Judson Press, 1923), 112; and B. F. Riley, *History of the Baptists of Alabama* (Birmingham: Roberts & Son, 1895), 206, 216.

25. Allen, *First 150 Years*, 56; *South Western Baptist*, 14 September 1854, 2; *South Western Baptist*, 12 June 1856, 2; and I. T. Tichenor to A. M. Poindexter, 22 July 1857, typed copy in Lawrence papers, box 10, file 33.

26. Allen, *First 150 Years*, 53–54; Flynt, *Alabama Baptists*, 96. For more on Curry see *J. L. M. Curry: Southerner, Statesman, and Educator* (New York: King's Crown Press, 1949).

27. Rogers and others, *Alabama*, 124; *Proceedings of the Alabama Baptist State Convention, 1852*, 3, 6, 13, 28, hereafter cited as *Proceedings, ABSC*; Flynt, *Alabama Baptists*, 94; *Proceedings, ABSC, 1853*, 4, 5, 9, 35–36; *Proceedings, ABSC, 1858*, 30; *South Western Baptist*, 8 January 1857, 2; *South Western Baptist*, 2 December 1858, 2; *Proceedings, ABSC, 1854*, 8, 14, 15, 23; *South Western Baptist*, 27 April 1854, 3; *South Western Baptist*, 22 June 1854, 4; *South Western Baptist*, 10 August 1854, 4; *Proceedings, ABSC, 1855*, 5, 6; *Proceedings, ABSC, 1856*, 5, 20–22; and *Proceedings, ABSC, 1857*, 5.

28. *Annual, SBC, 1853*, 3, 6, 16.

29. I. T. Tichenor to A. M. Poindexter, 5 June 1855, typed copy in Lawrence papers, box 10, file 33.

30. *South Western Baptist*, 31 July 1856, 2; I. T. Tichenor to A. M. Poindexter, 22 June 1857, 22 July 1857, 12 December 1858, 28 December 1858, and September 1859, typed copies in Lawrence papers, box 10, file 33.

31. Allen, *First 150 Years,* 60, 61.

32. *South Western Baptist,* 31 July 1856, 2; I. T. Tichenor to A. M. Poindexter, 12 December 1858, typed copy in Lawrence papers, box 10, file 33, emphasis is Tichenor's.

33. *Annual, SBC, 1855,* 12; Allen, *First 150 Years,* 59, 61–62.

34. *Annual, SBC, 1855,* 4, 5, 6; Allen, *First 150 Years,* 59.

35. Clifton Judson Allen and others, eds., *Encyclopedia of Southern Baptists* (Nashville: Broadman Press, 1958), s.v. "Landmarkism" by W. Morgan Patterson and "James Robinson Graves" by Homer L. Grice; Bill J. Leonard, ed., *Dictionary of Baptists in America* (Downers Grove, IL: Intervarsity Press, 1994), s.v. "Landmark Baptists" by H. Leon McBeth and "James Robinson Graves" by Marty G. Bell; William R. Estep, *Whole Gospel— Whole World: The Foreign Mission Board of the Southern Baptist Convention, 1845–1995* (Nashville: Broadman and Holman Publishers, 1994), 91–92; Baker, *Southern Baptist Convention and Its People,* 208.

36. Tichenor to Poindexter, 5 June 1855, Lawrence papers, box 10, file 33, question mark insertion is Tichenor's; Baker, *Southern Baptist Convention and Its People,* 218; and Tichenor to Poindexter, 8 March 1867, Lawrence papers, box 10, file 33.

37. Riley, *Memorial History,* 128; Allen, *First 150 Years,* 59, 63; *Proceedings, ABSC, 1859,* 13; *South Western Baptist,* 10 September 1857, 1; *South Western Baptist,* 28 May 1857, 1; and *South Western Baptist,* 10 May 1860, 2. Howard College is now Samford University. Tichenor's support of Southern Seminary did not end here. He was appointed to the chair when the convention went into session as a committee of the whole in 1873 and voted to move the seminary to Louisville and to set up an endowment for it. *Annual, SBC, 1873,* 17, 19. He spoke at the seminary's 1880 commencement. *Alabama Baptist,* 13 May 1880, 3. He also served as a trustee of the seminary from 1872 to 1889 and intermittently until 1899. See John R. Sampey, *Southern Baptist Theological Seminary: The First Thirty Years, 1859–1889* (Baltimore: Wharton, Barron & Co., 1890), 20; and William A. Mueller, *A History of Southern Baptist Theological Seminary* (Nashville: Broadman Press, 1959), 175.

38. Flynt, *Alabama Baptists,* 90; *Annual, SBC, 1857,* 6, 7, 10, 11; and *Annual, SBC, 1859,* 29.

39. *South Western Baptist,* 13 December 1860, 2; Allen, *First 150 Years,* 63; and Harold Tichenor, *Tichenor Families,* 441.

Chapter 2

1. Allen, *First 150 Years,* 58.

2. Dumas Malone and others, eds., *Dictionary of American Biography* (New York: Charles Scribner's Sons, 1928–1936), s.v. "Thomas Hill Watts" by Hallie Farmer and others, 204.

3. Charles F. Pitts, *Chaplains in Gray: The Confederate Chaplains' Story* (Nashville: Broadman Press, 1957), 39–41; Pamela Robinson-Durso, "Chaplains in the Confederate Army," *Journal of Church and State* (August 1991): 748, 750; Ron Ellison, "An Overview of Southern Baptists' Ministry to Confederate Soldiers," unpublished manuscript, 3, 4; and James W. Silver, *Confederate Morale and Church Propaganda* (Tuscaloosa, AL: Confederate Publishing Company, 1975), 77–78. Bill 102 stated, "There shall be appointed by the President such number of chaplains to serve with the armies of the Confederate States during the existing war as he may deem expedient; and the President shall assign

them to such regiments, brigades or posts as he may deem necessary; and the appointments made as aforesaid shall expire whenever the existing war shall terminate."

4. *South Western Baptist,* 21 November 1861, 2; Malcolm C. McMillan, *The Disintegration of a Confederate State: Three Governors and Alabama's Wartime Home Front, 1861–1865* (University, AL: University of Alabama, 1963), 31–33; W. W. McMillan, "History of the Seventeenth Alabama Regiment," file folders 4 and 5, Alabama Department of Archives and History, Montgomery, Alabama, hereafter cited as W. W. McMillan, "Seventeenth Alabama"; I. T. Tichenor, "Reminiscences of the Battle of Shiloh," 3, on Tichenor microfilm, copy at Southwestern Baptist Theological Seminary, hereafter cited as Tichenor, "Reminiscences"; Robinson-Durso, "Chaplains," 752; and Edward F. Witsell to Virgil Chapman, 20 July 1950, copy in KJ papers, box 1, file 5. See also Rogers and others, *Alabama,* 187, and Illene D. and Wilbur E. Thompson, *The Seventeenth Alabama Infantry: A Regimental History and Roster* (Bowen, MD: Heritage Books, 2001).

5. Robinson-Durso, "Chaplains," 752–57, 759; and Arthur L. Walker, "Three Alabama Chaplains," *Alabama Review* 16, no. 3 (1963): 176.

6. Larry J. Daniel, *Shiloh: The Battle That Changed the Civil War* (New York: Simon & Schuster, 1997), 61–63; W. W. McMillan, "Seventeenth Alabama," file 4, 6, 8; and Annie Kate Barnes to J. R. Rutland, n.d., copy in the KJ papers, box 3, file 166. For the strategic considerations involved in this concentration of forces and for background information on the battle of Shiloh, also see Daniel.

7. *South Western Baptist,* 10 April 1862, 3; W. W. McMillan, "Seventeenth Alabama," file 4, 6; *The War of Rebellion; Official Records of the Union and Confederate Armies,* series 1, 10 (Washington, DC: U.S. Government, 1880–1901), 463–70, 532–35, 553–56, hereafter cited as *OR;* and Grady McWhiney, *Braxton Bragg and Confederate Defeat* (Tuscaloosa: University of Alabama Press, 1969), 1:236–45. Second edition printed 1991.

8. Paul Harvey, "'Yankee Faith' and Southern Redemption," in *Religion and the American Civil War,* ed. Randall M. Miller, Harry S. Stout, and Charles Reagan Wilson (New York: Oxford University Press, 1998), 172.

9. Tichenor, "Reminiscences," 3–11; *Christian Index,* 8 May 1862, 3; *Religious Herald,* 1 May and 8 May 1862, 2; Tichenor to Thomas Watts, cited in undated newspaper clipping from *Richmond Whig* on Tichenor microfilm, Southwestern Baptist Theological Seminary; and James Lee McDonough, *Shiloh in Hell before Night* (Knoxville: University of Tennessee Press, 1977), 129. Kenneth Noe's paper (see chap. 1, n. 1) has questioned some of the details of this traditional account. See Noe, "Fighting Chaplain," 20–22.

10. *Christian Index,* 8 May 1862, 3; Riley, *History of the Baptists of Alabama,* 287; W. W. McMillan, "Seventeenth Alabama," 9–11; Willis Brewer, *Alabama: Her History, Resources, War Record, and Public Men* (Montgomery, AL: Willo Publishing, 1872), 617; and *OR,* 555.

11. *Religious Herald,* 8 May 1862, 2. See also Dill, *Tichenor,* 27–28.

12. Ibid. See also *Religious Herald,* 1 May 1862, 2.

13. Karen Fritz, *Voices in the Storm: Confederate Rhetoric, 1861–1865* (Denton, TX: University of North Texas Press, 1999), 7.

14. Noe, "Fighting Chaplain," 22, 25–26.

15. At Shiloh the Seventeenth Alabama suffered casualties of more than 33 percent of those engaged. W. W. McMillan, "Seventeenth Alabama," 9–11; Brewer, *Alabama,* 617; *Christian Index,* 8 May 1862, 3; and *OR,* 532, 555.

16. Daniel, *Shiloh*, 305, 313; Brewer, *Alabama*, 617; and W. W. McMillan, "Seventeenth Alabama," 12ff. See also Thomas L. Connelly, *Army of the Heartland: The Army of Tennessee, 1861–1862* (Baton Rouge: Louisiana State University Press, 1967); Thomas L. Connelly, *Autumn of Glory: The Army of Tennessee, 1862–1865* (Baton Rouge: Louisiana State University Press, 1971); James L. McDonough and Thomas L. Connelly, *Five Tragic Hours: The Battle of Franklin* (Knoxville: University of Tennessee Press, 1983); and Stanley F. Horn, *The Decisive Battle of Nashville* (1956; repr., Baton Rouge: Louisiana State University Press, 1984).

17. *OR*, 555; *Religious Herald*, 1 May 1862, 2; *South Western Baptist*, 1 May 1862, 2; Letter from Moses Burbank, February 1867, copy on Tichenor microfilm; and *South Western Baptist*, 28 July 1864, 1.

18. Robinson-Durso, "Chaplains," 762–63; I. T. Tichenor to John C. Breckinridge, 21 April 1862; I. T. Tichenor to G. W. Randolph, undated Veteran Record, Record Division, Rebel Archives, War Department, National Archives and Records Administration, Washington, D.C. Photocopies provided by Ron Ellison. The author gratefully acknowledges Mr. Ellison's research on this subject provided in an unpublished manuscript on Confederate chaplains, with Tichenor as a case study, and the photocopies of Tichenor's veteran's record that Ellison graciously provided.

19. Robinson-Durso, "Chaplains," 760; and Steven E. Woodworth, *While God Is Marching On: The Religious World of Civil War Soldiers* (Lawrence: University of Kansas Press, 2001), 151.

20. As cited in Robinson-Durso, "Chaplains," 760.

21. Brigadier General John K. Jackson's reply to letter from Tichenor to Randolph, approval of resignation, and accompanying endorsement to Braxton Bragg, 14 May 1862, in "I. T. Tichenor," Veteran Record, Record Division, Rebel Archives, War Department, National Archives and Records Administration, Washington, D.C., photocopies provided by Ron Ellison; Peter Cozzens, *This Terrible Sound: The Battle of Chickamauga* (Urbana and Chicago: University of Illinois Press, 1992), 155–56; and Peter Cozzens, *The Shipwreck of Their Hopes: The Battles for Chattanooga* (Urbana and Chicago: University of Illinois Press, 1994), 169.

22. Walker, "Three Alabama Chaplains," 179–80; Noe, "Fighting Chaplain," 22; Ellison, "Southern Baptists' Ministry," 31; and *South Western Baptist*, 4 December 1862, 2.

23. Woodworth, *God Is Marching On*, 157. See also Woodworth, 158 and 159, for information regarding other "fighting chaplains" in both the Union and Confederate armies.

24. Ibid., 157, 158.

25. *Christian Index*, 11 November 1862, 2; *South Western Baptist*, 15 January 1863, 2; and Allen, *First 150 Years*, 84–86.

26. Rogers, *Confederate Home Front*, 7–8, 10, 61.

27. Ibid., 57, 70, 71, 72, 73; and Harold S. Wilson, *Confederate Industry: Manufacturers and Quartermasters in the Civil War* (Jackson: University of Mississippi Press, 2002), xviii, 103.

28. I. T. Tichenor, "Fast Day Sermon," as cited in Dill, *Tichenor*, 88, 93, 106. See also *South Western Baptist*, 5 November 1863.

29. Tichenor, "Fast Day Sermon," in Dill, *Tichenor*, 88–89, emphasis is Tichenor's.

30. Ibid., 93–94.

31. Ibid., 94.

32. Ibid., 97, 98; and William C. Davis, *Look Away! A History of the Confederate States of America* (New York: Free Press, 2002), 211. See also Silver, *Confederate Morale,* 53–55.

33. Tichenor, "Fast Day Sermon," in Dill, *Tichenor,* 99, emphasis is Tichenor's.

34. Ibid., 99–100.

35. Davis, *Look Away,* 43.

36. Tichenor, "Fast Day Sermon," in Dill, *Tichenor,* 102. See also John B. Boles, "Evangelical Protestantism in the South," in *Religion in the South,* ed. Charles Reagan Wilson (Jackson: University Press of Mississippi, 1985), 28–34 and Mathews, *Old South,* 158ff.

37. Ibid.

38. Davis, *Look Away,* 130–37.

39. C. Vann Woodward and Elisabeth Muhlenfeld, eds., *The Private Mary Chesnut, The Unpublished Civil War Diaries* (New York: Oxford University Press, 1984), 42–43, entry dated 18 March 1861. See also Rogers et al., *Alabama,* 109–10.

40. Tichenor, "Fast Day Sermon," in Dill, *Tichenor,* 103–4, 106–7.

41. Woodworth, *God Is Marching On,* 273–86.

42. See Richard E. Beringer et al., *Why the South Lost the Civil War* (Athens, GA: University of Georgia Press, 1986), 366–72.

43. Paul M. Gaston, *The New South Creed: A Study in Southern Mythmaking* (New York: Alfred A. Knopf, 1970), 6–13.

44. Rogers et al., *Alabama,* 213, 214; Davis, *Look Away,* 370; Malcolm C. McMillan, *Disintegration of a Confederate State,* 82, 84–117 passim; Harold S. Wilson, *Confederate Industry,* 101.

45. *South Western Baptist,* 25 April 1861, 3; *Christian Index,* 9 September 1864; *South Western Baptist,* 15 September 1864, 1; Tichenor, *Tichenor Families,* 440, 441, 442; Whitner paper, 3 (see chap. 1, n. 12); and Joe W. Burton, *Road to Recovery* (Nashville: Broadman Press, 1977), 17–18.

46. *South Western Baptist,* 31 March 1864, 1; 28 April 1864, 1; 9 June 1864, 1; Emily L. Whitner to Mrs. Owens, n.d., KJ papers, box 1, file 5; and Davis, *Look Away,* 294–95. See also Whitner paper, 3. For more information of the siege of Atlanta, see James Lee McDonough and James Pickett Jones, *War So Terrible: Sherman and Atlanta* (New York: W. W. Norton & Company, 1987), 299–313 and Samuel Carter III, *The Siege of Atlanta, 1864* (New York: St. Martin's Press, 1973), 305–19.

47. *OR,* series 2, 8:166; Malcolm C. McMillan, *Alabama Confederate Reader* (Tuscaloosa: University of Alabama Press, 1863), 366–67; Malcolm C. McMillan, *Disintegration of a Confederate State,* 114; Rogers, *Confederate Home Front,* 97–98, 137; Woodworth, *God Is Marching On,* 284; and Silver, *Confederate Morale,* 55.

48. Rogers, *Confederate Home Front,* 143–44; Harold S. Wilson, *Confederate Industry,* 226–27; and Davis, *Look Away,* 186–87, 314.

49. Sam Duvall, "Incident at Hatcher's Run," *Alabama Heritage,* Winter 2002, 25; Malcolm C. McMillan, *Disintegration of a Confederate State,* 119; and Rogers, *Confederate Home Front,* 147. Troy's miraculous survival of his wounds and subsequent capture and recovery are thoroughly recounted in Duvall, 18–28. For more detail on the Battle of Hatcher's Run in the siege of Petersburg, see Arthur W. Bergeron Jr., "Three-Day Tussle at Hatcher's Run," *America's Civil War,* March 2003, 31–37.

50. Allen, *First 150 Years,* 86.

51. Annie Kate Barnes to J. R. Rutland, n.d., KJ papers, box 3, file 166.

Chapter 3

1. Harold S. Wilson, *Confederate Industry,* 227. For descriptions of these conditions and the turmoil that subsequently occurred see Eric Foner, *Reconstruction: America's Unfinished Revolution, 1863–1877* (New York: Harper & Row Publishers, 1988) and Hodding Carter, *The Angry Scar: The Story of Reconstruction* (Garden City, NY: Doubleday Press, 1959). For a description of the perspective of African Americans see Daniel W. Stowell, *Rebuilding Zion: The Religious Reconstruction of the South, 1863–1877* (New York: Oxford University Press, 1998), 65–79.

2. Walter L. Fleming, *Civil War and Reconstruction in Alabama* (New York: Columbia University Press, 1905; reprint, New York: Peter Smith, 1949), 253–61and Rogers et al., *Alabama,* 228–29.

3. Dan T. Carter, *When the War Was Over: The Failure of Self Reconstruction in the South, 1865–1867* (Baton Rouge: Louisiana State University Press, 1985), 23.

4. Ibid., 227.

5. Rufus B. Spain, *At Ease in Zion* (Nashville: Broadman Press, 1967), 17; Tichenor, "Fast Day Sermon," in Dill, *Tichenor,* 212, also 28–29; and H. Shelton Smith, *In His Image, But . . . : Racism in Southern Religion, 1780–1910* (Durham, NC: Duke University Press, 1972), 208–16.

6. *Annual, SBC, 1866,* 20, 85.

7. Foner, *Reconstruction,* 168 and *Annual, SBC, 1866,* 20, 85.

8. *Christian Index,* 17 February 1866, 2; *Minutes, Alabama Baptist Association, 1865,* 7, in Allen, *First 150 Years,* 87; and Allen, 87–88. See also Harvey, "'Yankee Faith,'" 39.

9. Katharine L. Dvorak, *An African-American Exodus: The Segregation of the Southern Churches* (Brooklyn: Carlson Publishing, 1991), 69.

10. Stowell, *Rebuilding Zion,* 80–87.

11. As cited in Dvorak, *African-American Exodus,* 70.

12. Minutes, First Baptist Church of Montgomery, 28 July 1867. Hereafter cited as Minutes, FBC.

13. Minutes, FBC, 15 August 1867; Allen, *First 150 Years,* 88–89; and Flynt, *Alabama Baptists,* 139.

14. Stowell, *Rebuilding Zion,* 87–99; Flynt, *Alabama Baptists,* 139–40.

15. Smith, *In His Image,* 228; Dvorak, *African-American Exodus,* 75, 76, 77, 114–19; and Stowell, *Rebuilding Zion,* 73, 76, 77, 78, 94.

16. *Alabama Baptist,* 1 June 1882, 3; I. T. Tichenor, "Jesse Goldthwaite: A Christian Slave," in Dill, *Tichenor,* 151–58; and Flynt, *Alabama Baptists,* 139.

17. Minutes, FBC, 29 December 1867; 17 January 1868; 25 January 1868; and Allen, *First 150 Years,* 91–92.

18. Minutes, FBC, 10 November 1867; 17 November 1867; 24 November 1867; 29 December 1867; 12 January 1868; and Joseph Squire diary, 14 January 1868, original copy in possession of Kenneth Penhale, Helena, Alabama. Squire diary, notebook, and papers hereafter cited as Joseph Squire papers, Penhale collection.

19. Minutes, FBC, 17 January 1868.

20. Ibid.

21. Ibid., 29 June 1868; Allen, *First 150 Years,* 92.

22. Tichenor, *Tichenor Families,* 440, 441, 442; Squire diary, 23 January 1868, Joseph Squire papers, Penhale collection.

23. Dill, *Tichenor,* 30; Allen, *First 150 Years,* 92; and Ray M. Atchison, *Baptists of Shelby County: History of the Shelby Baptist Association of Alabama* (Birmingham: Banner Press, 1964), 84, 148.

24. Deed Book N, 909, 910, 929 and Deed Book O, 616, 760, 765, Shelby County Court House, Columbiana, Alabama; Shelby County Abstract Book, Buck Creek Cotton Mill, Columbiana, Shelby County, Alabama, 1868–1871, Shelby County Museum and Archives, Columbiana, Alabama; Ethel Armes, *The Story of Coal and Iron in Alabama* (Birmingham: Birmingham Chamber of Commerce, 1910), 154–56; and James Sanders Day, "'Diamonds in the Rough'": A History of Alabama's Cahaba Coal Field" (Ph.D. diss., Auburn University, 2002), 9, 10, 14, 15, 32, 41, 54–75, 83, 84.

25. Squire diary, 27 January 1868, 28 January 1868, 31 January 1868, 1 February 1868, 6 February 1868, 7 February 1868, 11 February 1868, 17 February 1868, 22 April 1868, 9 May 1868, 25 May 1868, Joseph Squire papers, Penhale collection; Day, "'Diamonds in the Rough,'" 98.

26. Squire diary, 4 January 1868–21 July 1868, Joseph Squire papers, Penhale collection; Day, "'Diamonds in the Rough,'" 84, 85.

27. Saffold Birney, *Handbook of Alabama: A Complete Index to the State, 1878* (Mobile: Mobile Register Printing, 1878), 35–36; Glenn T. Miller, "Baptist Businessmen in Historical Perspective," *Baptist History and Heritage* 13 (1978): 58.

28. Rogers et al., *Alabama,* 278, 281; Day, "'Diamonds in the Rough,'" 134; and Harold S. Wilson, *Confederate Industry,* 284.

29. A more detailed definition of the New South movement will follow in the next chapter in the discussion of Tichenor's presidency at Alabama A & M.

30. Squire diary, entries 3 and 4, 5 January 1868, Joseph Squire papers, Penhale collection.

31. Ralph Lowell Eckert, *John Brown Gordon: Soldier, Southerner, American* (Baton Rouge: Louisiana State University Press, 1989), 11, 123–24, 239–40; Gaston, *New South Creed,* 18, 23–30, 32–35.

32. See letters from I. T. Tichenor to Joseph Squire, 8 December 1885 to 4 June 1902, Joseph Squire papers, Penhale collection.

33. Day, "'Diamonds in the Rough,'" 97–106; I. T. Tichenor to Joseph Squire, 2 September 1886, Joseph Squire papers, Penhale collection.

34. Day, "'Diamonds in the Rough,'" 108ff; Rogers et al., *Alabama,* 277, 285; J. Wayne Flynt, *Poor But Proud: Alabama's Poor Whites* (Tuscaloosa: University of Alabama Press, 1989), 114; and Edward L. Ayers, *The Promise of the New South: Life after Reconstruction* (New York: Oxford University Press, 1992), 110.

35. Charles Reagan Wilson, *Baptized in Blood: The Religion of the Lost Cause* (Athens: University of Georgia Press, 1980), 85–87.

36. Harold S. Wilson, *Confederate Industry,* 285–86 and Ayers, *Promise of the New South,* 109.

37. I. T. Tichenor to Joseph Squire, 4 June 1886 and 9 June 1886, Joseph Squire papers, Penhale collection; Day, "'Diamonds in the Rough,'" 100, 105, 106; and I. T.

Tichenor to Joseph Squire, 2 June 1887, 4 December 1899, and 4 June 1899, Joseph Squire papers, Penhale collection. See also, I. T. Tichenor to Joseph Squire correspondence, 2 January 1888 through 3 March 1891 and Day, "'Diamonds in the Rough,'" 98, 99, 101–4.

38. Allen, *First 150 Years,* 92–93; Dill, *Tichenor,* 30; and T. C. Boykin, "Montevallo," *Christian Index,* 22 July 1869.

39. Atchison, *Baptists of Shelby County,* 34, 84, 148, 150 and *Christian Index,* 4 November 1869.

40. Flynt, *Poor But Proud,* 120, 238.

41. *The Baptist,* 11 March 1871, 4; *Annual, SBC, 1871,* 6, 31; *The Baptist,* 27 May 1871, 5; and *The Baptist,* as cited in *Montgomery Daily Advertiser,* 15 May 1872, 1.

Chapter 4

1. John S. Brubacher and Willis Rudy, *Higher Education in Transition: A History of American Colleges and Universities,* 4th ed. (New Brunswick, NJ: Transaction Publishers, 1997), 59; John D. Pulliam, *History of Education in America,* 2nd ed. (Columbus, OH: Charles E. Merrill Publishing Company, 1976), 63, 64. Some examples of state universities developed in the late eighteenth and early nineteenth centuries would be the University of Pennsylvania, the University of Virginia, and the University of Georgia.

2. Brubacher and Rudy, *Higher Education in Transition,* 62; Dan R. Frost, *Thinking Confederates: Academia and the Idea of Progress in the New South* (Knoxville: University of Tennessee Press, 2000), 6; Pulliam, *History of Education,* 66; and Joel C. Watson, "Isaac Taylor Tichenor and the Administration of the Alabama Agricultural and Mechanical College, 1872–1882" (master's thesis, Auburn University, 1968), 1.

3. Frost, *Thinking Confederates,* 7–14.

4. At times in this work, Alabama A & M will be used interchangeably due to the fact that the university is now known as Auburn University and there is another institution with the name Alabama A & M.

5. William Warren Rogers, "The Founding of Alabama's Land Grant College at Auburn," *Alabama Review* 40 (January 1987): 14–16.

6. Ibid., 17–34.

7. Ibid., 20, 23, 34, 35 and Watson, "Tichenor and the Administration," 4.

8. Rogers, "Alabama's Land Grant College," 35, 36; Birney, *Handbook of Alabama,* 58–61; *Montgomery Daily Advertiser,* 10 March 1872, 1, and 27 March 1872, 2; *Auburn's First 100 Years* (Alabama Polytechnic Institute: Centennial Celebration, 1956) 7–12; *Christian Index,* 21 March 1872, 1; and *Western Recorder,* 6 April 1872, 2.

9. "Second Report of the President to the A & M Board of Directors, July 1873," no. 1 in "Reports of the President to the Alabama A & M Board of Directors," on Tichenor microfilm. Reports to the board are hereafter cited as "Report of the President." Apparently, there was no written record of Tichenor's first report, as it was delivered only orally.

10. *Christian Index,* 13 June 1872, 3, emphasis is Thornton's.

11. D. F. Davenport to J. R. Rutland, 28 April 1943, copy in KJ papers, box 3, file 166.

12. Nelly Thach to J. R. Rutland, n.d., copy in KJ papers, box 3, file 166, apparently the emphasis was Thach's.

13. Ibid.

14. J. E. D. Shipp to J. R. Rutland, 4 April 1943, copy in KJ papers, box 3, file 166.

15. Mrs. Reese Frazer to J. R. Rutland, n.d., KJ papers, box 3, file 166.

16. J. R. Rutland, "Dr. Tichenor as President of the Technological College at Alabama," Rutland papers, Auburn University, box 1, file 32.

17. "Second Report of the President, 30 July 1873," 1; "Fourth Report of the President, 12 July 1875," 22.

18. "Second Report of the President," 1, 4; "Third Report of the President, 6 July 1874," 12, 13; "Report of the President to the Alabama House of Representatives, 25 November 1874," 16; Gaston, *New South Creed*, 7; "Fourth Report of the President, 12 July 1875," 19, 21, 22; and "Fifth Report of the President, 8 January 1877," 32.

19. "Second Report of the President," 6–7; "Fifth Report of the President," 37; Frost, *Thinking Confederates*, 83–84; and Ayers, *Promise of the New South*, 420–22.

20. Frederick Rudolph, *The American College and University: A History* (Athens: University of Georgia Press, 1990), 241–306, 329–54 passim.

21. Gaston, *New South Creed*, 18, 48–49; Ayers, *Promise of the New South*, 21; Joel Chandler Harris, ed., *Life of Henry W. Grady: Including His Writings and Speeches* (New York: Haskell House Publishers, 1972), 60–68, 77–80; Henry Grady, "The New South," in Harris, 83–93; and Harold S. Wilson, *Confederate Industry*, 281–82. See also Grady, "The South and Her Problems," in Harris, 94–120.

22. Gaston, *New South Creed*, 7, and Ayers, *Promise of the New South*, 56. See also Frost, *Thinking Confederates*.

23. Frost, *Thinking Confederates*, 39–64. See also Emory M. Thomas, *Robert E. Lee: A Biography* (New York: W. W. Norton, 1995), 399–401 and Herman Hattaway, *General Stephen D. Lee* (Jackson: University Press of Mississippi, 1976), 178–92.

24. "Sixth Report of the President, 25 June 1877," 59, 60.

25. See Frost, *Thinking Confederates*; Gaston, *New South Creed*; Gaines Foster, *Ghosts of the Confederacy: Defeat, the Lost Cause, and the Emergence of the New South, 1865–1913* (Baton Rouge: Louisiana State University Press, 1987); and Charles Reagan Wilson, *Baptized in Blood*. See also Bill J. Leonard, *God's Last and Only Hope: The Fragmentation of the Southern Baptist Convention* (Grand Rapids, MI: William B. Eerdmans, 1990).

26. "Second Report of the President," 6; "Fifth Report of the President," 38, 46, 47; "Seventh Report of the President, 24 June 1878," 33, 36, 37; and Birney, *Handbook of Alabama*, 78.

27. "Sixth Report of the President," 58, 59, 60.

28. Frost, *Thinking Confederates*, 51.

29. Rudolph, *American College*, 264, 265; "Sixth Report of the President," 57, 58.

30. "Sixth Report of the President," 48; "Tenth Report of the President, 27 June 1881," 98, 99; Frost, *Thinking Confederates*, 79, 81; and "Fifth Report of the President," 41, 42. See also Frost, 78–82.

31. "Seventh Report of the President, 24 June 1878," 76, 77; Frost, *Thinking Confederates*, 60–64; "Sixth Report of the President," 56, 64, 66; and "Fifth Report of the President," 32, 33. See also D. F. Davenport to J. R. Rutland, 28 April 1943, and J. E. D. Shipp to J. R. Rutland, 4 April 1943, copies in Johnson papers, box 3, file 166.

32. "Sixth Report of the President," 67, 68.

33. Frost, *Thinking Confederates*, 78–82.

34. "Third Report of the President," 10; "Report to the Speaker of the House, 25 November 1874," 15, 16, on Tichenor microfilm; "Tenth Report of the President," 97, 102; and "Ninth Report of the President, 29 June 1880," 88, 91.

35. "Fourth Report of the President, 12 July 1875," 19; "Eighth Report of the President, 23 June 1879," 82; "Ninth Report of the President," 88; "Tenth Report of the President," 97; and "Eleventh Report of the President, 26 June 1882," 117.

36. Davis, *Look Away*, 205–6; "Fourth Report of the President," 26; "Sixth Report of the President," 53; Frost, *Thinking Confederates*, 103–5; and "Tenth Report of the President," 107.

37. Frost, *Thinking Confederates*, 97–98, and "Seventh Report of the President," 77, 78.

38. "Second Report of the President," 4; "Report to the Speaker of the House, 25 November 1874," 17, 18; "Fourth Report of the President," 23, 24, 26, 27; "Fifth Report of the President," 32, 33; "Sixth Report of the President," 49; and "Seventh Report of the President," 73, 74, 80.

39. "Report to the Governor, 10 October 1876," 43, on Tichenor microfilm; "Sixth Report of the President," 54; "Tenth Report of the President," 100, 102; and Frost, *Thinking Confederates*, 99.

40. "Report to the Governor," 46.

41. "Tenth Report of the President," 102.

42. Ibid., 104–6.

43. Ibid., 106–8.

44. Ibid., 108–11.

45. Ibid., 112–14.

46. Ibid., 115.

47. Frost, *Thinking Confederates*, 51–52; Gaston, *New South Creed*, 67–71; and Charles Reagan Wilson, *Baptized in Blood*, 92, 93.

48. Brubacher and Rudy, *Higher Education in Transition*, 253–55; Rudolph, *American College*, 275–86, 290–306; Walter Crosby Eells, *The Junior College* (Boston: Houghton Mifflin Company, 1931), 45–64; Carl E. Seashore, *The Junior College Movement* (New York: Henry Holt and Company, 1940), 4; Jesse Parker Bogue, *The Community College* (New York: McGraw-Hill Book Company, Inc., 1950), 77–92; James W. Thornton Jr., *The Community Junior College* (New York: John Wiley & Sons, Inc., 1966), 46–49; and James L. Ratcliff et al., *Community Colleges* (Needham Heights, MA: Simon & Schuster Custom Printing, 1994), 14–17.

49. Tichenor, *Tichenor Families in America*, 441, 442; *South Western Baptist*, 10 February 1876, 2, and 17 February 1876, 3; and John Jeffers, *The Auburn First Baptist Church, 1838–1988* (Auburn, AL: The Gnu's Room, 1990), 18.

50. Jeffers, *Auburn First Baptist*, 14–15. For examples of Tichenor's continued participation in denominational issues during his tenure as Alabama A & M president, see *South Western Baptist*, 25 May 1875, 2; 1 June 1875, 2; 8 June 1875, 3; 5 October 1875, 1; 24 February 1876, 2; 23 March 1876, 1; and *Alabama Baptist*, 4 April 1878, 3; 25 July 1878, 2; 25 August 1878, 1; 28 November 1878, 2; 24 July 1879, 3; 31 July 1879, 1; 22 April 1880, 3; 29 April 1880, 3; 17 June 1880, 3; 24 June 1880, 3; 8 July 1880, 3; 21 October 1880, 1; 2 December 1880, 2; and 17 March 1881. For articles about A & M, see *Alabama Baptist*, 27 March 1879, 3; 12 August 1880, 3; and 26 August 1880, 3.

51. *Annual, SBC, 1879*, 14, 25–26; *Annual, SBC, 1895*, 41; Robert A. Baker, *A Baptist Source Book* (Nashville: Broadman Press, 1966), 158–59; Burton, *Road to Recovery*,

85–86; *Alabama Baptist,* 22 May 1879, 2; A. T. Robertson, *Life and Letters of John Albert Broadus* (Philadelphia: American Baptist Publication Society, 1910), 314; and *Alabama Baptist,* 23 May 1895, 2, and 30 May 1895, 1.

52. *Minutes, ABSC, 1880,* 20, 21; Flynt, *Alabama Baptists,* 182; and A. H. Reid, *Baptists in Alabama: Their Organization and Witness* (Montgomery: Alabama State Convention, 1967), 120, 121.

53. Watson, "Tichenor and the Administration," 96–97; J. R. Rutland to J. E. D. Shipp, 22 April 1943, and J. R. Rutland to Daniel F. Davenport, 1 May 1943, Rutland papers, box 1, file 6; and "Seventh Report of the President," 75. See also Rod Andrew Jr., "Soldiers, Christians, and Patriots: The Lost Cause and Southern Military Schools, 1865–1915," *Journal of Southern History* 64 (November 1998): 677–710.

54. "Sixth Report of the President," 77; "Eighth Report of the President," 84; and Frost, *Thinking Confederates,* 80. For information on the work of George Washington Carver, see Rackham Holt, *George Washington Carver: An American Biography* (Garden City, NY: Doubleday, Doran, and Company, 1943) and Lawrence Elliott, *George Washington Carver: The Man Who Overcame* (Englewood Cliffs, NJ: Prentice Hall, 1967).

55. Burton, *Road to Recovery,* 59.

56. *Alabama Baptist,* 2 May 1895, 2.

57. *Glomerata, 1910* (Richmond: Edward Woddey Co., published by the senior class, 1910), 12.

Chapter 5

1. Mark A. Noll, *A History of Christianity in the United States and Canada* (Grand Rapids, MI: Eerdmans Publishing, 1992), 344–53, 360–62.

2. *Annual, SBC, 1882,* 29; *Alabama Baptist,* 1 June 1882, 2; Patti Stephenson, "Journey to Atlanta, One Hundred Years," *Missions USA* 53 (Sept./Oct. 1982): 36; and Home Mission Board minutes, 22 May 1882, 113, 114, on microfilm at the Southern Baptist Library and Archives, Nashville, Tennessee, hereafter cited as HMB minutes.

3. *Annual, SBC, 1882,* 29; J. B. Lawrence, *History of the Home Mission Board* (Nashville: Broadman Press, 1958), 64; *Annual, SBC, 1880,* 72; and Barnes, *Southern Baptist Convention,* 77–78.

4. HMB minutes, 23 May 1882, 114.

5. HMB minutes, 3 July 1882, 118; *Annual, SBC, 1883,* I, II.

6. B. F. Riley, *History of the Baptists of Texas,* (Dallas: by the author, 1907), 270.

7. Harvey, "'Yankee Faith,'" 90, 144, 201, 204.

8. Alan Trachtenberg, *The Incorporation of America: Culture and Society in the Gilded Age* (New York: Hill and Wang, 1982), 3–5.

9. HMB minutes, 1 August 1882, 121–22 and Fletcher, *Southern Baptist Convention,* 92–93.

10. HMB minutes, 25 September 1882, 124.

11. B. F. Riley, *History of Baptists in Southern States East of the Mississippi* (Philadelphia: American Baptist Publication Society, 1898), 226; *Annual, SBC, 1884,* appendix A; *Annual, SBC, 1892,* XI; and *Annual, SBC, 1899,* LXXV. In 1884 under Tichenor's leadership, the Home Mission Board had established the Church Building Fund. See McBeth, *Baptist Heritage,* 429.

12. Ayers, *Promise of the New South,* 22.

13. Miller, "Baptist Businessmen," 58.

14. Fletcher, *Southern Baptist Convention*, 94–95 and Patricia R. Hill, *The World Their Household: The American Woman's Foreign Mission Movement and Cultural Transformation* (Ann Arbor: University of Michigan Press, 1985), 53–54.

15. Bobbie Sorrill, *Annie Armstrong: Dreamer in Action* (Nashville: Broadman Press, 1984), 59, 70, 87–91, 123; *Alabama Baptist*, 5 October 1893, 2; 30 May 1895, 1; 8 August 1895, 1; 5 September 1895, 1; and 6 August 1896, 2.

16. Sorrill, *Annie Armstrong*, 128, 139, 166–68; Fletcher, *Southern Baptist Convention*, 103–4.

17. H. Leon McBeth, *Texas Baptists: A Sesquicentennial History* (Dallas: Baptistway Press, 1998), 13, 14, 15, 19, 20, 22, 28, 42.

18. Rupert N. Richardson, Adrian Anderson, and Ernest Wallace, *Texas: The Lone Star State*, 6th ed. (Englewood Cliffs, NJ: Prentice Hall, 1993), 240, 254.

19. McBeth, *Texas Baptists*, 64.

20. J. M. Carroll, *A History of Texas Baptists* (Dallas: Baptist Standard Publishing Co., 1923), 664–65.

21. McBeth, *Texas Baptists*, 70.

22. *Annual, SBC, 1892*, 10; McBeth, *Texas Baptists*, 65, 66, 67. See McBeth, *Texas Baptists*, 67-83 for a description of these various bodies.

23. HMB minutes, 3 July 1882, 119; *Proceedings of the Baptist General Association of Texas, 1882*, 18, hereafter cited as *Proceedings, BGA of Texas;* HMB minutes, 1 August 1882, 121. Riley, *Baptists of Texas*, 270, reports that Tichenor was at the July 1882 BGA meeting at Sulphur Springs, Texas, where these overtures were made. However, the author was unable to find any record of Tichenor's attendance at a BGA meeting until the following year at Cleburne, Texas. See *Proceedings, BGA of Texas*, 6, 13.

24. *Minutes of the Baptist State Convention of Texas, 1882*, 5, 22, 42, hereafter cited as *Minutes, BSC of Texas;* HMB minutes, 6 November 1882, 127–28; 25 September 1882, 124; 12 January 1885, 194; and 4 December 1893, 312.

25. HMB minutes, 25 September 1882, 125; McBeth, *Texas Baptists*, 84–87; Carroll, *History of Texas Baptists*, 576–77, 665; and Robert A. Baker, *The Blossoming Desert: A Concise History of Texas Baptists* (Waco: Word Books Publisher, 1970), 143.

26. *Minutes, BSC of Texas, 1883*, 6; *Minutes, BSC of Texas, 1884*, 5; *Proceedings, BGA of Texas, 1883*, 7, 9, 13; and *Proceedings, BGA of Texas, 1885*, 8.

27. HMB minutes, 25 May 1885, 201–2; *Minutes, BSC of Texas, 1885*, 22.

28. Carroll, *History of Texas Baptists*, 664–65; *Annual of the Baptist General Convention of Texas, 1887*, 8; *Annual, BGCT, 1889*, 9; *Annual, BGCT, 1891*, 9; *Annual, BGCT, 1894*, 33; *Annual, BGCT, 1895*, 11; and Alan J. Lefever, *Fighting the Good Fight: The Life and Work of Benajah Harvey Carroll* (Austin: Eakin Press, 1994), 59.

29. Lefever, *Fighting the Good Fight*, 59, 60; B. H. Carroll, "Speech to the SBC in Richmond," 12 May 1888, appendix III in Lefever, 145.

30. Lefever, *Fighting the Good Fight*, 60.

31. *Annual, SBC, 1892*, xii.

32. *Annual, SBC, 1894*, 42–43.

33. McBeth, *Texas Baptists*, 95.

34. Richardson, Anderson, and Wallace, *Texas*, 256–57, 263–65; Roy R. Bradley et al., eds. *The New Handbook of Texas*, vol. 2 (Austin: Texas State Historical Association, 1996), s.v. "Census and Census Records."

35. Carroll, *History of Texas Baptists,* 665.

36. Penrose St. Amant, *A Short History of Louisiana Baptists* (Nashville: Broadman Press, 1948), 19–20.

37. *SBC Annual, 1882,* 26–27. See also John Frank Gibson, "Isaac Taylor Tichenor: Southern Baptist Statesman," (Th.D. diss., New Orleans Baptist Theological Seminary, 1955), 81-85.

38. Glenn Lee Greene, *House Upon a Rock, about Southern Baptists in Louisiana* (Alexandria, LA: Executive Board of Louisiana Baptist Convention, 1973), 170; May Detharge, ed., *Highlights of the History of the First Baptist Church of New Orleans* (New Orleans: First Baptist Church of New Orleans, 1968), 8; and HMB minutes, 23 May 1882, 114.

39. HMB minutes, 1 August 1882, 122; *Annual, SBC, 1883,* viii; and HMB minutes, 29 January 1884, 163.

40. *Annual, SBC, 1883,* viii; HMB minutes, 31 May 1883, 143, and 29 January 1884, 162.

41. HMB minutes, 5 August 1884, 182, and 10 November 1884, 186; *Annual, SBC, 1886,* ix; and *Annual, SBC, 1887,* XXXVIII. See also Gibson, "Isaac Taylor Tichenor," 81–96 and I. T. Tichenor, *Phases of Home Board Work, Southern Baptist Convention* (Baltimore: Baptist Mission Rooms, 1898), 5.

42. Tichenor, *Phases of Home Board Work,* 4–5.

43. Ibid., 5, 6.

44. Tichenor, *Phases of Home Board Work,* 5 and *Annual, SBC, 1898,* LXIX, Emphasis is Tichenor's.

45. David R. Goldfield, "Pursuing the American Urban Dream: Cities in the Old South," in *The City in Southern History: The Growth of Urban Civilization in the South,* ed. Blaine A. Brownell and David R. Goldfield (Port Washington, NY: Kennikat Press, 1977) 52–91 passim; Howard N. Rabinowitz, "Continuity and Change: Southern Urban Development, 1860–1900," in Brownell and Goldfield, *City in Southern History,* 92–122 passim; and Don Harrison Doyle, *New Men, New Cities, New South: Atlanta, Nashville, Charleston, Mobile, 1860–1910* (Chapel Hill: University of North Carolina Press, 1990,) 87.

46. *Annual, SBC, 1892,* VII.

47. Ibid.

48. *Annual, SBC, 1894,* LIX.

49. Doyle, *New Men,* 15, 31, 46, 49, 88–89, 95, 136–58.

50. *Annual, SBC, 1898,* LXIX.

51. Ibid.

52. Ibid.

53. *Annual, SBC, 1883,* viii. See also I. T. Tichenor, *Phases of Home Board Work,* 10.

54. I. T. Tichenor, *Home Missions* (Baltimore: Baptist Mission Rooms, 1898), 5.

55. HMB minutes, 22 May 1882, 114; *Annual, SBC, 1855,* 32–34; *Annual, SBC, 1859,* 6; and *Annual, SBC, 1882,* 43. For the origins of SBC work among the Chinese of California, see also J. B. Lawrence, *History of the Home Mission Board,* 43.

56. HMB minutes, 18 December 1882, 13.

57. *Annual, SBC, 1884,* XII, XIII, XIV. Emphasis is Hartwell's.

58. *Annual, SBC, 1890,* 16.

59. Ibid., 16–17. Emphasis mine.

60. Ibid., 17.

61. Ibid.

62. Ibid.

63. Social control as used here and throughout the remainder of this work is utilized from a "macro-social perspective." Such control may be defined as being established by power groups either through laws and legal systems and norms or through the adoption of either spoken or unspoken customs or norms. Social control as utilized here also means the manipulation and management of a society or subgroups by informal means so that the ruling class or group can maintain its power without serious disruption to that power or to the status quo. Such social control "may appear humane and benign, but is in reality oppressive." (See Robert Keel on-line, University of Missouri, St. Louis, http://www.umsl.edu/~rkeel/200/socontrl.html, "Sociology at Hewett," http://www.hewett.norfolk.sch.uk/curric/soc/crime/s_contro.htm, and *Wikipedia: The Free Encyclopedia,* "Social Control," http://en.wikipedia.org/wiki/Social_control.)

64. Harper, *Quality of Mercy,* 23–24.

65. HMB minutes, 11 June 1888, 254; *Annual, SBC, 1892,* iii.

66. *Annual, SBC, 1894,* lv–lvi; Tichenor, *Phases of Home Board Work,* 11. See also Tichenor, *Home Missions,* 5.

Chapter 6

1. *Annual, SBC, 1882,* 46; *Annual, SBC, 1883,* iv; *Annual, SBC, 1887,* xxxii; and *Annual, SBC, 1892,* ii, xiii.

2. *Annual, SBC, 1885,* x; *Annual, SBC, 1887,* xxxviii; and Una Roberts Lawrence, *Cuba for Christ* (Atlanta: Home Mission Board, 1926), 145–50.

3. *Annual, SBC, 1886,* 21–22, 28–29, ix–x.

4. Una Lawrence, *Cuba,* 151. For more on the debate regarding Cuba see the *Alabama Baptist,* 23 December 1886, 6 January 1887, and 13 January 1887.

5. Annie Kate Barnes to Una Roberts Lawrence, 31 March 1945, Lawrence papers, box 10, file 34; HMB minutes, 12 July 1886, 225; *Annual, SBC, 1887,* xxxviii; and *Alabama Baptist,* 8 July 1886, 1; 23 February 1888, 1; 3 May 1888, 1; 13 December 1888, 1.

6. HMB minutes, 6 February 1888, 247, 249; HMB minutes, 11 June 1888, 254; HMB minutes, 23 January 1889, 261; *Our Home Field* 1 (August 1888): 6; and *Alabama Baptist,* 15 March 1888, 1. See also J. B. Lawrence, *History of the Home Mission Board* (Nashville: Broadman Press, 1958), 76–77.

7. *Alabama Baptist,* 3 January 1889, 2; 17 January 1889, 1; 20 February 1890, 1; 17 July 1890, 2; 4 September 1890, 2; 22 January 1891, 2; 8 October 1891, 2; 21 January 1892, 3; HMB minutes, 8 December 1892, 12 December 1892, 25 December 1892; *Alabama Baptist,* 5 January 1893, 1; *Annual, SBC, 1893,* lxx; *Alabama Baptist,* 2 May 1895, 2; and Una Lawrence, *Cuba,* 82–83.

8. *Annual, SBC, 1895,* lxvi; *Alabama Baptist,* 3 October 1895, 1; HMB minutes, 11 January 1896, 361; HMB minutes, 8 April 1896, 362; *Alabama Baptist,* 23 April 1896, 2; and Una Lawrence, *Cuba,* 85–86.

9. H. W. Brands, *The Reckless Decade: America in the 1890s* (New York: St. Martin's Press, 1995), 308–14; Tichenor, *Home Missions,* 6–7; and *Annual, SBC, 1899,* lxxx–lxxxi. On the conflict between the Home Mission Board and the American Baptist Home Mission Society, see chapter eight below.

10. *Annual, SBC, 1899,* lxxxi.

11. Brands, *Reckless Decade,* 287, 288.

12. Ahlstrom, *Religious History,* 733–34, 798–99, 849–50; Brands, *Reckless Decade,* 288–90; and Daniel G. Reid et al., eds., *Dictionary of Christianity in America* (Downer's Grove, IL: Intervarsity Press, 1990), s.v. "Evangelical Alliance" by R. R. Mathisen and "Josiah Strong" by R. T. Handy.

13. *Annual, SBC, 1896,* lxv; *Annual, SBC, 1890,* 17; and James F. Love as quoted in Paul Harvey, *Redeeming the South: Religious Cultures and Racial Identities among Southern Baptists, 1865–1925* (Chapel Hill: University of North Carolina Press, 1997), 203.

14. HMB minutes, 28 July 1896, 368, and 3 October 1896, 373.

15. Porter King to A. J. Diaz, 9 December 1898, Lawrence papers, box 6, file 31. Porter King was chairman of the Home Mission Board committee on Cuba. At the time Tichenor was debilitated by rheumatism. See Diaz's response to Tichenor regarding King's letter in A. J. Diaz to I. T. Tichenor, 3 January 1899, Lawrence papers, box 6, file 31.

16. Philip S. Foner, *The Spanish-American War and the Birth of American Imperialism, 1895–1902* (New York: Monthly Review Press, 1972), 453–56, 462–64, 466–83, 559–77; Emily S. Rosenberg, *Spreading the American Dream: American Economic and Cultural Expansion, 1890–1945* (New York: Hill and Wang, 1982), 7.

17. A. J. Diaz to I. T. Tichenor, 3 January 1899, Lawrence papers, box 6, file 31. Emphasis is Diaz's.

18. J. William Jones to A. J. Diaz, 4 January 1899, Lawrence papers, box 6, file 29, emphasis is Jones's.

19. Jones to Diaz, 4 January 1899, and I. T. Tichenor to A. J. Diaz, 8 February 1899, Lawrence papers, box 6, file 29.

20. Rosenberg, *Spreading the Dream,* 28, 32, 33.

21. Porter King, F. H. Kerfoot, I. T. Tichenor, and E. L. Connally to A. J. Diaz, 22 April 1901, Lawrence papers, box 6, file 29.

22. Emphasis is mine.

23. Philip Hamburger, *Separation of Church and State* (Cambridge, MA: Harvard University Press, 2002), 77–78. See also "Jefferson and the Baptists," in Hamburger, 169ff.

24. I. T. Tichenor to A. J. Diaz, 16 May 1901, Lawrence papers, box 6, file 29; I. T. Tichenor to A. J. Diaz, 21 May 1901, 7 June 1901, 26 July 1901, Lawrence papers, box 6, file 31; HMB minutes, 9 September 1901; George Hilyer to A. J. Diaz, 6 January 1902, I. T. Tichenor to A. J. Diaz, 15 January 1902, A. J. Diaz to I. T. Tichenor, 3 March 1902, Lawrence papers, box 6, file 31.

25. *Annual, SBC, 1903,* 154.

26. *Annual, SBC, 1885,* xi. For a similar definition of Appalachia see John C. Campbell, *The Southern Highlander and His Homeland,* rev. ed. (Lexington: University Press of Kentucky, 1969), 10–11.

27. *Annual, SBC, 1892,* vi; *SBC, Annual, 1893,* lxvi.

28. Henry D. Shapiro, *Appalachia on Our Mind: The Southern Mountains in the American Consciousness, 1870–1920* (Chapel Hill: University of North Carolina Press, 1978), xi, xiii, 34, 39; Dwight B. Billings, Mary Beth Pudup, and Altina L. Waller, "Taking Exception with Exceptionalism: The Emergence and Transformation of Historical Studies of Appalachia," in *Appalachia in the Making,* ed. Dwight B. Billings, Mary Beth Pudup, and Altina L. Waller (Chapel Hill: The University of North Carolina Press, 1995),

1, 2; Deborah Vansau McCauley, *Appalachian Mountain Religion: A History* (Urbana: University of Illinois Press, 1995), 20–26; Campbell, *Southern Highlander,* 165, 169–70, 172; and Rodger Cunningham, *Apples on the Flood: Minority Discourse and Appalachia* (Knoxville: University of Tennessee Press, 1987), xxv, 100.

29. Tichenor, *Home Missions,* 9.

30. Tichenor, *Home Missions,* 9; Leonard, *Dictionary of Baptists,* s.v. "Antimission Movement" by H. Leon McBeth; McBeth, *Baptist Heritage,* 371–77; Shapiro, *Appalachia on Our Mind,* 39; and McCauley, *Mountain Religion,* 405–7.

31. *Annual, SBC, 1897,* lxxix. See also Shapiro, *Appalachia on Our Mind,* 39, and Tichenor, *Phases of Home Missions,* 9, 10.

32. *Annual, SBC, 1885,* xi; *Annual, SBC, 1892,* vi; and David Whisnant, *All That Is Native and Fine: The Politics of Culture in an American Region* (Chapel Hill: University of North Carolina Press, 1983), 10. For an example of early twentieth-century philanthropic efforts in the Appalachians, see Whisnant on the Hindman Settlement School, 17–101.

33. Paul Salstrom, "Newer Appalachia as One of America's Last Frontiers," in *Appalachia in the Making,* ed. Pudhap, Billings, and Waller, 90, 91; Shapiro, *Appalachia on Our Mind,* 158, 159, 161, 184; Harry M. Caudill, *Night Comes to the Cumberlands: A Biography of a Depressed Area* (Boston: Little, Brown and Company, 1962), 75, 76; Harper, *Quality of Mercy,* 87; and McCauley, *Mountain Religion,* 342, 343, 399.

34. Tichenor, *Phases of Home Mission Work,* 9, 10; Shapiro, *Appalachia on Our Mind,* 40, 41, 42.

35. McCauley, *Mountain Religion,* 398.

36. Harper, *Quality of Mercy,* 72–76.

37. Harper, *Quality of Mercy,* 76; Baker, *Southern Baptist Convention and Its People,* 263.

Chapter 7

1. Spain, *At Ease in Zion,* 11 (see chap. 3, n. 5); *Annual, SBC, 1890,* xi.

2. Robert A. Baker, *Relations Between Northern and Southern Baptists* (Fort Worth, TX: Evans Press, 1948), 104–5, 126–27, 133–38; *Annual, SBC, 1890,* x, xi. For more discussion of these efforts by the American Baptist Home Mission Society, see other portions of Baker.

3. Walter B. Shurden, *The Sunday School Board, Ninety Years of Service* (Nashville: Broadman Press, 1981), 16, emphasis is Shurden's.

4. Fletcher, *Southern Baptist Convention,* 93, 94; Loftis, "Southern Baptist Identity," 259, 138; and Baker, *Relations,* 143.

5. Tichenor, "Fast Day Sermon," in Dill, *Tichenor,* 94, 103.

6. Presentation by Robert A. Baker to Baptist Theologians seminar and conversation with author, Southwestern Baptist Theological Seminary, 23 October 1991; Michael E. Williams, "Visionary and Optimistic: The Preaching of I. T. Tichenor," *Alabama Baptist Historian* 32, no. 1 (January 1996): 31.

7. J. B. Hawthorne as cited in Kimball Johnson, "A Biography of Isaac Taylor Tichenor" (Ph.D. diss., Southern Baptist Theological Seminary, 1955), 61.

8. John R. Sampey, *Memoirs* (Nashville: Broadman Press, 1947), 13–14.

9. Interview with W. O. Carver, cited in Johnson, "Biography," 62.

10. W. B. Crumpton, *A Book of Memories, 1848–1920* (Montgomery, AL: Baptist Mission Board, 1921), 277.

11. Interview with Annie Kate Barnes, in KJ papers, box 2, file 104, Auburn University Archives. See also Tichenor, "Fast Day Sermon," in Dill, *Tichenor,* 88–108.

12. Barnes interview; Tichenor, "Fast Day Sermon," in Dill, *Tichenor,* 88–108; and Tichenor sermons on Tichenor microfilm, Southern Baptist Historical Library and Archives.

13. Letter from Annie Kate Barnes to Una Lawrence, 31 March 1945, Lawrence papers, box 10, file 34; Barnes interview, KJ papers, box 2, file 104; Dill, *Tichenor,* 12; interview with Mrs. J. S. Dill by Joseph W. Burton, 31 May 1944, Lawrence papers, box 10, file 34; and J. B. Hawthorne as quoted in Dill, *Tichenor,* 25.

14. As quoted in Dill, *Tichenor,* 25.

15. *Annual, SBC, 1885,* xiii, xvi, xvii.

16. *Annual, SBC, 1887,* xlii.

17. I. T. Tichenor, *Foreign Missions Journal* 22, no. 1 (August 1890): 27.

18. *Annual, SBC, 1890,* 14, emphasis is mine.

19. *Annual, SBC, 1883,* i; I. T. Tichenor, *Our Home Field,* 1, no. 8 (April 1889): 4.

20. Spain, *At Ease in Zion,* 26.

21. Spain, *At Ease in Zion,* 26–28; "Report on the Death of Jefferson Davis" and a poem about Davis written by Mrs. J. William Jones, wife of the assistant corresponding secretary of the Home Mission Board in *Our Home Field* 2, no. 5 (January 1890): 1.

22. Spain, *At Ease in Zion,* 25; Wilson, *Baptized in Blood,* 58–78.

23. *Annual, SBC, 1891,* xl–xliv; *Annual, SBC, 1903,* 153, emphasis is mine. See also I. T. Tichenor, "Our Country; Its Resources and Opportunity," in Dill, *Tichenor,* 109–32. In the Tichenor memorial given at the 1903 SBC, F. C. McConnell identified Tichenor as "a Southerner of Southerners."

24. *Annual, SBC, 1893,* lxx.

25. J. B. Hawthorne as quoted in Prince Emmanuel Burroughs, *The Story of the Sunday School Board of the Southern Baptist Convention: Forty Years of Growth and Ministry, 1891–1931* (Nashville: Sunday School Board, 1931), 29; Wilson, *Baptized in Blood,* 39.

26. Ahlstrom, *Religious History,* 720.

27. See chapter three.

28. Harper, *Quality of Mercy,* 90–91, 93, 96–97. See also Joel Williamson, *The Crucible of Race: Black-White Relations in the American South since Emancipation* (New York: Oxford University Press, 1984).

29. Tichenor, "Uncle Ben's Golden Wedding," in Dill, *Tichenor,* 139–50.

30. Tichenor, "Jesse Goldthwaite: A Christian Slave," in Dill, *Tichenor,* 154–56.

31. Wilson, *Baptized in Blood,* 102–6.

32. *Annual, SBC, 1890,* iii.

33. *Annual, SBC, 1891,* xxxvi.

34. H. Leon McBeth, *A Sourcebook for Baptist Heritage* (Nashville: Broadman Press, 1991), 283.

35. I. T. Tichenor, *Work of Southern Baptists Among the Negroes* (Atlanta: Home Mission Board, n.d.), 2–5.

36. Ibid., 6–7; Wilson, *Baptized in Blood,* 108; and Harvey, *Redeeming the South,* 178, 180, 183, 184.

37. *Annual, SBC, 1898,* lxxviii; *Annual, SBC, 1883,* 37, ix; *Annual, SBC, 1884,* 15, xiv; *Annual, SBC, 1885,* vii–viii; *Annual, SBC, 1886,* xiv; and "Interview with Mrs. J. S. Dill," Lawrence papers, box 10, file 34.

38. Ayers, *Promise of the New South,* 322–26; Harvey, *Redeeming the South,* 178, 187, 229; and Booker T. Washington, "Speech at the Atlanta Exposition" and "What I Am Trying to Do" in *Great Documents in Black American History,* ed. George Ducas (New York: Praeger Publishers, 1970), 154–64.

39. Gaston, *New South Creed,* 211–13.

40. Doyle, *New Men,* 260. See also Harper, *Quality of Mercy,* 101.

41. Winthrop D. Jordan, *The White Man's Burden: Historical Origins of Racism in the United States* (London: Oxford University Press, 1974), 225.

42. Ibid. For further elaboration of these ideas in the antebellum period, see Winthrop D. Jordan, *White Over Black: American Attitudes Toward the Negro, 1550–1812* (Chapel Hill: University of North Carolina Press, 1968). For post-Reconstruction racial attitudes, see C. Vann Woodward, *The Strange Career of Jim Crow,* 3rd ed. (New York: Oxford University Press, 1974).

43. *Annual, SBC, 1890,* viii.

44. *Annual, SBC, 1893,* lxxi; *Annual, SBC, 1896,* lxix. Both of these reports reveal significant concepts in Tichenor's viewpoints regarding race relations. His ideas were not unique but demonstrate more fully how completely he was influenced by his culture.

Chapter 8

1. Tichenor, "Reminiscences," 5–10; "Letter to Thomas Watts" quoted in the *Richmond Whig,* undated newspaper clipping on Tichenor microfilm.

2. *Annual, SBC, 1892,* xi.

3. Robert G. Torbet, *A History of the Baptists,* 3rd ed. (Valley Forge, PA: Judson Press, 1987), 251, 286; Baker, *Relations,* 125.

4. Ibid., 128–32.

5. Ibid., 132.

6. *Annual, SBC, 1883,* x, 30.

7. HMB minutes, 11 June 1883, 147; *Alabama Baptist,* 23 May 1895, 2, and 30 May 1895, 1; *Annual, SBC, 1885,* vi; HMB minutes, 1 August 1884, 181; and Lawrence, *History,* 74. See also HMB minutes, 9 July 1883, 151, and 3 September 1883, 153.

8. *Annual, SBC, 1895,* 34, lxviii; Lansing Burrows, *Tichenor Memorial of the Church Building Loan Fund* (Baltimore: Women's Missionary Union, 1903), on Tichenor microfilm, 5–16; Mrs. B. D. Gray, *A Life Sketch of I. T. Tichenor* (Atlanta: Home Mission Board, n.d.), 12–13; and Lawrence, *History,* 74.

9. Basil Manly Jr. to I. T. Tichenor, 7 August 1888, Basil Manly Jr. letters, copy in KJ papers, box 3, file 155; Ron Chernow, *Titan: The Life of John D. Rockefeller, Sr.* (New York: Random House, 1998), 241, 309, 354, and 362.

10. *South Western Baptist,* 22 September 1859, 2; 24 November 1859, 2; and 14 June 1860, 2; Robert A. Baker, *The Story of the Sunday School Board* (Nashville: Convention Press, 1966), 14–26; *Annual, SBC, 1873,* 29; *Annual, SBC, 1866,* 6; *Annual, SBC, 1867,* 6; and *Annual, SBC, 1871,* 6.

11. *Annual, SBC, 1885,* vii, 25. See also Baker, *Sunday School Board,* 34–36, and Shurden, *Sunday School Board,* 14–17.

12. Basil Manly Jr. to I. T. Tichenor, 7 August 1888, copy in KJ papers, box 3, file 155; *Alabama Baptist,* 29 April 1886, 1; *Annual, SBC, 1886,* xii; *Annual, SBC, 1887,* xxxix–xl; and HMB minutes, 2 March 1886, 215.

13. See Baker, *Sunday School Board,* 36–37; Baker, *Southern Baptist Convention and*

Its People, 36–37; Fletcher, *Southern Baptist Convention,* 97; and McBeth, *Baptist Heritage,* 437.

14. James M. Frost, *The Sunday School Board of the Southern Baptist Convention: Its History and Work* (Nashville: Sunday School Board, n.d.), 9, 10.

15. Ibid., 10–11. Robert Baker suggests that this meeting came during the 1889 Alabama State Convention meeting. See Baker, *Sunday School Board,* 38.

16. Baker, *Sunday School Board,* 38–39.

17. *Annual, SBC, 1890,* 9–10, 23–25, vii–viii; HMB minutes, 26 May 1890, 277.

18. *Annual, SBC, 1891,* 22–23, 31; Robertson, *John Albert Broadus,* 394; Fletcher, *Southern Baptist Convention,* 99; and Baker, *Southern Baptist Convention* (Nashville: Broadman Press, 1974), 274–76, emphasis (on *Southern*) is Bell's.

19. *Annual, SBC, 1885,* 25; Burton, *Road to Recovery,* 66; and McBeth, *Baptist Heritage,* 643–44.

20. Baker, *Sunday School Board,* 32–33; Baker, *Relations,* 159–64; Herbert C. Jackson, "Henry Lyman Morehouse: Statesman of the Baptist Denomination in the North" (Ph.D. diss., Yale University, 1954), 93; Baker, *Southern Baptist Convention;* and McBeth, *Baptist Heritage,* 429, 437.

21. "Tribute to Dr. Morehouse," *Missions* 8 (September 1917): 646–47. See also Jackson, "Morehouse" and Lathan A. Crandall, *Henry Lyman Morehouse: A Biography* (Philadelphia: American Baptist Publication Society, 1919).

22. Barnes, *Southern Baptist Convention,* 77–78; Lawrence, *History,* 64; McBeth, *Baptist Heritage,* 429, 431; *Annual, SBC, 1892,* 10; and Baker, *Relations,* 128–32.

23. Baker, *Relations,* 127, 139, 140–41.

24. *Annual, Missouri Baptist General Association, 1879,* 12, hereafter cited as *Annual, MBGA; Annual, MBGA, 1880,* 10; *Annual, MBGA, 1881,* 13; and *Annual, MBGA, 1882,* 7, 10, 26, 35.

25. *Annual, MBGA, 1884,* 31, 37, 38, 43, 59; *Annual, MBGA, 1885,* 43, 47, 49.

26. *Annual, SBC, 1888,* viii.

27. *Annual, MBGA, 1889,* 40–41. See also HMB minutes, 21 December 1888.

28. I. T. Tichenor and Henry McDonald to H. L. Morehouse, 28 February 1889, H. L. Morehouse papers, American Baptist Historical Society. Hereafter cited as Morehouse papers. See also *Annual, SBC, 1889,* xlix.

29. H. L. Morehouse to Henry McDonald and I. T. Tichenor, 6 May 1889, Morehouse papers.

30. *Annual, MBGA, 1889,* 42.

31. E. W. Stephens to H. L. Morehouse, 20 December 1889, and E. W. Stephens to H. L. Morehouse, 25 October 1889, Morehouse papers. This author has assumed that the "Missouri Plan" was communicated to the Home Mission Board, although no direct correspondence from Stephens to Tichenor was located.

32. *Baptist Home Mission Monthly* 12 (December 1890): 357.

33. Baker, *Relations,* 141.

34. Allen et al., eds., *Encyclopedia of Southern Baptists,* s.v. "J. S. Murrow" by William A. Carleton and "E. L. Compere" by Amy Hickerson Compere; HMB minutes, 3 December 1878, 57; and William A. Carleton, "'Not Yours but You,' the Life of Joseph Samuel Murrow" (Th.D. thesis, Southwestern Baptist Theological Seminary, 1945), 77–86, 133–41.

35. J. S. Murrow to E. L. Compere, 15 February 1882, E. L. Compere papers, box 8, file 2, Southern Baptist Historical Library and Archives, hereafter cited as Compere papers; J. S. Murrow to E. L. Compere, 14 March 1882, Compere papers, box 8, file 2; E. L.

Compere to H. F. Buckner, 10 October 1882, Compere papers, box 8, file 2; and I. G. Vore to E. L. Compere, 23 December 1882, Compere papers, box 5, file 5, emphasis is Vore's.

36. Baker, *Relations,* 142; Carleton, "'Not Yours but You,'" 85.

37. I. T. Tichenor to E. L. Compere, 5 March 1886, box 8, file 1, and I. T. Tichenor to E. L. Compere, 5 March 1886, box 8, file 1, both in Compere papers. See also I. T. Tichenor to E. L. Compere, 16 November 1883, Compere papers, box 8, file 1.

38. E. L. Compere to I. T. Tichenor, n.d., E. L. Compere letters book, Compere papers, box 7, file 9. See Compere letters book, 21–22. Likewise, Tichenor and Jones consistently corresponded with Compere, notifying him of support and providing encouragement. See I. T. Tichenor to E. L. Compere, 18 June 1883, box 7, file 8; Tichenor to Compere, 16 November 1883, box 8, file 1; Tichenor to Compere, 19 June 1885, box 7, file 8; Tichenor to Compere, 2 January 1886, box 7, file 8; Tichenor to Compere, 16 June 1887, box 8, file 1; Tichenor to Compere, 25 June 1887, box 7, file 8; Tichenor to Compere, 25 July 1887, box 7, file 8; J. William Jones to Compere, 27 September 1888, box 7, file 8; and Tichenor to Compere, 17 October 1888, box 7, file 8, all located in Compere papers, as representative letters for this correspondence.

39. Carleton, "'Not Yours but You,'" 86.

40. Ibid., 87.

41. Fletcher, *Southern Baptist Convention,* 101–2; Allen et al., eds., *Encyclopedia of Southern Baptists,* s.v. "Gospel Missionism" by John F. Gibson; and Leonard, *Dictionary of Baptists in America,* s.v. "Gospel Mission Controversy" by W. R. Estep and "Tarleton Perry Crawford" by H. Leon McBeth.

42. E. L. Compere to John William Jones, 20 June 1890, 4–5, Compere papers, box 8, file 2, emphasis is Compere's. See also J. M. Gaskin, *Baptist Milestones in Oklahoma* (Oklahoma City: Baptist General Convention of Oklahoma, Good Printing Co., 1966), 143; G. W. Hyde to E. L. Compere, 21 July 1890, box 7, file 9; Hyde to Compere, 23 July 1890, box 7, file 9; Compere to Hyde, 29 July 1890, box 8, file 2; J. William Jones to Compere, 30 July 1890, box 8, file 2; Hyde to Compere, 2 August 1890, box 7, file 9; Jones to Compere, 5 August 1890, box 8, file 2; Hyde to Compere, 8 September 1890, box 7, file 9; and Jones to Compere, 30 October 1890, box 7, file 9, all located in Compere papers.

43. Gaskin, *Baptist Milestones,* 120–23.

44. Ibid., 123, 136, 138.

45. J. William Jones to E. L. Compere, 19 December 1890, Compere papers, box 7, file 9. The author was unable to discern whether the emphasis was Jones's or was added later by Compere as he read the letter.

46. J. William Jones to E. L. Compere, 24 March 1891, Compere papers, box 8, file 2.

47. Copies of the letters may be found in Carleton, "'Not Yours but You,'" 135–41, 142–47; Baker, *Relations,* 143; and HMB minutes, 4 August 1891, 284, 285.

48. J. William Jones to E. L. Compere, 19 August 1891, Compere papers, box 8, file 2, emphasis is Jones's.

49. J. William Jones to E. L. Compere, 29 September 1892, Compere papers, box 8, file 3; R. J. Hogue to I. T. Tichenor, 3 October 1892, Compere papers, box 8, file 3; and Gaskin, *Baptist Milestones,* 145–51.

50. J. William Jones to E. L. Compere, 12 August 1891, Compere papers, box 8, file 2. Emphasis is Jones's.

51. Ibid, emphasis is Jones's.

52. *Annual, SBC, 1894,* 16.

53. *Annual, SBC, 1891,* xxxvi; *Annual, SBC, 1893,* lxv, lxvi; McBeth, *Baptist Heritage,* 429–31; and Baker, *Relations,* 120–22.

54. *Annual, SBC, 1895,* 14–16.

55. Minutes of the meeting of the joint committee from the Southern Baptist Home Mission Board and Northern Baptist Home Mission Society, 12–13 September 1894, 2, 4, 5, copy in the Morehouse papers.

56. *Baptist Home Mission Monthly* 17 (July 1895): 221.

57. McBeth, *Sourcebook,* 290–91; *Home Mission Monthly* 17 (July 1895): 221.

58. Baker, *Relations,* 176–77; McBeth, *Baptist Heritage,* 429.

59. *Annual, SBC, 1879,* 14; *Annual, SBC, 1895,* 41; and Baker, *Source Book,* 158–59.

60. Harvey, *Redeeming the South,* 183–85.

61. Ayers, *Promise of the New South,* 310, 324–26, 328–32, 338.

62. HMB minutes, 24 September 1894, 331–32; I. T. Tichenor to T. J. Morgan, 25 September 1894, Morehouse papers; Tichenor to H. L. Morehouse, 5 July 1895, Morehouse papers; Undated and unsigned list attached to the Tichenor letter to Morehouse, Morehouse papers; HMB minutes, 2 October 1895, 355; and HMB minutes, 26 November 1895, 357. For other correspondence regarding cooperative work between the HMB and the HMS, see Tichenor to Morehouse, 28 January 1898, 2 February 1898, and 6 April 1898, Morehouse papers.

63. HMB minutes, 1 November 1898, 441, 6 December 1898, 1–2; and Tichenor to Morehouse, 6 March 1899, 1–2, Morehouse papers.

64. Tichenor to Morehouse, 6 March 1899, 2, 4, Morehouse papers.

65. Morehouse to Tichenor, 22 March 1899, 3–4, Morehouse papers.

66. Ibid., 4, 5, 7.

67. Morehouse to Tichenor, 22 March 1899, 8; I. T. Tichenor to H. L. Morehouse, 27 March 1899, Morehouse papers.

68. Baker, *Relations,* 178–200; and Allen et al., *Encyclopedia of Southern Baptists,* s.v. "Comity Agreements" by William A. White.

69. Wilson, *Baptized in Blood,* 38, 74, 85, 86, 90, 94–96, 100–101; Ayers, *Promise of the New South,* viii, 322–26, Harvey, *Redeeming the South,* 42; and Gaston, *New South Creed,* 130–33. For an excellent discussion of the "Lost Cause Critique of the New South," see Wilson, *Baptized in Blood,* 79–99.

Conclusion

1. Burton, *Road to Recovery,* 160; *Alabama Baptist,* 9 September 1897, 2.

2. Dill, *Tichenor,* 70–71; Burton, *Road to Recovery,* 161–62.

3. *Annual, SBC, 1900,* 12, appendix B.

4. Dill, *Tichenor,* 72–74; Burrows, *Tichenor Memorial.*

5. *Annual, SBC, 1903,* 154. See also J. B. Hawthorne, "I. T. Tichenor, D.D.: An Oration Delivered before the SBC in Savannah, Georgia," *Baptist Argus,* 30 July 1903, 3–4.

6. As cited in Barnes, *Southern Baptist Convention,* 78.

7. *Annual, SBC, 1883,* xi. See also HMB minutes, 19 May 1884, 169, and 15 June 1885, 204.

8. *Minutes, ABSC, 1880,* 20–21; *Annual, SBC, 1886,* xi; and HMB minutes, 22 June 1897, 386.

9. *Annual, SBC, 1903,* 154.

10. Burton, *Epochs,* 77.

11. Robert A. Baker, "The Cooperative Program in Historical Perspective," *Baptist History and Heritage* 10 (July 1975): 172. See Albert McClellan, "The Origins and Development of the SBC Cooperative Program," *Baptist History and Heritage* 10 (April 1975): 71. See also *Alabama Baptist,* 18 February 1886 and 10 June 1886 for examples of Tichenor's pleas for a systematic approach to support for missions.

12. Barnes, *Southern Baptist Convention,* 69–70, 78; Lawrence, *History,* 81; Baker, *Southern Baptist Convention,* 264; John Franklin Loftis, "Factors in Southern Baptist Identity as Reflected in Ministerial Role Models, 1750–1925" (Ph.D. diss., Southern Baptist Theological Seminary, 1987), 138; and McBeth, *Baptist Heritage,* 428.

13. *Annual, SBC, 1897,* 35.

14. Walter B. Shurden, "The Southern Baptist Synthesis: Is It Cracking?" *Baptist History and Heritage* 16 (April 1981): 2–11; H. Leon McBeth, "The Texas Tradition: A Study in Baptist Regionalism," *Baptist History and Heritage* 19 (January 1991): 37–57.

15. Martin Marty, *Righteous Empire* (New York: Dial Press, 1970), 134.

Bibliographic Essay

The author found a number of sources helpful while compiling this work on Isaac Taylor Tichenor. Unfortunately, many of Tichenor's personal papers were apparently in his family's possession and were lost decades ago. There are, however, a number of primary source materials and collections that proved useful in reconstructing his life and understanding his thought.

Tichenor published little with the exception of a few small pamphlets while Home Mission Board corresponding secretary. There are also five of his writings published at the end of a short biography by his son-in-law that are valuable resources. The most important is his "Fast Day Sermon" that he originally delivered to the Alabama legislature in 1863. Another excellent resource is a collection of interviews done by a family member at the end of his life, and a short diary Tichenor kept as a young man that includes a few sermon notes, both of which are on Tichenor microfilm. One of the most important resources are copies of the annual reports he issued to the trustees and the governor of Alabama during his tenure as president of the Agricultural and Mechanical College of Alabama. No study of his presidency in Auburn is complete without careful analysis of these reports. The Tichenor diary, a typed copy of the interviews, and many of these annual reports are available at the Southern Baptist Historical Library and Archives in Nashville, Tennessee. This resource is also available on microfilm.

Southern Baptist Convention annuals are an especially good resource, most notably for Tichenor's Home Mission Board reports, which he gave annually throughout his tenure at the board. The Alabama State Convention annuals are important in understanding Tichenor's Alabama years. Some of Tichenor's writings can be found in publications of the Home Mission Board, most notably *Our Home Field*. Several Baptist newspapers provide important information as well, especially the *Alabama Baptist,* the *Christian Index,* and the *South Western Baptist.*

There are several collections of personal papers that include either correspondence by or to Tichenor, interviews of Tichenor contemporaries or relatives, and other pertinent Tichenor information. These include the Una Roberts Lawrence papers and E. L. Compere papers at the Southern Baptist Historical Library and Archives, Nashville, Tennessee; the Kimball Johnson papers and J. R. Rutland papers at the Auburn University Archives, Auburn, Alabama; the Henry Lyman Morehouse collection at the American Baptist Historical Society Archives, Valley Forge, Pennsylvania; and the Joseph Squire papers in the private collection of Kenneth Penhale, Helena, Alabama. The minutes of the First Baptist Church of Montgomery from 1867–68 are also a good resource. The minutes of the Home Mission Board provide an excellent source for Tichenor's tenure at the board. I utilized the microfilm copy of these minutes at the Southern Baptist Historical Library and Archives in Nashville, Tennessee.

A number of secondary sources proved very helpful in understanding Tichenor, his world, and his contributions to that world. For his years in Montgomery, Lee Allen's *The First 150 Years: Montgomery's First Baptist Church, 1829–1979* (Birmingham, AL: Oxmoor Press, 1979), is an excellent local church history with an entire chapter and a portion of another devoted to Tichenor and his years as pastor. To better understand the battle of Shiloh, Larry Daniel, *Shiloh: The Battle That Changed the Civil War* (New York: Simon and Schuster, 1997) and James Lee McDonough, *Shiloh in Hell Before Night* (Knoxville: University of Tennessee Press, 1977) are recommended. For an accurate picture of Civil War Montgomery, W. W. Rogers Jr., *Confederate Home Front: Montgomery During the Civil War* (Tuscaloosa: University of Alabama Press, 1999) is a tremendous resource. Likewise, Steven Woodworth's recent *While God Is Marching On: The Religious World of the Civil War Soldiers* (Lawrence: University of Kansas Press, 2001) gives a clear understanding of the religious motivations and concerns of the men serving in the Civil War.

In recent years a number of secondary sources have been published that are essential to understanding the postbellum South. First and foremost is Paul M. Gaston's *The New South Creed: A Study in Southern Mythmaking* (New York:

Alfred A. Knopf, 1970). While now more than thirty years old, Gaston's arguments are extremely significant in understanding Tichenor's context. Furthermore, many other valuable secondary sources have been published since Gaston, works that aid in understanding postwar southern culture and religion, including Charles Reagan Wilson, *Baptized in Blood: The Religion of the Lost Cause* (Athens: University of Georgia Press, 1980); Henry D. Shapiro, *Appalachia on Our Mind: The Southern Mountains in the American Consciousness, 1870–1920* (Chapel Hill: University of North Carolina Press, 1978); Edward L. Ayers, *The Promise of the New South: Life after Reconstruction* (New York: Oxford University Press, 1992); Paul Harvey, *Redeeming the South: Religious Cultures and Racial Identities among Southern Baptists, 1865–1925* (Chapel Hill: University of North Carolina Press, 1997); J. Wayne Flynt, *Alabama Baptists: Southern Baptists in the Heart of Dixie* (Tuscaloosa: University of Alabama Press, 1998); Keith Harper, *The Quality of Mercy: Southern Baptists and Social Christianity, 1890–1920* (Tuscaloosa: University of Alabama Press, 1996); Dan R. Frost, *Thinking Confederates: Academia and the Idea of Progress in the New South* (Knoxville: University of Tennessee Press, 2000); and Daniel W. Stowell, *Rebuilding Zion: The Religious Reconstruction of the South, 1863–1877* (New York: Oxford University Press, 1998). Two slightly lesser known but significant works that are helpful are Katherine L. Dvorak, *An African-American Exodus: The Segregation of the Southern Churches* (Brooklyn: Carlson Publishing, 1991) and Don Harrison Doyle, *New Men, New Cities, New South: Atlanta, Nashville, Charleston, Mobile, 1860–1910* (Chapel Hill: University of North Carolina Press, 1990). The most important unpublished work is James Sanders Day's fine dissertation on the origins of the Alabama mining industry, "'Diamonds in the Rough': A History of Alabama's Cahaba Coal Field" (Ph.D. diss., Auburn University, 2002). Significant portions of Day's work focus upon Alabama mining during the years of Tichenor's direct association with Alabama's coal fields, especially Tichenor's relationship with mining pioneer Joseph Squire and his continued interest in Alabama mining long after his direct involvement ceased.

Index